D0344755

# HYPOTHESES AND EVIDENCE

# HYPOTHESES AND EVIDENCE

*William N. Stephens*
FLORIDA ATLANTIC UNIVERSITY

THOMAS Y. CROWELL COMPANY
*New York* *Established 1834*

Library of Congress Catalog Card Number: 68-13387

Designed by Barbara Kohn Isaac

Manufactured in the United States of America

# *Preface*

This book sets forth what might be termed a theory of evidence: a general epistemological scheme, an overall frame of reference in which particular methodological problems may be placed. The scheme is given in the second chapter; later chapters elaborate on various parts of it.

Theoretically, the scheme has a wide range of applicability. In fact, all the examples are drawn from the social or behavioral sciences. The book itself is a part of the social science tradition. It focuses on judging hypotheses about human behavior, on doing and evaluating research in sociology, psychology, political science, and anthropology.

I have done something here which, I think, many social scientists have already done for themselves. All of us, in the course of doing and thinking about research, pick up a body of "methodological knowledge": various points, considerations, desiderata to be kept in mind when judging an hypothesis or a study; numerous principles, criteria, taboos, in the light of which we frame our own work and judge others' work. Each discipline and research specialty has its own lore. Each of us, depending on the direction and extent of his professional growth, comes to acquire several of these lores, or parts of them. One "learns something about" sampling and scaling and the design of surveys and experiments. Depending on his ability to do so, one may gain some control over various of the mathematical elaborations of methodology. One may branch out in another direction, and

read the philosophers of science. The methodologies sprawl in many directions; the individual must somehow systematize—for himself—what he "knows." We make this synthesis for ourselves. Each of us accumulates lore and evolves for himself some general orientation to give it order and sense. This book represents such a general orientation. How positively (or negatively) a given professional reader will react to it would hinge, I imagine, to a considerable extent on how closely it corresponds to the overall scheme which he has already worked out for himself.

Any approach to epistemology, or to research methodology, is necessarily segmental. The writer focuses on a certain part of the spectrum, and allows the rest to remain out of focus. He writes on an "area" or a "problem" or a particular technique, or on a selected number of these. He pursues his arguments and his analyses to a certain point and then lets them rest, even though some of them could be extended further. No treatment is all-encompassing. This is even true for broad-based, orientation-giving treatments like the present one. Any such treatise is limited, in part, by the writer's own limitations. The field is broad; he cannot hope to control all of it. Also, such a book must have a definite point of departure and a language of its own. Depending on the syntax that one chooses, some "problems" and "points" are better handled than others.

The point of departure here is the single hypothesis. The "theory of evidence" is a series of "points" which might be kept in mind when judging an hypothesis for likelihood of truth. The points have to do with (1) the nature of any evidence and (2) characteristics of the hypothesis itself—what will be termed, in Chapter 2, "sources of doubt."

The present work might be viewed as standing between philosophy of science, on the one hand, and the mathematically based methodologies, on the other. It never drifts very far toward either pole. Some attention is given to philosophic fine points; but such treatments are customarily dropped at a point when an Ayer or a Kaplan would wish to pick them up and carry them much further. It comes close to being a methodology sans math. Tests of significance, multivariate analysis, scaling techniques, and the like are given an overall rationale by the scheme; but they are not really delved into. No formulas are given. The reasoning never becomes mathematical.

Once the writer of such a book has been able to locate and fix his subject matter, decide what he will discuss and what he will ignore or gloss over, the next question is: Whom is he writing *to?* What is the prospective audience? Colleagues? Students? On what "level" should the discussion be? Should it be slow-moving, repetitive, peppered with examples, for the benefit of the person without background? Or should it be more condensed, fast-moving, for the convenience of the professional? I have attempted a compromise. I have tried to write so that a lay person with no background in methodology or social science can follow the discussion. At the same time, I have tried to proceed rapidly enough so that the professional reader will not be bored. This is easier said than done; the "level" does wander a bit. For example, the first part of Chapter 1 is strictly for the beginner. In other places, the pace quickens.

It is, perhaps, appropriate that the style of the book itself should reflect an imperfect compromise between the conflicting needs of professional and amateur reader. Conflicts and compromise, dilemmas, ambiguities: these will occupy much of our attention in the pages to come.

April, 1968 W. N. S.


# *Acknowledgments*

There are many contributors to this book: colleagues, former teachers, students; the lines of influence are myriad. Four persons were particularly helpful with the manuscript as it went through its revisions. For criticism, advice, and encouragement, special thanks to Carl Peck and Dan Ragle at the University of Kansas, to Mark Stephens at Purdue, and, most especially, to Ray Cuzzort at the University of Colorado.

For permission to publish quotations, thanks are due to the

following: the *American Political Science Review* and Anatol Rapoport for permission to quote from his article, "Various Meanings of 'Theory' "; the *Journal of Philosophy* and Abraham Kaplan for permission to quote from his article, "Definition and Specification of Meaning"; John Wiley & Sons for permission to quote from *The American Voter* by Angus Campbell *et al.*, from *Theory and Methods of Scaling* by Warren Torgerson, and from *The Handbook of Experimental Psychology* by S. S. Stevens (ed.); the Liveright Publishing Corporation for permission to quote from *General Introduction to Psychoanalysis* by Sigmund Freud; to Holt, Rinehart & Winston for permission to quote from *Society* by Robert M. MacIver; the Blaisdell Publishing Company for permission to quote from *Social Causation* by Robert M. MacIver; the Open Court Publishing Company for permission to quote from *An Analysis of Knowledge and Valuation* by C. I. Lewis; the Humanities Press for permission to quote from *The Logic of Social Enquiry* by Quentin Gibson; and Harcourt, Brace & World for permission to quote from *Human Behavior: An Inventory of Scientific Findings* by Bernard Berelson and Gary Steiner.

# *Contents*

# HYPOTHESES AND EVIDENCE

## *Chapter 1*

# BUILDING BLOCKS

All attempts to describe reality in words we shall call "hypotheses." Thus what others have termed, in other contexts, "descriptions," "facts," "laws," "propositions," also "guesses," "hunches" and "speculations": all such statements will here bear the common rubric "hypothesis."

An hypothesis is a small unit of description, the smallest possible. It presumes to describe just one "fact," one thing. It can usually be stated in a single sentence. Those "descriptions" which take up entire paragraphs, pages, books—for example, theories, arguments, narratives, ramified explanations—are compounded of many hypotheses. The hypothesis is the essential unit, or building block, out of which the more complicated descriptions are made.

For some examples of hypotheses, we might take these: "Slums breed crime." "It is a cold day." "Economic development facilitates democratic government." "The older you are when you marry, the better your chances of making a go of it." "The earth is flat." Here is a longer sentence which is crammed with eight hypotheses: "Women, as compared with men, are more active in church but less active in politics; mature earlier; live longer; drive fewer miles and have fewer accidents; threaten suicide more often but actually commit suicide less often."

Some hypotheses must be true; others are no doubt false. That is, some accurately describe that segment of reality which they pretend to describe; while others distort, falsify, misrepresent reality.[1] How can we know if an hypothesis "matches" or "agrees with" that part of reality which it tries to describe? Our notions of what is "real," what is "out there," come by way of mental images and sense impressions. We perceive—see, listen, touch, and so forth—and introspect, and, through the media of our sensory apparatus, we receive presumed "messages" from reality. We may believe an hypothesis because it agrees with a perception. For example, one might believe the hypothesis "It is a cold day" upon looking at a thermometer. Also, we may believe some hypotheses because other people report that they have made observations which agree with or support these hypotheses.

In a sense, our contact with the external reality is indirect. We can only assume that these "messages" that come in are faithful descriptions of what is "out there." Since there is this assumptive gap between sense impressions and reality, it has become unfashionable to speak of "proving" or "disproving" hypotheses (Carnap 1936; Stevens 1951:3; Ayer 1956; Mehlberg 1957:27–28; Nagel 1961:81–84; Kemeny 1959:122–124). Here we shall follow the fashion and speak of "evidence"—which may be present or absent, strong or weak—and not of "proof."

An hypothesis, then, is a statement which tries to describe reality. Before it is examined further, it should be differentiated from other sorts of statements, which do *not* try to describe reality.

First of all, there is the *analytic statement*, sometimes termed a priori statement (Ayer 1956) or tautology (Popper 1959). The analytic statement differs from the hypothesis in that it *can* be proved to be true or false; proof or disproof devolves merely upon definition. Examples would be: "All husbands are married." "If all men are mortal, and if Socrates is a man, then Socrates is mortal." An analytic statement may usually be phrased, "If . . . then. . . ." "If this and this are true, then that must be true." "If this stands for this, and that stands for that, then this must follow." In other words, an analytic statement merely says some-

[1] Some, too, may be "near the truth," approximating the truth, "have some truth in them." This will be an awkward point for us.

thing about the defined mutual relations of symbols. It is a rather esoteric sort of statement, and is seldom met with outside the realms of mathematics and formal logic.

Hypotheses and analytic statements, then, are both statements of supposed fact. Hypotheses presume to describe the external reality, and are ordinarily considered as not subject to proof—only to partial and tentative verification, "evidence," through the medium of people's sensory apparatus. Analytic statements are subject to proof, and they are concerned only with the defined mutual relations of symbols, as with the mathematician's formula and the philosopher's syllogism.

Now we turn to three other types of statements, which are not statements of supposed fact.

*Definitions*, or labeling statements, are statements which say what various terms mean. A definition may always be phrased, "By . . . , I mean. . . ." "By 'rain,' I mean water coming down out of the sky." "By 'culture,' I mean the sum total of gear and learned habits possessed by a group of people." "By 'population density,' I mean number of persons per square mile." [2]

If we think of reality as composed of various things or entities, which have various traits, attributes, or characteristics, then definition is a process by which we "hang labels on" what we perceive as things and traits of things. Definition must have occurred, of course, before we can "start talking about reality"; that is, before we can start stating hypotheses.

Labeling, or naming, is arbitrary. A given perceived object may have many names, and a term may refer to a variety of perceived objects or traits—as is attested by the dictionary, with its multiple definitions of words. Names may change. St. Petersburg may become Leningrad. Since definitions are mere arbitrary assignments of labels, they are not "true" or "false" in the same sense as hypotheses are. A term can mean anything one says it means.[3]

[2] A definition of a definition is: "A logical equivalence between the term specified and an expression whose meaning has already been specified" (Kaplan 1946).

[3] "A definition is a kind of statement, but one which neither requires nor can have any verification by recourse to sense experience. . . . The use of linguistic symbols is indeed determined by convention and alterable at will.

*Value statements* might be set aside as still another type of statement. These express moral and aesthetic judgments, and preferences of all sorts. Examples would be: "Debussy was the foremost impressionist composer." "This steak is delicious." "The ends do not justify the means." "Communism is evil."

Value statements might all be construed as beginning: "I like . . ."; "I abhor . . ."; "I condone . . ."; "I disapprove . . ."; or as "I want *you* to like, abhor, condone, or disapprove. . . ." They can be considered "true" or "false" in only a very limited sense. If they are *truthful* expressions of the speaker's preferences, only in this sense are they true. Like labeling statements, they express the speaker's choices; they do not describe the external reality.

This is a controversial point, of course. It would be contested by moralists and by art critics. As a working principle, no doubt none of us could accept it without reservations; probably all of us cling to certain statements of preference as obvious truths and facts. For our purposes here, it is enough merely to set value statements aside, distinguishing them from hypotheses. Thus "Debussy is a great composer" is a statement of preference; and it is not the sort of statement which can be tested against evidence. "Debussy never wrote a symphony" is an hypothesis, and it can be tested against evidence.

Having outlined hypotheses, analytic statements, definitions and value judgments, we are left with one residual type, a miscellaneous category. This type includes commands, greetings, exclamations, and various verbal fragments: "Workers of the world, unite!" "Hello." "Goodbye." "My stars!" "Gracious sakes!" We shall call these *nondescriptive statements*, for want of a better name.

This concludes the five-fold typology of statements. Only two of these—hypotheses and definitions—will receive any more attention in this book. Since hypotheses are phrased in words, definition and specification of meaning become crucial at many

---

Also what classifications are to be made, and by what criteria, and how these classifications shall be represented, are matters of decision" (Lewis 1945:25, 97).

points when one considers the problems involved in relating hypotheses to evidence.

To repeat: only hypotheses *can* be related to evidence. Questions on the order of, What is Truth? What is Beauty? What is emotion *really?* would be construed as definitional questions, asking not for observations or research findings, but merely for agreement as to the meaning of terms. Likewise, questions on the order of, Is contraception wrong? Are we better off Red or dead? Are the Alps more beautiful than the Jersey marshes? are asking for value statements.

## Variables and Cases

All hypotheses will be construed as assigning *variables* to *cases.* The "case" is the entity or thing that the hypothesis talks about. The "variable" is the characteristic, trait, or attribute which, in the hypothesis, is imputed to the case. Thus a national economy (case) might be characterized as diversified, stable, fast-growing (all variables). A person (case) might be described as labile, outgoing, energetic, decisive (all variables). The international situation (case) is precarious (variable). The city of New York (case) has grave budget problems (variable).

In ordinary discourse, which is frequently vague, variables are merely assigned to cases: thus the above examples, "fast-growing," "energetic," "precarious," "has grave budgetary problems." When the hypothesis is a report of measurement, on the other hand, the case may be assigned some specified amount of the variable: "He weighs 187 pounds." "The city has 7,854,320 residents." "Her I.Q. is 140." Variables can always be construed as continua of magnitude. A case may "have" or exhibit much, little, or none of a particular variable. Some hypotheses make the "how much" designation precise; others leave it vague.

In hypotheses about human behavior, the case is often a person or some type of person—student, American, child, or whatever. The variable is "something about" the person, or something he does, or something that happens to him. "He was naughty. He got a spanking. Afterward he cried for a while."

Some hypotheses mention only one case. Others cite more than one. These are termed *generalizations* or comparisons; here, they will all be called generalizations. Examples: "The world's illiteracy rate is steadily decreasing" (the case is a person). "The New Math has been adopted by a majority of our nation's primary schools (the case is a primary school). "There are now five nations producing thermonuclear weapons" (the case is a nation).

Some hypotheses cite only one variable. Others cite two. Rarely, more than two variables are mentioned in a single hypothesis. Hypotheses citing more than one case—that is, generalizations—which also mention more than one variable, will be termed *correlation statements.* An hypothesis may report a positive correlation, a negative correlation, or a zero correlation.[4] A correlation is a "relationship," or covariance, between a pair of variables. In a positive correlation, the two variables tend to "go together": cases exhibiting one variable also tend to exhibit the other; cases "having a lot" of one variable also tend to "have a lot" of the other. Conversely, cases which "don't have" one variable tend not to have the other; cases exhibiting a low magnitude of one variable tend also to show a low magnitude of the other.

As an example, let us take: "Crime tends to occur in slums." This is a generalization about neighborhoods. Two variables are mentioned: degree of "slumminess" and crime rate. The hypothesis says that the slummier neighborhoods tend to have higher crime rates. In other words, cases (neighborhoods) high on one variable (slumminess, "badness" of neighborhood) tend to be high on the other (crime rate). Cases low on one variable tend to be low on the other; the non-slums have fewer crimes.

A negative correlation says just the opposite: cases which exhibit one variable tend not to exhibit the other, or, cases low on one variable tend to be high on the other. An example would be

[4] Many correlations are in fact curvilinear. However the curvilinear correlation is ill-described in words. It is best pictured in a graph. We shall not concern ourselves with curvilinear correlations.

the above hypothesis worded in reverse: " 'Good' neighborhoods tend to have low crime rates." The better the neighborhood, the lower its crime rate tends to be.

Suppose that all the evidence we have in support of this hypothesis is summarized in the following table, Table I. Suppose

TABLE I

RELATIONSHIP BETWEEN WEALTH OF NEIGHBORHOOD AND CRIME RATE

| | *Number of crimes per 1,000 inhabitants in 1967* | | |
|---|---|---|---|
| Average dwelling unit is assessed at | Over 5 | Between 1 and 5 | Less than 1 |
| over $50,000 | 1 | 1 | 7 |
| between $10,000 and $50,000 | 1 | 1 | 16 |
| between $2,000 and $9,999 | 2 | 4 | 10 |
| under $2,000 | 12 | 3 | 1 |

further that all we mean by how "good" a neighborhood is, is how rich it is; i.e., for how much the property in it is assessed. Table I divides the neighborhoods into four groups as regards "goodness" or expensiveness: neighborhoods where the average dwelling unit—be it house or apartment—is assessed at over $50,000 (there are 9 of these neighborhoods in our imaginary sample); neighborhoods where the average assessment of dwelling units is somewhere between $10,000 and $50,000 (there are 18 of these neighborhoods in the sample); 16 poorer neighborhoods, where the average assessment is between $2,000 and $10,000; and 16 really poor neighborhoods—"slums," let us call them—where the average dwelling unit is valued at less than $2,000.

The table makes a threefold division as regards crime rate:

neighborhoods having over 5 crimes per 1,000 persons (16 of these); those having between 1 and 5 crimes per 1,000 persons (9 of these); and those having less than 1 crime per 1,000 persons (34 of these in the sample).

The table, therefore, shows scores on two variables: "goodness" or "richness" or assessed valuation of the neighborhood, represented on a 4-point scale; and crime rate, on a 3-point scale. The table has 12 cells, 12 possible categories into which a neighborhood may fall. ($4 \times 3 = 12$.) The numbers in the cells represent tallies of cases. Thus for example, one neighborhood scored highest on both variables—assessed valuation over $50,000, and over 5 crimes per 1,000; 12 neighborhoods scored lowest on property valuation, while scoring highest on crime rate; and so forth.

This is the usual sort of table employed to represent correlations in accounts of social research; it is the type of table we shall use here. The number of scale points for each variable—and hence the number of cells in the table—of course varies from one table to the next. The cutting point—dividing one scale point from the next—is frequently a matter of arbitrary choice. With equal justification we could have made the lowest point on the property-valuation scale "under $1,000" or "under $5,000" rather than "under $2,000." The number of scale points is often arbitrary too. If we had wanted to, we could have represented both variables on 100-point scales; this would have yielded a 10,000-cell table. Or we might collapse Table I into a $2 \times 2$, 4-cell table—again, making the cutting points anywhere we wished. This is done in Table II. In this transposition no cases have been lost. In Table II, as in Table I, there are 59 neighborhoods in the sample.

The $2 \times 2$ or 4-celled table is the minimal size for representing a correlation. It simply divides the cases into "highs" and "lows" with respect to each of the two variables. For simplicity's sake, tables in this book will generally be $2 \times 2$.

As stated previously, with a positive correlation cases "high" on one variable tend to be "high" on the other; cases "low" on one variable tend to be "low" on the other. A negative correlation means the reverse: "highs" on one variable tend to be "lows" on the other. In order to "see" the negative correlation in Table II, it is merely necessary to ask oneself, "Of the 'highs' on property valuation, how many were also 'high' on crime rate?" The answer is 10 out of 43, or about 23 percent. And, "Of the 'lows' on property valuation, how many were 'high' on crime rate?" The answer is 15 out of 16, or about 94 percent. The "lows" on one variable—more than the "highs" on that variable

TABLE II

RELATIONSHIP BETWEEN WEALTH OF NEIGHBORHOOD AND CRIME RATE

| | *Number of crimes per 1,000 inhabitants in 1967* | |
|---|---|---|
| Average dwelling unit is assessed at | Over 1 ("high" crime rate) | Less than 1 ("low" crime rate) |
| over $2,000 | 10 | 33 |
| under $2,000 | 15 | 1 |

—tend to be "highs" on the other variable. The greater the difference between these two percentages, then the stronger the correlation.[5] Imagine that the correlation was perfect, with no exceptions: all 43 (100 percent) of the relatively wealthy neighborhoods had low crime rates; none (0 percent) of the poor neighborhoods had low crime rates. Imagine again that the correlation was maximally weak—for all practical purposes, a zero correlation: 21, or about half of the 43 wealthy neighborhoods (49 percent) had low crime rates; 8, or half the poor neighborhoods (50 percent) had low crime rates.

Whether one construes a table as showing a positive or negative correlation depends merely on choice of words. Tables I and II show a negative correlation between wealth, property valua-

[5] Of course various statistical tests are available, if one desires a more precise estimate of strength-of-correlation.

tion, "goodness" of neighborhood, or whatever one wishes to call it, and crime rate. It might also be construed as showing a negative correlation between poverty and lawfulness. It shows a positive correlation between poverty and crime rate. It could also be said to show a positive correlation between property valuation and lawfulness.

Hypotheses which state *zero* correlations merely say that some relationship was *not* found, or does *not* occur: "Negroes are not naturally inferior to whites." "Technological development does not lead to an overall increase in human happiness." [6]

To summarize: if an hypothesis cites more than one case, it will be termed a generalization. If it cites more than one case and more than one variable, it will also be termed a correlation statement. An hypothesis may describe a positive, negative, or zero correlation. Most of the examples throughout this book will be hypotheses stating positive correlations; when evidence is offered in support of these, it will be given in $2 \times 2$ tables.

## Relating Hypotheses to Evidence

An hypothesis reports on observations. These "observations" are sense impressions, "messages" from the sensory apparatus about things and events seen, heard, and otherwise experienced. We might also include people's "observations" of their own mental states: intentions, thoughts, preferences, and so forth.[7] Once made, the observation is noted or stored in the mind's eye, in memory, or on paper: "I saw a rainbow yesterday"; "We have

[6] In the first example, the case is a person. The variables are (1) Negroness, or white-ness, or race and (2) inferiority. In the second example, it is not clear what the case is. Let us call it a country. The variables are (1) degree of technological development and (2) degree of overall human happiness. This is a cause-effect hypothesis—or rather, one which states the absence of a cause-effect relationship. The cause-effect hypothesis is a special subtype of correlation statement.

[7] Examples: "I intend to vote Democrat"; "I believe in a life after death"; "I want to make more money."

three children"; or as when, in response to the questionnaire item "Age?" the questionnaire-respondent answers, "19."

Such a notation of a single observation will be called an *observer-report*. Ordinarily it is given in words or can be easily translated into words ("I am nineteen years old"). Actually, of course, observer-reports are summaries of sense impressions—editing, condensing, leaving much out, no doubt distorting at times what was actually experienced or what was actually "there."

An observer-report, then, is a little hypothesis in its own right, and its truth or accuracy is problematic. Some will be more readily believed than others ("I am nineteen years old" as compared with "I have seen a flying saucer").

If an hypothesis is a presumed description of reality, and if it is true when it accurately describes what it pretends to describe, then *evidence* that the hypothesis is true must be in the form of sense impressions—experienced by someone—which "match" or "agree with" the hypothesis. And if these sense impressions are to be available for use as evidence, they must be noted, expressed, recorded, in the form of observer-reports.

If an hypothesis "has evidence to support it," this means that observer-reports are available which "agree with it." In other words, the hypothesis can be related to "agreeing" observer-reports. "Agreeing" is put in quotations because often the agreement is not literal, but logical, in a narrow and conservative sense. For example, suppose a teacher asked his students how old they were, and got the following answers: "18," "18," "19," "20," "20," "20," "21," "21," "23," "24," and "30." He concludes, "Most of you are under 21. The observer-reports—what we shall call the evidence—are in the form of reports of single cases, "I am 18," "I am 23," etc. These are not literally identical to his conclusion (the generalization "Most of you are under 21"), but this is what they add up to. In this sense, these observer-reports agree with the hypothesis "Most of you are under 21."

If an hypothesis cites only a single case, then it may be literally identical to its supporting observer-report(s) (example: "The U.N. General Assembly convened today"). If it generalizes about many cases, then ordinarily each supporting observer-report describes a single case, many such observer-reports are cited as evidence, and the hypothesis says something about how these observer-reports "add up," as in the above example concerning students' ages.

Hypotheses of interest to science, those tested in research, are with few exceptions generalizations. For evidence, they require that many observer-reports, each describing a single case, be brought together, or collated. This collating process can be orderly and systematic, with observer-reports being written down as they are received by the collator. An example is the teacher who asks each student his age, writes the answer on the blackboard, and proceeds thus until each student's age is noted in a simple table:

| | |
|---|---|
| Under 21 | six students |
| Over 21 | five students |

Or, the collating process may be slipshod and subject to the vagaries of the collator's memory, as it usually is in everyday life (example: "When I want very much to do well, I usually do badly").

For a given hypothesis, there may be much evidence, little evidence, or none. How much evidence there is depends on how many supporting observer-reports are presented to the person who is asked to believe the hypothesis.[8]

Also, the evidence may be strong or weak. The strength of the evidence is its degree of persuasiveness: how successful it is in dispelling doubts about the truth of the hypothesis. This depends on two general factors: how confident one feels about the accuracy of the observer-reports, and the nature of the hypothesis itself. Many hypotheses present what we shall term "sources of doubt"; these are special reasons why an hypothesis might be

[8] As we shall see, just how many supporting observer-reports there are —even whether there is any evidence at all—is sometimes unclear and ambiguous and subject to argument. This difficult problem will dog us continually as we proceed in our consideration of evidence. It will be introduced toward the end of Chapter 2, it will receive more attention in Chapter 3, and it will continue to assert itself in Chapters 4 and 5.

false, even though it is supported by perfectly accurate observer-reports. This will be discussed in Chapter 2.

"Much evidence" is quite different from "strong evidence." For some hypotheses, a single observer-report is quite persuasive: "It is raining." "He is smoking a pipe." "I am nineteen." For other hypotheses, myriad observer-reports still leave unanswered doubts: "Education dispells prejudice." "Severe sex training engenders anxiety about sex." "Anticipating a subsequent use increases retention, even of uncongenial material."

Evidence may be favorable or unfavorable to a particular hypothesis. In the example of the students' ages, the assembled observer-reports were favorable to the hypothesis "Most of you are under 21." They gave unfavorable evidence for such hypotheses as "All of you are under 21" or "Most of you are over 21."

In the example of the students' ages, the professor first gathered and collated the observer-reports and then stated his general hypothesis. In other words, he first observed—or rather, "observed" the students' own self-observations—and then drew a conclusion. We shall call this observation-then-conclusion sequence *induction:* first the observer-reports are collated, then the generalization is made which says how they "add up." In behavioral science research, usually the hypothesis is stated first, and then observer-reports are gathered. Sometimes the hypothesis is phrased as a question. The professor might have asked himself, "Are most of them under 21?" and then gathered evidence in order to answer the question. Sometimes this is termed testing the hypothesis. He might first state, or predict, "Most of you are under 21"; then he could ask his question of each student, put the answers in his table, and relate this evidence back to his hypothesis.

Judging an hypothesis on the basis of evidence, then, involves gathering observer-reports and then relating them to the hypothesis. The evidence thus gathered may be favorable or unfavorable to the hypothesis, and it may be strong or weak. How to assess the strength or persuasiveness of the evidence—and hence the likelihood of truth of the hypothesis—is a difficult issue. In fact, it gives rise to an entire complex of issues, some of them controversial, subject to alternative formulations and various shadings of opinion. Before we get into this, a word should be said about other, and radically different, methods of judging hypotheses.

## Alternative Criteria for Judging Hypotheses

We shall start with two criteria for belief which, I suspect, we all apply frequently in our everyday lives: these are the criterion of *faith* and the criterion of *reasonableness.*

First, faith. Many hypotheses are believed merely because the person who states the hypothesis is trusted. Sometimes this simply devolves on a judgment as to the speaker's honesty. If the listener decides the report is truthful, then he believes the hypothesis. This sort of faith we could ill do without, since so much of our picture of the world and of our surrounding milieu comes to us secondhand. Even science depends on this sort of faith. In research, the primary observations are often not made by the investigator himself, but rather by laboratory assistants, respondents, or other persons; the research depends on some faith in the truthfulness of these observer-reports. Sometimes a check on their truthfulness and accuracy is possible, in the form of consensual validation from other observers; but often this is not done or is not possible.

We are more or less forced, then, to have some faith in the veracity of reported observations—those made by friends, acquaintainces, and family members and those that come through the news media, in history books, on road maps, and various other written sources. It is also hard not to accept many of the more difficult and ambitious hypotheses—those which explain, interpret, forecast, those which, in the terms of this book, present various sources of doubt—merely on the basis of faith. Faith, here, often reposes in some authority or expert: the doctor, the learned professor, the agronomist, the TV repairman, someone who "knows better than I" about his particular specialty. If the malaise is diagnosed as anemia, or a nitrogen deficiency in the soil, or a burned-out picture tube, if the proposed cure is iron pills, or nitrogen supplement, or a new tube, how can the listener, the customer, the non-expert, possibly check on the truth and accuracy of the expert's pronouncements? In most cases, the only way would be to consult another expert.

In terms of strength of evidence and likelihood of truth, sometimes faith is well founded, but often it is not. For some of the simpler reports of observations, the only serious source of doubt is the speaker's veracity. For these, the criterion of faith is fairly appropriate. The more "difficult" hypotheses, on the other hand, do demand evidence of a special sort; for these, much more is involved than the reporter's truthfulness. Sometimes these "special demands" or "sources of doubt" have been well handled by supporting research, sometimes not. In any event, when one accepts such an hypothesis on faith, he generally does so without knowledge of the actual state of the evidence.

Reasonableness, the other criterion for belief which is in common use in everyday life, involves accepting incoming hypotheses which seem to agree with previously held beliefs. The exact mental process involved is vague and shadowy. Perhaps Leon Festinger captures part of its essence, in *A Theory of Cognitive Dissonance* (1957). The person who decides to believe or disbelieve a particular hypothesis according to whether or not it "seems reasonable" may feel that he is "checking it against his experience," or seeing if it "jibes with experience." However, this "experience" is seldom mere observation. Rather, I suspect, it is usually a rather complex jumble of hypotheses and impressions, some ill documented; it often includes various preferences and value positions, plus rather vague feelings about logical coherence; and the listener's awareness of much of this "experience" is dim. In short, the process is generally intuitive and disorderly in the extreme. It is far removed from the process of relating an hypothesis to evidence, in the manner described in the previous section.

Another way to judge hypotheses is according to their *success at prediction.* On the basis of an hypothesis, one predicts as yet unobserved events. Then one makes the observations necessary to check on the accuracy of the predictions: one tests the predictions. If the predictions are generally confirmed, then the hypothesis is viewed as "good," prestigeful, useful. If a good many predictions do not match with subsequent observations—in other words, if tests fail to confirm predictions—then the prestige of the hypothesis suffers, it is considered less "good," not "valuable." Also, the greater the precision of the predictions—the lower the margin for error—the more prestigeful, powerful, useful is the hypothesis. This criterion of success at prediction is attractive to some scientists and philosophers of science, since it does not demand that one make any assumptions about the existence of the external reality, or about observers' ability to perceive and report that reality accurately. Considerations of "true" and "false" and likelihood of truth no longer apply. "Evidence" is merely the correspondence between predictions and the subsequent observer-reports made in the predictive tests; the term no longer denotes assurances that the hypothesis accurately describes reality. Officially, at least, hypotheses are no longer believed or doubted (although they may continue to be, in the scientist's secret heart); rather they are tentatively "entertained," ranked in prestige, according to their demonstrated predictive utility.

If one seriously applies this criterion of predictive utility to a particular hypothesis, makes and gathers predictive tests, sees how well the predictions correspond to the predicted observer-reports, one often finds that the process is exceedingly awkward.[9] For one thing, it is usually a matter of arbitrary choice, and not a matter of "simple logic," what sorts of predictions "follow from" a particular hypothesis and what sorts do not. How successful an hypothesis is at predicting depends not solely on the hypothesis, but also on who does the predicting, that is, on what sorts of predictions are judged appropriate. Collating evidence, then, becomes a messy business and somewhat arbitrary; the final

[9] This is not meant as an unfavorable comparison with the alternative method, judging hypotheses for likelihood of truth. That method can be exceedingly awkward too.

rating of the hypothesis as regards success at predicting can be subject to wide differences of opinion.

The criterion of predictive utility is usually applied to entire systems of statements—theories, models, complex explanations —rather than to single hypotheses. Such a system ordinarily contains several hypotheses, along with definitions (defining the terms in the hypotheses), and analytic statements which are meant to "join" some of the hypotheses to each other logically. The term "system of statements" is hardly appropriate, since generally in the natural sciences—and increasingly in the behavioral sciences—these theories and models are stated in mathematical formulae and not in words. There seems to be a fair amount of agreement among philosophers of science that, while at least some single hypotheses may be judged for likelihood of truth, these complex systems defy such a judgment. Prestige, usefulness, or success at prediction is the only feasible criterion by which to judge them.[10]

Of course, hypotheses are often judged as parts of systems—rather than singly—outside the higher reaches of science, and the judgment arrived at is in terms of likelihood of truth, not mere "success at prediction." When we decide to accept a statement on the basis of whether or not it "seems reasonable," this statement is often not a single hypothesis, but rather an entire narrative or account or a complex explanation. While this judgmental process is generally slipshod, in some fields—such as law, history, epidemiology and medical diagnosis—there has been some attempt to bring a modicum of order into it. Thus a jurist or an historian may weigh several alternative narratives or accounts of "what happened" at a particular time and place in order to decide which story seems the most plausible. Each of the competing accounts of "what happened" is a series of hypotheses. Some "evidence" is available. This may be in the form of observer-reports which can be directly related to some of the hypotheses in the

[10] Also mentioned as criteria are the purely formal properties of the theory or model: its elegance, syntactical "tightness" or clarity; the ratio of assumptions to "explained facts" (Kaplan 1964; Marx 1963; Nagel 1961:47–152; Popper 1959; Rapoport 1958; Weaver 1961).

accounts, in the manner described in the previous section; or, in a less direct and less clear way, it may lend weight to one or another account's plausibility or "reasonableness." The process of relating the stories to evidence is much more complicated, problematic, and uncertain than when only a single hypothesis must be judged by itself. The jurist or historian scans the stories for contradictions—contradictions between the various hypotheses or parts within each story and contradictions between parts of the story and reported observations. Whichever account seems to "hang together best"—is felt to be most consistent within itself, with the evidence, and with previously held beliefs—will be chosen as the most plausible one.

Sometimes, when something needs to be explained, there is, or is thought to be, only a finite number of possible explanations. If evidence can be brought to bear which, to the explainer's satisfaction, disposes of all possible explanations but one, then the remaining explanation is considered well documented and probably true. This process of elimination may be brought to bear on competing hypotheses, or it may be used to sort out competing stories or hypothesis-series. It is also used by the historian and the jurist, as well as by the detective, the physician, the auto mechanic, all manner of diagnosticians. Berton Roueche (1965) describes how a public health officer goes through this process of elimination as he checks out possible causes for an epidemic of neuromyasthenia. Is the disease carried by an insect? No, the public health officer decides, he has persuasive evidence that it is not. Is it caused by contamination of the city water, the milk, the beaches, the food supply? No. Does it come from a toxic product, like some cosmetic? No, probably not. Is it simply a psychosomatic outbreak, mass hysteria? No, it does not seem to be. The highest incidence of the disease is among hospital personnel, so it must be an infectious disease, transmitted from person to person. What sort of organism causes the disease? It must not be one of the rickettsia or bacteria, because these would have been found in laboratory tests; nothing showed up in the tests, so the causal agent must be some sort of virus. There the explanation must end, because of lack of evidence; it is not final and complete, but the field of possibilities has been considerably narrowed.

We have probably not reviewed all possible bases for judging hypotheses, but here we shall stop. Aside from the criterion of faith and, in special instances, the method of finite possibilities, all these methods are very complicated. They are hard to do justice to in a brief description. They cannot be conceptualized or comprehended with any precision. In special circumstances each is necessary, for want of any other method. We shall leave these other approaches now, and have nothing more to say about them through the remainder of this book.

The only method to be discussed here involves relating a single hypothesis to observer-reports, in order to arrive at an estimate of likelihood of truth. It is a relatively simple method, although even it can get complicated enough. Relative to the other methods, it is fairly orderly, systematic, rigorous—or it can be, at any rate. But even this way leaves much to be desired in the way of precision and closure. I think there is some loose consensus among scientists about what should be considered when an hypothesis is judged on the basis of evidence. However, when one moves into the details of the process, one finds much room for alternative formulations, shifting emphases, marginal differences of opinion. We are now ready to consider one possible formula for judging a single hypothesis' truth-value on the basis of evidence.

## *Selected References*

Here, and at the end of subsequent chapters, are listed more intensive treatments and elaborations of a few of the topics covered. The references are offered as a service to the interested student who would like to continue reading and "branching out" in this general area. For all readings that are cited, full references are given in the bibliography at the end of the book.

Tables—reading them, making them, moving back and forth between verbal hypotheses and data given in tabular form:

Hans Zeisel, *Say It with Figures.*

"Reasonableness" as a criterion for deciding what to believe:

Leon Festinger, *A Theory of Cognitive Dissonance.*

Harold Garfinkel, *Studies in Ethnomethodology.*

Criteria used for rating theories for "goodness" or "prestige":

Ernest Nagel, *The Structure of Science*, pp. 47–152.

Judging hypothesis-sequences, i.e., "stories," against evidence, as in history, archaeology, geology, jurisprudence:

Quentin Gibson, *The Logic of Social Enquiry*, pp. 184–185.

# *Chapter 2*

# A SYSTEM FOR JUDGING EVIDENCE

To repeat what was outlined in Chapter 1: when an hypothesis is related to evidence, various observer-reports—reports of single observations—are collated or brought together, in order to see whether they agree or disagree with the hypothesis. If, on balance, the observer-reports agree with the hypothesis, then the evidence is favorable; we have some reason to believe the hypothesis. If the observer-reports disagree with the hypothesis, evidence is unfavorable; the hypothesis is probably untrue. The example was the teacher who asked his students how old they were, wrote each student's answer (each observer-report) down on the blackboard, and then, having thus brought together the evidence, could relate it (as favorable evidence) to the hypothesis "Most of you are under 21" and could relate it (as unfavorable evidence) to such hypotheses as "Most of you are over 21."

For a particular hypothesis, then, evidence may be present or absent, favorable or unfavorable. If we confined ourselves to judging hypotheses solely on the basis of evidence, we would conclude that unless favorable evidence is presented, we have no reason to believe an hypothesis: if the evidence is unfavorable, we ought not to believe the hypothesis; if there *is* no evidence, we have no grounds for believing it either.

If we are shown favorable evidence, the question then arises: how strong is the evidence? How persuasive is it of the truth of the hypothesis? Or, in the light of the evidence, what is the hypothesis' likelihood of truth?

Likelihood of truth depends in part on the nature of the evidence, but it also has much to do with characteristics of the hypothesis itself. Some hypotheses are much more "difficult," ask for much more in the way of supporting observer-reports, than do others. A given assembly of data may give strong support to one of the easier hypotheses and considerably weaker support to one of the more difficult hypotheses. An example would be the age data on the blackboard as evidence for "Most of you are under 21" and "Most of you are immature."

These special demands which some hypotheses make, we shall term *sources of doubt*. The core of the "system for judging evidence" to be reviewed here is eight sources of doubt. Six of these reside in the hypothesis itself. The other two sources of doubt concern the nature of the evidence. Here they all are:

A. The hypothesis may be a prediction.
B. It may be a generalization beyond known cases.
C. It may cite an inferred variable.
D. It may state a cause-effect relationship.
E. It may cite a necessary cause.
F. It may be a compound hypothesis.

The final two sources of doubt, having to do with the nature of the evidence or supporting observer-reports, are:

G. *Is* there any evidence? That is, how clear is it that any observer-reports mustered in support of the hypothesis are actually *relevant* to the hypothesis?
H. Is the evidence right? Or rather: is the evidence spuriously favorable to the hypothesis?

A particular hypothesis may pose one, several, all, or none of the sources of doubt A through F. Source-of-doubt H is always present for every hypothesis if we concur, with the philosophers of science, that it is never absolutely certain that observers' reports accurately mirror the reality they try to describe; however, in some instances, observer-error is a much more serious possibility than it is in others. Source-of-doubt G is sometimes completely absent—as it is in the example of the students' ages—and it is often present in varying degrees of seriousness.

The sources of doubt having to do with the nature of the hypothesis—A through F—once they arise, can never be completely dispelled. They can, however, be partly "answered"—with varying degrees of assurance—by the sort of special evidence which they demand. A generalization beyond known cases, for example, can be documented with evidence for a representative sample; a cause-effect statement can be supported by an experiment.

At this point I shall briefly describe what I mean by each of the sources of doubt.

A. A *prediction*, of course, describes something which has not yet been observed. Eventually the predicted observation may be made, and the prediction then can be directly tested. Prior to that time, the prediction may be less directly documented by evidence for a past trend. The prediction "You will die" would seem well documented in this way, since we have evidence for a past trend: all men die. The evidence here seems convincing. Yet, theoretically at least, it is not quite so strong as it would be after the predicted event had occurred and had been observed; the fact that a trend has been observed to remain perfect in the past does not assure that it will hold perfect in the future (Kaplan 1963:20). A prediction, then—prior to the time when it can be directly tested—presents a source of doubt. With the strongest of evidence for the strongest of past trends, the predicted event still might not come true.

With the "You will die" example, this caution might seem academic; the past trend has been observed to be perfect, exceptionless. Predictions, however, are often based on *imperfect* past trends. One consideration, when judging evidence in support of the prediction, is the observed strength of the past trend. Obviously "You will marry," "You will have children," and "You will draw Social Security" rate lower on likelihood of truth than does "You will die."

Another determinant of the strength of evidence for a prediction is: Just how clear can we be about what the past trend *is?* And, whatever it is, does the predicted event actually "fit" it? In many everyday predictions about human behavior, the "fit" to a past trend is problematic, to say the least. Examples: "There will not be a serious recession during the next five years." "Candidate X will be elected." "He will be a doctor when he grows up." Some predictions are based on *intent.* "I am going to be a doctor." "How do you know that?" "Because that is what I intend to be." Here, of course, it is a matter of opinion what the past trend is. Perhaps it is "People who want to become doctors, tend to become doctors." Maybe it is something else: "People who want to become doctors, are male, do well in pre-med, and have the money for medical school, tend to become doctors." Perhaps several past trends are being invoked. But whatever they are, we do not know. Quite likely the speaker does not know either. In all cases such as this, where the prediction does not clearly and obviously "fit" some particular trend, the relation of the prediction to anything which could be called "evidence" becomes rather tenuous and uncertain, and likelihood of truth suffers a decline.

A final consideration when judging a prediction is: How strong is the evidence for the statement-of-trend on which the prediction is based? In other words, does the past trend which was "observed" actually exist? Following this line of inquiry would turn our attention to the other possible sources of doubt. For one thing, the statement-of-trend which enables the prediction always is—or can be construed to be—a generalization beyond known cases. It is to this type of hypothesis that we now turn.

B. A *generalization beyond known cases* bears some similarity to a prediction. In both instances, an observed trend is projected, said to hold for cases which have not yet been observed. A prediction often pertains to a single (future) case. A generalization beyond known cases is, of course, a generalization; it pertains to many cases. Typically, it projects some trend observed in a group of events to the entire *class* to which those events are said to belong. One function of generalizations beyond known cases is to serve as the basis for prediction; they state that trends noted in observed cases also hold for cases not observed (including future events), thus enabling prediction. In the previous example, the prediction "You will die" was based on the generalization beyond known cases "All men die."

Evidence for a generalization beyond known cases comes from observation of a number of cases in the class specified, a sample. Research findings can ordinarily be stated in alternate forms. They can be mere "statements of findings" confined to the samples studied; in other words, they can be stated as generalizations *not* beyond the known cases. ("In our sample, a greater percentage of delinquents than of nondelinquents came from broken homes." "Of the 'cured' addicts we followed, all relapsed into addiction." "Of the mothers we studied, *post partum* depression was more frequent after the first parturition than it was after subsequent births.") Or they can take the form of the generalization beyond known cases, which goes beyond the subjects studied to state general laws or trends that hold (it is hoped) for the entire class or population to which the cases are said to belong. ("Delinquents tend to come from broken homes." "Drug addiction can only be temporarily 'cured'." "*Post partum* depression is most frequent after the first birth.")

The mere statement of findings is of course safer than the bolder option, the generalization beyond known cases. What the researcher found in his sample might be true enough; still, the sample may not be a faithful picture-in-microcosm of the population to which the generalization beyond known cases refers. Maybe some other addicts *have* been permanently cured. Maybe, if all delinquents could be studied, they would *not* show a tendency to come from broken homes.

The trouble with the conservative statement of findings is that it is usually trivial. In order for the research to be of any value—for planning, or prediction, or with respect to theoretical significance—someone must draw a generalization beyond known cases from it. As soon as this step is taken, of course, likelihood of truth declines.

Minimal evidence for a generalization beyond known cases comes from a sample of *some* kind. A group of cases must have been observed, not just one or two or several. The ideal sample is not only fair-sized, but also one in which the method of sample selection is such that each case in the population has, at the outset, an equal chance of being included in the sample. This—what we shall term "evidence for a representative sample"—is the ideal; unfortunately, it is seldom attainable. Lacking this, evidence for a generalization beyond known cases can be strengthened somewhat by replications: several samples, drawn from several subgroups of the population to which one wishes to generalize. All of this will be discussed in Chapter 6.

Generalizations beyond known cases are necessary because they are required for prediction. Prediction, in turn, is required for any sort of planning (either private or public), any decision making, all attempts to build things, to fix things, to influence the future to our own liking. We must predict. To predict, we must generalize. This is one of the many conflicts between significance (of an hypothesis) and likelihood of truth.

C. *Inferred variables* are variables which are inferred to be present (or are inferred to be present in some particular magnitude) on the basis of other variables which are reported by the sensory apparatus. A child has a tantrum; you observe the tantrum; you infer anger. A fire burns in the fireplace across the room; you see the flames; you infer heat. A man drives by in a Cadillac; you see the Cadillac; you infer wealth.

An hypothesis which cites an inferred variable is problematic on at least two counts. First, source-of-doubt H, always present: Did the observer "see" what was "there?" Is his mental image, and any subsequent report of it, faithful to that aspect of reality he is trying to describe? Did the tantrum, the flames, the Cadillac, really "happen"? Second, the source of doubt peculiar to the inferred-variable hypothesis: Did he infer correctly concerning the "meaning" of the sense impressions—the presence of anger, heat, wealth?

In other words, variables which can be directly observed—throwing a tantrum, emitting flames, driving a Cadillac—are taken by the observer as "signs" of other variables which were not actually seen or heard by the observer. In the examples, these were feeling angry, emitting heat, being wealthy. The resulting inferred-variable hypotheses are "He is angry," "The fire is hot," "He is wealthy." For any of these to be true, the observation must be accurate, and the "sign" must have been "read right."

These examples are rather atypical of inferred-variable hypotheses, since each of these variables can, in another context, be directly observed. A squalling child can introspect and "observe" his own anger. One may touch a flame. Somewhere census data must be available which give the correlation between Cadillac-ownership and annual income. So it would be possible to get very good evidence as to the trustworthiness of these signs. How "good" these signs are would hinge on how strong the correlation is between the sign and what it supposedly signifies. Flame, surely, would turn out to be a perfectly reliable indicator of heat. A tantrum as signifying anger might be just slightly less trustworthy. And Cadillac-ownership would be a less good sign of wealth; here, the correlation would be much less strong, with a goodly percentage of exceptions.[1]

These "signs" will be termed *indices*. Any evidence that the sign signifies rightly, we shall call evidence for the validity of the sign or index. For flames as an index of heat, we could get very strong evidence that the index is very valid or trust-

[1] In these particular examples we are concerned with only one kind of exception: the poor Cadillac owner, non-angry child, cool flame. We would not count exceptions of the other type: rich non-Cadillac owner, quietly angry child, hot substance which emits no flame.

worthy. For tantrum as an index of anger, we could get somewhat less strong evidence [2] that the index is also fairly valid, reasonably trustworthy. For Cadillac as index of wealth, we would probably find good evidence that the sign is somewhat valid—more often right than wrong.

The usual inferred variable, however, can never be directly observed; therefore, whatever its index, no direct test for probable validity is possible. Various roundabout tests are resorted to, but they are doomed to be considerably weaker than the example-tests just referred to. Inferred variables, indices, the validity problem, and evidence for validity are discussed in Chapter 5.

A particular hypothesis may cite one or more inferred variables. Each or any inferred variable in the hypothesis may be counted as a separate source of doubt. Inferred variables again pose the conflict between significance and likelihood of truth. The higher reaches of science—high-level laws, theories well up on the hierarchy of generality—are phrased in terms of inferred-variable hypotheses. Much of the more interesting discourse about human behavior—concerning motives, aptitudes, personality traits, attitudes—likewise takes the form of inferred-variable hypotheses. If they could be eliminated by fiat, one's "information" and picture of the world would shrivel drastically; and some branches of social science would practically disappear.

D. A *cause-effect hypothesis* says that one variable is a cause for another; it helps make it happen; or the magnitude of the effect-variable is contingent, to some degree, on the magnitude of the cause-variable. The effect is, in part, a result of the cause. The cause is ordinarily seen as coming first in time. A case first "gets" or is subjected to or acquires an increment of the cause-variable; then, as a result, the case acquires or shows an increment of the effect-variable. An example would be: "Broken homes are a cause for juvenile delinquency." If a boy lives in a broken home, this makes him more likely (after experiencing the broken home) to become a delinquent.

[2] Here the evidence runs into some minor problems with respect to sources-of-doubt G and H.

Minimal evidence for a cause-effect statement comes from a correlation (ordinarily positive) between the presumed cause-variable and effect-variable. If it is true that broken homes are a cause for delinquency, then if we studied a sample of boys, we should expect to find a positive correlation between these two variables. The delinquents should show a higher rate of coming-from-broken-homes than should the nondelinquents. Furthermore, if our cause-effect statement is true, it must be generally true, in whatever population we are talking about, that delinquents show a higher rate of broken homes.

Any such correlational evidence in support of a cause-effect hypothesis must jump two other hurdles before it becomes really strong. If variables *A* and *B* are positively correlated, there are three possible reasons, excluding mere coincidence, for the correlation. *A* is a cause for *B* (as our example-hypothesis says). *B* is a cause for *A* (the presumed effect is actually the cause). Some third variable or group of variables —let us call this *C*—is acting as a cause for both *A* and *B* in such a way as to make them covary. (Actually, several of these possibilities could combine to produce the correlation between *A* and *B*.) The *B*-causing-*A* possibility can be eliminated if we have before-after conditions; that is, if the presumed cause-variable precedes the presumed effect-variable in time. In the above example this is not absolutely clear-cut; but we might be able to make out a fair case that *first* some of the boys lost father and/or mother, and *later* some of the boys turned to crime. The other possibility, which might be represented as

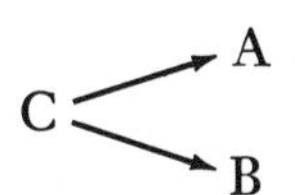


can be strongly handled by an experiment in which the presumed cause-variable is under the control of the experimenter; he "gives" it to some cases, withholds it from others, and then measures the effect-variable. In our example, this would involve depriving some boy of parents, making sure that other boys in the sample kept their parents, and then later noting whether each boy turned to crime. Of course this is impossible; it often is, with hypotheses about human behavior. If an experiment is not feasible, a much weaker alternative is to "hold constant" certain possible "variable-C's," either in the sample selection or by means of "statistical controls" and multivariate analysis. This, along with the general topic of cause and effect, is discussed in Chapter 7.

At any rate, assessing a cause-effect hypothesis for likelihood of truth involves first looking for the minimal evidence, the correlation. Then, how nearly source-of-doubt D has been "answered" depends on how well the other two possibilities regarding the direction of causation have been dealt with: Are there before-after conditions? Was the correlation derived from an experiment or, lacking that, were some holding-constant operations performed? Also, of course, the hypothesis may present some other sources of doubt besides D. For one thing, it will always be a generalization beyond known cases.

The causal hypothesis, then, makes very special demands on the evidence. Its more modest counterpart, the noncausal correlation statement which merely says, "Delinquents tend to come from broken homes," could very well be true, while the more ambitious "Broken homes are a cause for delinquency" was false.

Cause-effect statements are needed to express the consequences of human actions. In order to answer such questions as "What will this policy lead to?" and "What must we do to achieve that state of affairs?" we must invoke causation. Again, significance collides with likelihood of truth.

It might be mentioned in passing that sources-of-doubt B, C, and D are fairly standard in the social sciences. The usual hypothesis which the psychologist, sociologist, political scientist, or economist tries to document through research is a generalization beyond known cases, *and* an inferred variable hypothesis, *and* a cause-effect statement. Predictions (documented solely on the basis of past trends), necessary-cause statements, and compound hypotheses receive relatively little attention.

E. What was just discussed under source-of-doubt D was actually the most modest and undemanding type of cause-effect statement. It did not say that *A* was *the* cause for *B*, or that *B* always resulted from *A*, or that *A* was necessary before *B* could happen. It merely said that *A* was one cause for *B*, that *A* "helps make *B* happen." Therefore, such a statement can be true, even if some cases are found which "experience" *A* yet fail to exhibit *B*, and "show" *B* without "experiencing" *A*. In our example, a fairly weak correlation between broken homes and delinquency could stand as favorable evidence for an hypothesis of this type, since the hypothesis makes allowance for exceptions: some delinquents from intact homes, and some nondelinquents from broken homes.

One may, of course, state one of the more ambitious causal hypotheses. A *necessary-cause hypothesis* says that *A* is necessary before *B* can happen; no child becomes delinquent unless he has experienced a broken home. The sufficient-cause hypothesis is the mirror image of the necessary-cause: all children from broken homes become delinquent. These two assertions can even be combined into a necessary-and-sufficient-cause-effect hypothesis: all those—and only those—children who come from broken homes become delinquent.

All causal hypotheses demand, as minimal evidence, an observed correlation between cause-variable and effect-variable. While the more modest causal hypothesis—what we shall term the non-necessary-cause-effect hypothesis—leaves room for exceptions, these more ambitious hypotheses rule out exceptions of certain types; hence, they leave themselves more vulnerable to unfavorable evidence.

If a necessary-cause hypothesis is true, we should find no cases who exhibit *B* and did not experience *A*: no delinquents who did not come from broken homes. If the correlational evidence does include any cases of this sort, the evidence is unfavorable to the necessary-cause hypothesis (even though it may be favorable to the less stringent non-necessary-cause hypothesis).[3]

If a sufficient-cause hypothesis is true, exceptions of the opposite type should be absent: no children from broken homes who fail to become delinquent. Finally, the necessary-and-sufficient cause demands a perfect correlation; any exception constitutes unfavorable evidence.

Even if available evidence for one of these more stringent causal hypotheses is favorable, there is still no assurance that future samplings of the population being generalized about might not turn up the wrong kind of exceptions; if this were to happen, the assembled evidence might still be favorable to the non-necessary-cause hypothesis, but it would now be unfavorable to the necessary- or sufficient-cause hypotheses.

Therefore, if one wishes to add up sources of doubt for a particular hypothesis, he can credit it with at least one source of doubt if it is a cause-effect hypothesis of any sort. If it is either a necessary- or sufficient-cause statement, another source of doubt can be added. If it is necessary-and-sufficient, two more sources of doubt must be added.

In the exact sciences some of these more stringent causal statements are actually stated and tested. We in the social sciences, on the other hand, deal routinely with "statistical trends," exception-ridden and imperfect correlations. The human subject matter is notoriously ill-behaved, as compared with the regular habits of stars, planets, and other physical objects. Hence it is the rare social scientist who has the temerity to state a necessary- or sufficient-cause hypothesis.

One important qualification must be made of this last statement. A special type of necessary-cause statement does receive heavy use in everyday life and in speculative writings about human affairs. That is, social scientists, and everyone else, use it regularly. This is the *explanation for a single case.* This cites a reason for one event: "World War II would not have occurred if it had not been for Hitler's madness." "The Castro

[3] There is a qualification to this, which will be made in a moment.

revolution would have failed, had it not been for the unpopularity of the Batista regime." "He caught cold because he went out without his rubbers." "Acquisition of horses from the south made possible the flowering of Plains Indian culture."

All single-case explanations should be construed as necessary-cause statements, since they say that *B* (the effect) would not have happened if *A* (the presumed cause) had not occurred. *A* was necessary for this case before *B* could happen.

The single case can never "explain itself"; rather, all single-case explanations refer back to causal generalizations (Gibson 1960:29–42; Popper 1959:60; Kemeny 1959:49). If it is true that he caught cold because he went out without his rubbers, then it must be true that going out without one's rubbers is one reason why people catch cold. If the explanation for the Cuban revolution is right, then it must be true that the unpopularity of a regime tends to cause the regime to be overthrown. (For the other two examples, what the appropriate causal generalization should be is unclear.)

Likelihood of truth for a single-case explanation depends on the strength of the evidence for whatever causal generalization is invoked; it also depends, like any necessary-cause statement, on the presence of exceptions in the supporting data. Its demands for evidence are similar to, but not quite so stringent as, the demands of the other type of necessary-cause statement, the necessary-cause generalization. To illustrate this, as well as the evidence-demands of all types of causal statements, let us consider Table III. The data in this table are fictitious. However, Seymour Lipset (1960) and Philips Cutright (1963) have given real evidence on the relationship between economic development and democratic government. Stable and successful democracy tends to occur in relatively rich and industrially developed countries.

Table III shows a pronounced positive correlation between economic development and presence of stable democracy. The trend is followed by 82 countries; there are 19 exceptions. It gives minimal[4] but favorable evidence for the more modest causal hypothesis (i.e., an hypothesis which does not state a necessary or sufficient cause), which merely states, "Industrial development makes stable democracy more likely."

TABLE III

FICTITIOUS CORRELATION BETWEEN DEGREE OF ECONOMIC DEVELOPMENT AND PRESENCE OF STABLE DEMOCRATIC GOVERNMENT

| | *Degree of industrial development* | |
|---|---|---|
| | "High," well advanced | "Low," underdeveloped |
| Stable democracy present | 32 countries | 4 countries |
| Stable democracy absent | 15 countries | 50 countries |

Table III gives *un*favorable evidence for the necessary-cause generalization, "industrial development is a *prerequisite* of stable democracy." The 4 countries in the upper right-hand cell of the table, underdeveloped but stable democracies, give the lie to the notion that economic development is absolutely necessary. Likewise, the 15 exceptions in the lower left-hand cell refute the sufficient-cause statement that industrial development always eventuates in stable democracy. And all 19 exceptions stand as unfavorable evidence for the necessary-and-sufficient hypothesis.

A single-case explanation might be on the order of "The United States would not have achieved stable democracy if it had not been economically developed." Here, I think, evidence is favorable. The causal generalization which must be invoked, "Economic development aids democratic government," gets support from the table. Also, the table gives odds, in a sense, for the truth of the single-case explanation. Of the

[4] The data do not come from an experiment, and before-after conditions cannot be demonstrated.

54 underdeveloped nations in the table, 4 are stable democracies. It suggests that the odds are rather long, perhaps less than 1 to 10, against an underdeveloped country's having stable democratic government. For this reason, I think, the table gives evidence favorable to this single-case explanation.

This "looking for exceptions" which necessary- and/or sufficient-cause hypotheses demand, we might term *tests for negative cases*. The "something extra" which an hypothesis of this sort requires—in addition to the positive correlation and to evidence regarding direction of causation—is a test for negative cases. For the necessary-cause generalization (and for the sufficient-cause, and the necessary-and-sufficient), the test for negative cases is most stringent. *Any* exception of the "wrong sort" constitutes unfavorable evidence. For the single-case explanation the test for negative cases is more lenient; here, it devolves on a calculation of odds.

Still, the single-case explanation, like any other necessary-cause statement, presents an extra source of doubt. In the example above, it might be true that economic development aids democratic government; and yet, in spite of the long odds, the United States might have been one of those rare countries which could have achieved democracy in the absense of economic development.

In closing, it might be mentioned that the necessary-cause generalization, if true, is a particularly useful and powerful type of hypothesis. It enables prediction statements that tell us how to build systems which will work: motors, electric circuits, football plays, well-performed symphonies. The non-necessary-cause hypothesis will not yield this sort of useful prediction.

F. A *compound hypothesis* states three or more interdependent relationships; usually, these are phrased (or may be construed) in cause-effect terms. It is most commonly used to explain further a cause-effect relationship by citing a "reason" for it, or by stating a mechanism through which it operates.

An example Zeisel gives is: "Women have fewer accidents

because they drive less (1957:192)." The reason sex is a cause for accident rate is that sex is a cause for rate of miles driven, and rate of miles driven is a cause for accident rate. The more you drive, the more likely you are to have an auto accident; men drive more than women; this is why (or one reason why) men have more accidents. Construed in this way, Zeisel's hypothesis breaks down into three cause-effect statements. In order for the entire compound hypothesis to be true, each of the three part-hypotheses must be true.[5] Hence, sources of doubt have been multiplied.

Compound hypotheses are discussed in Chapter 7.

This concludes the preliminary review of the six sources of doubt that may reside in the hypothesis itself. When judging a particular hypothesis for likelihood of truth, one must first "construe" or interpret the hypothesis for himself—decide what it "means" to him—and then, when this is done, count how many sources of doubt the hypothesis presents. A given hypothesis, depending on how it is construed, may show none of these sources of doubt, or it may present one or several. Its likelihood of truth depends on how many sources of doubt are present, and to what extent the judge decides the sources of doubt have been "answered" or dispelled by the sorts of special evidence which they "ask for."

Likelihood of truth, of course, depends not simply on what the hypothesis "says," but also on the nature of any observer-reports which have been marshaled as supporting evidence. This remains to be discussed under remaining sources-of-doubt G and H. Also, one final characteristic of the hypothesis, which weighs heavily in any estimate of likelihood of truth, remains to be treated. This is the margin for error which the hypothesis provides. This becomes crucial when one considers the possible effect of observer-error on any favorable evidence which has been presented, and it is discussed under source-of-doubt H.

[5] Actually, evidence is needed for only two of them. If it is true that sex is a determinant of rate of miles driven, and that rate of miles driven is a cause for accident rate, then it follows that sex is a real—if remote—cause for accident rate.

Before we get into this, let us retrace our steps, and consider the sources-of-doubt notion from different angles.

## An Inductive Example

Numerous studies show a positive correlation between level of education and voting. People with many years of schooling are more inclined to vote than are people with few years of schooling. This evidence can be used in support of a variety of conclusions. If we took any one of the surveys which supply this evidence, the safest conclusion would be the cautious statement of findings, in such form as, "In our sample, we found a positive correlation between years of schooling and voting turnout." For this hypothesis there is just one source of doubt, H—the residual doubt, always present to some extent, about the accuracy of the observer-reports. Or the conclusion could be stated as, "People with many years of schooling are more inclined to vote than are people with few years of schooling." Now another source of doubt has been added. Presumably, this hypothesis talks about some population of voters from which any studies have merely sampled; it is a generalization beyond known cases. Conceivably, the correlation might emerge from any samples studied, and yet not obtain in the population at large; in other words, perhaps the favorable evidence was simply the result of biased samples.

We might get more ambitious and make a cause-effect conclusion: "Education promotes voting." Another source of doubt has been added. Even if it were generally true that the better educated were more inclined to vote, this still might having nothing to do with education's causing or promoting the inclination to vote. Perhaps the correlation stems from some "variable *C*," which might be something to do with social class or parents' income and which acts as a determinant for both years of schooling *and* proneness to vote, thus producing the correlation.

We might go further and add inferred variables: "The ignorant are less inclined to vote." This has one inferred variable, ignorance, as represented by the years-of-schooling index. Or we might put two inferred variables in the conclusion, thus raising two more sources of doubt: "The ignorant tend to be less interested in politics." Finally, we could also add the causal inference to this: "Ignorance alienates people from politics." Now we have a generalization beyond known cases, a cause-effect statement, and two inferred variables: four sources of doubt, in addition to source-of-doubt H.

Sources of doubt can be viewed as special inferences which can be made from the data. Thus, starting with the observed correlation, we made a generalizing inference (to a larger population), and then a causal inference, and then inferences about unobserved variables ("ignorance" and "disinterest" or "alienation"). Each such inference can be viewed as a special reason why the hypothesis might not be true, even in the presence of the minimal favorable evidence.

## The Principle of Multiple Contingency

This term refers to a more formal, and fancier, way of rationalizing the sources-of-doubt notion. Let us start with a convention —what we shall call the *strong-condition/weak-condition convention*—in which an hypothesis that presents a particular source of doubt is matched against another hypothesis, similar to it in all respects but one: it does *not* present this source of doubt. This is exemplified in the paradigm on page 39.

Thus the weak condition presents the source of doubt in question, while its strong-condition counterpart does not. The weak condition "says more" than its strong-condition mate. For it to be true, other things must be true. We might say that its truth depends on the truth of other, subsidiary, hypotheses. Or we might say that the supporting evidence it requires refers back to evi-

| Source of doubt | Strong condition | Weak condition |
|---|---|---|
| A. Prediction | "Poorly educated people are less likely to vote." | "In the next election, the poorly educated people will be less inclined to vote." |
| B. Generalization beyond known cases | "In our sample, the poorly educated people were less likely to vote." | "Poorly educated people are less likely to vote." |
| C. Inferred variable | "Poorly educated people (i.e., with few years of schooling) are less likely to vote." | "Ignorant people are less likely to vote." |
| D. Cause-effect | "Ignorant people are less likely to vote." | "Ignorance causes people not to vote." |
| E. Necessary cause (single case) | "Ignorance causes people not to vote." | "He didn't vote because he is ignorant." |
| F. Compound hypothesis | "Ignorance causes people not to vote." | "Ignorance causes people not to vote because it makes them less likely to see the importance of voting." |

dence in support of other, subsidiary, hypotheses. One of these subsidiary hypotheses is its strong-condition counterpart.

Actually, what subsidiary hypotheses are invoked by a particular source of doubt is to some extent open to argument. One possible rundown of subsidiary hypotheses for each source of doubt might go as follows:

A. The *prediction* depends, first of all, on the statement of a trend which has been observed in the past; the trend may be more or less strong, and more or less solidly documented. "Poorly educated people are less likely to vote." Also, perhaps, it hinges on another subsidiary hypothesis which says "This trend will continue into the future," and still another which says "The predicted event(s) will conform to the trend." Put another way: any evidence in support of a prediction—short of actually checking it, in the future—comes from a past trend. If such a trend is invoked, it becomes problematic whether the trend actually exists and whether—if it does exist —it will continue into the future, and whether the predicted future event(s) will conform to it.

B. The *generalization beyond known cases* requires two subsidiary hypotheses. One is the statement of sample findings—the statement which gives any evidence in support of the generalization beyond known cases—in other words, its "strong condition": "In our sample, the poorly educated people were less likely to vote." The other subsidiary hypothesis is the assumption necessary to extend the sample findings to a population: "In the rest of the population, not studied, this trend holds," or something of the sort.

C. The *inferred-variable hypothesis* likewise rests on a subsidiary hypothesis which states any supporting evidence. "Amount of schooling is positively correlated with voting turnout." It also demands another statement which links the index (i.e., the observed variable) with the inferred variable: "Little schooling is a 'good sign' or a 'valid index' of ignorance," or "The evidence is not spuriously favorable because of the low correspondence between years of schooling and degree of ignorance," or something of this nature.

D. The *cause-effect statement* demands, first of all, a correlation between the presumed cause-variable and effect-variable. In other words, its weak-condition counterpart must be true. One could say that it needs one more subsidiary hypothesis which says, "The reason variables $A$ and $B$ correlate is that $A$ is a cause for $B$." However, the business of trying to "answer" the source of doubt raised by the cause-effect statement—that is, furnishing evidence with respect to the direction of causation—actually involves documenting *three* additional subsidiary hypotheses: "The correlation between *A* and *B* is not simply due to the fact that *B* is a cause for *A*." "Neither is it simply due to the fact that some third variable or group of variables, *C*, acts as a cause for both *A* and *B* so as to make them covary." "Neither is it due to a combination of these two possibilities." As mentioned before, the "strong" test of a causal hypothesis is an experiment; it can furnish fairly good evidence in support of all three subsidiary hypotheses.

E. As the representative of the more stringent and exacting forms of causal statements, let us take an explanation for a single case, one species of *necessary-cause* hypothesis. "He didn't vote because he is ignorant." This refers back to a causal generalization, "Ignorance is a cause for nonvoting." It requires one more subsidiary hypothesis, something in the nature of "This principle accounts for the case in question."

F. The *compound hypothesis* breaks down into part-hypotheses. If the example in the paradigm is true, it must be true that ignorance is a cause for nonvoting (the compound hypothesis' strong condition form), ignorance is a cause for not seeing the importance of voting, and not seeing the importance of voting is a cause for not voting—three subsidiary hypotheses here. Also, to give the compound hypothesis any chance of being true, we should probably word it more conservatively: "*One reason* why ignorance causes people not to vote is because it makes them less likely to see the importance of voting."

To sum up: the truth of any hypothesis presenting one of these sources of doubt hinges on the truth of several subsidiary hypotheses. Operating within the strong-condition/weak-condition convention: for the weak-condition form of any hypothesis, one of its subsidiary hypotheses is its strong-condition counterpart. If the strong condition is not true, then the weak condition is not true either. If evidence for the strong condition is lacking or unfavorable, the same holds for the weak condition. But the strong condition may be true, although the weak condition is untrue. For the weak condition to be true, *all* subsidiary hypotheses—inferences or assumptions—on which it rests must be true.[6]

With this fixed in mind, let us turn back to the dictum of the philosophers of science: *No* hypothesis can be proved. Evidence for any hypothesis comes from observer-reports, and we can never be absolutely certain that the observer-reports "match" the reality they try to describe. Because of this assumptive gap, then, between reality and any descriptions of it, evidence is never air-tight. It may be very strong and persuasive, but never absolutely certain. Thus, if the likelihood of truth of hypotheses could be stated numerically, they might be rated .20 ("Chances are 1 to 4 it is true"), .50 ("This coin, when flipped, will come up heads"), .99 ("You will die"), and so forth; but no hypothesis' truth-value could ever be rated 1.00, absolutely certain.

If we accept the dictum that no hypothesis can be proved, this gives us our *principle of multiple contingency*. Each subsidiary hypothesis which a statement requires can be viewed as a special reason why the statement may be untrue. The more of these "reasons" there are, the lower the statement's likelihood of truth. Furthermore, the statement's likelihood of truth is always less than the truth-value of any of its subsidiary hypotheses. (Thus, the weak condition is always less likely to be true than the strong condition; the strong condition is just one of several subsidiary hypotheses on which the weak condition rests.)

The statement's truth-value is some function of the truth-values of each of its subsidiary hypotheses; perhaps it is a multiple of them. For example, if the statement rests on two subsidiary hypotheses, each of which has a truth-value of .50, it would seem that the statement's likelihood of truth is $.50 \times .50$ or .25. An analogy would be the forecast, "The next two times you flip the coin it will come up heads." For this to be borne out, two little forecasts must both be true: "The first flip will yield heads," and

[6] Actually, a few special instances can be found where this breaks down. For example, "Poorly educated people are less likely to vote" might conceivably be true, even though its subsidiary hypothesis, "In our sample, the poorly educated people were less likely to vote" were untrue.

"The second flip will yield heads." Each, presumably, has a 50–50 chance of success; the total forecast will come true 1 time out of 4.

The likelihood of truth of an hypothesis, then, depends first of all on how many subsidiary hypotheses it requires: how many chances it has of being wrong. Secondly, it depends on the likelihood of truth of the subsidiary hypotheses. For these, likelihood of truth depends on strength of supporting evidence. If the subsidiary hypotheses are well documented, then the entire statement may have a fairly high likelihood of truth, short of certainty. Thus some of the more "difficult" hypotheses, which depend on numerous subsidiary statements, are more likely true than some simpler hypotheses which rest on no subsidiary hypotheses. An example would be "A gun won't fire unless it is loaded," as compared with "I have smiled 8,537,690 times in my life." [7]

Using the strong-condition/weak-condition convention, it is possible to arrange tests, of a sort, of some of the principles in our epistemological scheme. The strong-condition/weak-condition convention involves setting two hypotheses side by side; these two hypotheses are identical in all respects but one. One of them, the weak condition, presents a particular source of doubt; the other, the strong condition, does not. When this is done, then:

A. The *prediction* is less likely true than its strong-condition form, which does not predict.

B. The *generalization beyond known cases* is less likely true than its strong-condition form, which does not generalize beyond known cases.

C. The *inferred-variable hypothesis* is less likely true than its strong-condition form, which does not cite an inferred variable.

[7] Observer-reports, the substance of evidence, are of course little hypotheses in their own right. In a sense, they too are "subsidiary" to whatever hypothesis for which they stand as evidence. However, as we shall see when we reach a consideration of source-of-doubt H, many an hypothesis may be true even though some of the supporting observer-reports are untrue; the extent to which this is so depends on the margin for error provided by the hypothesis. Such is not the case for the species of "subsidiary hypotheses" we have been considering here. If any one of these is untrue, then the statement that rests on it is likewise untrue.

D. The *cause-effect statement* is less likely true than its strong-condition form, which merely states a correlation between the variables in question.
E. The *necessary-cause hypothesis* is less likely true than its strong-condition form, which merely states a non-necessary causal relationship.
F. A *compound hypothesis* is less likely true than its strong-condition form, which cites no mechanism or intervening variable.

# Testing the Sources-of-Doubt Notion

What I have done above is to state the sources-of-doubt notion in hypothesis form. Now each of these six hypotheses may be tested. The tests are rather peculiar, unusual for our treatment here, since they do not involve relating an hypothesis to evidence in order to rate it for likelihood of truth. Rather, they involve pitting the strong condition against the weak condition, to see which will enable the more successful prediction. The tests might go like this:

A. *The prediction is less likely true than its strong-condition counterpart, which does not predict.*

TEST 1. Coin flipping.

CASE: A series of two flips of a coin.

SAMPLE: 100 of these two-flip series.

Condition of the past-time statement (the strong condition): For each series, you flip the coin once, note whether it comes up heads or tails, then forecast whether or not both flips in the series will come up heads.

Condition of the prediction statement (the weak condition): For each series, before the first flip you predict whether it will come up heads or tails; then on this basis you forecast whether or not both flips in the series will come up heads.

On this test, the strong condition should yield better forecasts of consecutive-heads series than should the weak condition.[8]

TEST 2. Ball dropping.

CASE: You hold a rubber ball out a fourth-story window and release it.

SAMPLE: 100 of such trials.

Condition of the past-time statement (the strong condition): You release the ball and note whether or not it falls toward the ground. Then, on the basis of this observation (which you report to yourself, in a private observer-report) you forecast whether or not the ball will bounce within the next five seconds.

Condition of the prediction statement (the weak condition): Each time, before you release it, you predict whether the ball will fly downward (toward the ground) or not. On the basis of this prediction, you then forecast whether or not the ball will bounce within five seconds of release.

On this test the strong condition and weak condition should "tie," do equally well. Tests of each of the other sources-of-doubt hypotheses have been chosen in the same way, one test in which strong condition and weak condition should approach a tie; another test in which the strong condition should enable better forecasts. Each source-of-doubt hypothesis could be subjected to many such tests. If this were done, there should be some ties, some instances where the strong condition did better, and *no* (or practically none) tests where the weak condition forecast better; overall, the strong-condition form would have a better batting average.

B. *The generalization beyond known cases is less likely true than its strong-condition form, which does not generalize beyond known cases.*

[8] Qualification: if, in this particular test, the weak-condition player *never* predicted a consecutive-heads series, then he should do as well as the strong-condition player: about 75 percent successful forecasts.

TEST 1.

Strong condition (not a generalization beyond known cases): You count number of men and women for each of 100 towns. Then, for each town, you predict whether more or less than half the adult population will admit to wearing dresses.

Weak condition (generalization beyond known cases): For each of the 100 towns, you sample 10 percent of the population, noting whether there are more men or women in your sample. On the basis of your sample findings, you guess whether each town contains more men or women. Then, for each town, you forecast whether more or less than half the adult population will admit to wearing dresses.

TEST 2.

Strong condition (not a generalization beyond known cases): You observe 1,000 pigs and note, for each pig, whether or not he has wings. Then you predict how many of the pigs can fly.

Weak condition (generalization beyond known cases): You observe 100 of the 1,000 pigs, noting, for each pig you observe, whether or not he has wings. On the basis of your sample findings, you guess about how many of the 1,000 pigs have wings. Then you predict how many of them can fly.

C. *The inferred-variable hypothesis is less likely true than its strong-condition form, which does not cite an inferred variable.*

TEST 1.

Strong condition (no inferred variable): In a deck of playing cards, the backs of the cards are in 4 different colors, with each suit having its own color. All hearts are red, all diamonds are pink, all spades are black, and clubs are grey. You know this. On each of 100 trials, 5 cards are dealt out, face down. It is your task, on each trial, to say (or "predict") whether or not a flush has been dealt, on the basis of whether or not all 5 cards are the same color.

Weak condition (inferred variable). In this deck of playing

cards, the backs of the cards are in alternating colors; some red, others black. You know that all hearts and diamonds have red backs, and all clubs and spades have black. On each of 100 trials, 5 cards are dealt out, face down. It is your task, on each trial, to guess whether or not a flush has been dealt, on the basis of whether or not all 5 cards are the same color (either all red or all black).

TEST 2.

Strong condition (no inferred variable): You observe 100 naked children. For each child, you predict whether or not he or she will ever give birth to a baby.

Weak condition (inferred variable): You observe 100 fully clothed children. For each, you predict whether or not he or she will ever give birth.

D. *The cause-effect statement is less likely true than its strong-condition form, which merely states a correlation between the variables in question.*

TEST 1.

Strong condition (noncausal statement of correlation): You survey 100 men, asking each if he owns a new car. For each new-car owner, you predict he will earn over $10,000 during the coming year. For each old-car owner, you predict he will earn less than $10,000 during the coming year.

Weak condition (cause-effect statement): You present 50 of the men with new cars; the other 50 don't receive new cars. For each man who was given a new car, you predict he will earn over $10,000 during the coming year. For each man who was not given a new car, you predict he will earn less than $10,000 during the coming year.

TEST 2.

Strong condition (noncausal): You survey 100 men, asking each how much he earned during the past year. For each man who says he earned over $10,000, you predict he will buy a new car during the coming year. For each who says he earned less than $10,000, you predict he will not buy a new car during the coming year.

Weak condition (cause-effect): To half of the men you give some substantial sum of money—say, $5,000. You predict that each of those who was given the money will buy a new car during the coming year, and each of those who was not given $5,000 will not buy a car during the coming year.

E. *The necessary-cause hypothesis is less likely true than its strong-condition form, which merely states a non-necessary causal relationship.*

TEST 1.

You select 100 boys and give them golf lessons at age 12. When the boys reach 18, you note how many have average golf scores below 100. You select a second group of 100 boys and see to it that they do *not* have golf lessons at (or before) age 12. When they reach 18, you also note how many shoot below 100.

The strong-condition hypothesis (non-necessary-cause statement) predicts: There will be a positive correlation between golf lessons at age 12 and shooting below 100 at age 18.

The weak-condition hypothesis (necessary-cause statement) predicts: None of the boys without golf lessons at 12 will be shooting below 100 at 18.

TEST 2.

During 100 trials, you load a gun, cock it, and press the trigger. During a second 100 trials, you do *not* load the gun, but you cock it and press the trigger.

The strong condition hypothesis (non-necessary-cause statement) predicts: the gun will more often fire when it is loaded.

The weak condition hypothesis (necessary-cause statement) predicts: the gun will never fire when it is not loaded.

F. *A compound hypothesis is less likely true than its strong-condition form, which cites no mechanism or intervening variable.*

TEST 1.

A sample of 500 college students is measured for 3 variables: (1) sex (male versus female), (2) grade-point average, and (3) hours spent studying the previous week (by questionnaire).

The non-compound hypothesis (strong-condition statement) predicts: The girls will be found to have the higher grade-point average.

The compound hypothesis (weak-condition statement) predicts: (1) The girls will have the higher grade-point average; (2) the girls will have spent more hours studying; and (3) there will be a positive correlation between hours spent studying and grade-point average (i.e.: "Girls make better grades because they study more").

TEST 2.

A sample of 500 college students is measured for 3 variables: (1) sex, (2) school (Engineering versus Liberal Arts), and (3) hours spent studying the previous week.

The non-compound hypothesis predicts: The boys, on the average, studied more the previous week.

The compound hypothesis predicts: (1) The boys studied more; (2) the boys are more likely to be in Engineering School; and (3) those in Engineering School tend to study more ("The boys study more because they are more apt to be in Engineering").

If we wished, we could apply these tests to other principles in the epistemological scheme. We could "test" sources-of-doubt G and H in this fashion. We could "test" subsidiary points, which say what is required partially to "answer" or "overcome" particular sources of doubt—for example, that any supporting evidence is in less danger of being spuriously favorable if the hypothesis allows a good-sized margin for error, or that a generalization beyond known cases is more likely true if the supporting data come from a fair-sized sample.

These "tests," along with the principle of multiple contingency, require rather complicated reasoning. For this reason, perhaps, they should be taken with a grain of salt. In all instances of complex verbal arguments, given the imprecision of words themselves, there may be many a slip 'twixt the cup and the lip. They do represent alternative ways of rationalizing the sources-of-doubt notion. The simpler way of viewing sources of doubt is merely that they are special reasons why certain hypotheses may be untrue, even in the presence of favorable evidence.

The term "evidence" has been used repeatedly, but really very little has been said about it so far. Later chapters treat the special evidence called for by some of the sources of doubt. Thus Chapter 6 discusses sampling (for generalizations beyond known cases). Chapter 7 treats evidence for causal hypotheses and discusses evidence for compound hypotheses. Chapter 5 mentions some of the difficulties, puzzles, and controversial issues which arise if one tries to document an inferred-variable hypothesis. There is also the matter of the observer-reports themselves. Are they true? Is any evidence favorable simply because the observer-reports are not accurate? And finally, when do we have *any* evidence? How clear is it that any observer-reports which might be offered are even relevant, as evidence, to a particular hypothesis? We shall get into these questions in the middle of Chapter 3, and continue with them through Chapters 4 and 5. At this point they will be introduced in a discussion of the last two sources of doubt, G and H, those having to do not with the form of the hypothesis, but with the nature of any observer-reports which are offered as evidence.

## Sources of Doubt in the Evidence

In rather oversimplified version, these are G: Is there any evidence? and H: Is it right? Source-of-doubt H hinges on two general considerations: (1) What assurance do we have that there were not extensive observer-errors? and (2) How large is the margin for error allowed for in the hypothesis? Source-of-doubt G has to do with various gaps and lacunae which may enter in, between the point of observation and the point of evidence-judging; the seriousness of this source of doubt hangs on the clarity or vagueness of reports of observations, and the orderliness of the collating process, and the clarity of the hypothesis itself. Thus the last sentence in the preceding paragraph is not quite true. Even when we consider evidence as such, the form of the hypothesis is still crucial.

## SOURCE-OF-DOUBT G: IS THERE ANY EVIDENCE?

If an hypothesis is to be judged on the basis of evidence, it must be related to observer-reports. In Chapter 1, the example of this relating process was the students' ages. The teacher asked each student his age, put the answers into a table on the blackboard, and used the assembled answers to document the hypothesis "Most of you are under 21." The observer-reports were furnished by the students. Each student "observed" and then classified himself with respect to the variable—age. The person who collated the evidence was the teacher. He brought together the observer-reports, put them in a little table, and then related them to an hypothesis—his conclusion. Here, source-of-doubt G has been completely dispelled. The reported observations, in sum, clearly "agree" with the teacher's conclusion. They are relevant as evidence, no doubt about that. Source-of-doubt H still remains; the hypothesis might be untrue because some of the students lied. But for this example, we can forget about source-of-doubt G.

The raw material of evidence is reported observations, made by someone. In order for these observer-reports to stand as evidence for some hypothesis, they must be brought together, collated by someone and then "related back" to the hypothesis. If, on balance, they "agree with" the hypothesis, evidence is favorable. If they "disagree with" the hypothesis, evidence is unfavorable to the hypothesis. In the absence of this relating process, we might say that the hypothesis has no evidence to support it, or to indicate that it is true.

So far, this is simple enough. But source-of-doubt G turns out to be a difficult one. For many hypotheses, it is not clear whether anyone has gone through this relating process, or who the collator was, or what and how many cases were observed, or how the cases were classified. The assembled observations—whatever they might be—are not neatly brought together in a table or a data sheet. We may not know who the observers were (if there were any), or by what rules or judgments the cases were given scores on the variable in question.

In other words, for some hypotheses there is obviously relevant evidence ("Most of you are under 21"). For other hypotheses, there clearly is not ("Arthritis is caused by orgone deficiency"). But many other hypotheses are in a twilight zone, neither clearly documented nor undocumented. For these, it is to some extent a matter of opinion and arbitrary choice as to whether evidence is available or not.

In fact, one's decision about source-of-doubt G always hinges on his philosophic starting point and hence is to some extent arbitrary. When do we actually have evidence? Or, when can a person—we shall call him Ego—who entertains a particular hypothesis actually relate it to observations, in order to judge it on the evidence? One possible answer is: "Only when he saw it." Only when Ego himself is the observer and the collator, can Ego actually relate an hypothesis to observations.

Operating under this stricture, one could still document many of the everyday and generally trivial hypotheses which he states to himself mentally: "My pipe is lit," "She is coughing a lot tonight," "The speedometer reads 55," and so forth. Ego is the observer. When collating is necessary, he is also the collator. For many of these homely little hypotheses, no collating is required. The hypothesis concerns a single case. It is not a generalization. The observer-report (which Ego makes to himself) *is* the hypothesis. It is not related (as evidence) to some other hypothesis.

Of course, if we were faithful to this stricture, there would be a number of drastic consequences—the elimination of science, for one. The abolition of the news media might be another. Even ordinary conversation, or the reception of it, would take a new and peculiar form. Thus a more lenient philosophic starting point is more or less forced on us, if we wish to relate a wider range of descriptive statements to sense impressions. This one says: "Hypotheses *may* be related to observations, even if Ego is not the observer, and even if Ego is not the collator of any evidence." All of us, I am sure, do operate under this assumption.

In practice, sometimes Ego is the observer, sometimes not. The observations are passed on to him by someone else, as with the teacher who is told by his students, "I am 18," "I am 20," and so forth. Sometimes Ego is presented with a set of presumed observations, one or several of which were made by him and others of which come secondhand: as with any student in the teacher's class, who can "observe" his own age (in a sense, at least), but must be told the other students' ages. In everyday life, many generalizations on the order of "Rats have whiskers," "Big cities have heavy traffic," and "Smiles do not necessarily indicate happiness" are "documented" in this fashion.

Sometimes Ego is the collator, as was the teacher. The students were in on the collating process too; they sat in the classroom, gave their ages, saw the evidence go up on the blackboard, and then could relate the data in the table to the teacher's conclusion. Often Ego is neither the observer nor the collator. An hypothesis is simply presented to him, with some allusion to (or implication of) evidence: "The literacy rate in Puerto Rico is on the rise." "We have a stockpile of $x$ number of Polaris missiles." "Slum clearance reduces the rate of tuberculosis." "Economic development enables successful democratic government."

When this happens, Ego himself does not really "have" evidence that he can relate to the hypothesis. The question "*Is* there any evidence?" hangs on whether the author of the hypothesis —or someone—has assembled observer-reports and has related them to the hypothesis. The statement or implication that "evidence is available" must be accepted on faith, if it is accepted at all; and this goes for the hypothesis itself. Of course, this faith-judgment may take the form of a sophisticated guess, weighing the possibility that supporting observations were actually made, and that any observer-reports could be clearly stated, and that the collating process was orderly.

Sometimes, when Ego is presented with an hypothesis, he is "given some evidence" in support of it. This "supporting evidence" is some kind of account of something that was done in the observing or collating process. It may be more or less explicit and detailed, more or less complete. At one end of the continuum is the generalizer who cites an example to "prove his point." At the other end is the German experimentalist who, in the report of his study, gives pictures of his laboratory apparatus, explains his method of measurement and the experimental conditions in some detail, describes his experimental animals down to such details as sex, age, weight, and their individual names, and reports the collating process in data sheets, tables, and charts.

When presumed evidence is given in some detail, Ego is in a better position to judge whether there is any relevant evidence. Even though he did not "see" the evidence—it comes to him secondhand—he can better judge whether someone else *did* "see" it. In other words, he can better judge whether the relevance of presumed observations to the hypothesis, as evidence, is at all problematic: whether the "fit" between observer-reports and hypothesis is obvious and neat—as with "Most of you are over 21"; or whether, due to the vagaries of observation, or collating of observations, or the hypothesis itself, the "fit" is not at all obvious—as with "The popularity of existential philosophy stems from the identity crisis of Modern Man."

We are now ready to consider this fit. It depends on three factors: (1) the clarity of observer-reports, (2) the orderliness of the collating process, and (3) the clarity of the hypothesis itself. We will start with the second factor, the manner of collating.

Much of the special persuasiveness of "research," measurement-based studies, comes from orderly collating. Ordinarily a written record is kept of how many cases fell under observation and how each case was classified by the observer. The measurement yields numerical scores, which are written down. If discrete observations are combined to give summary scores to cases—in other words, if "scaling" is done—then the scaling convention is explicitly stated, [9] and it is presumed to have been applied in a standard

[9] Whether or not the scaling convention is explicitly stated in the research report, the researcher is at least presumed to have an explicit scaling convention in hand when he gives cases their scale scores.

manner to all cases in the sample. All the cases' scores can be "pulled together" on data sheets or IBM cards. The quantified data can be summarized in tables, graphs, or statistics, all according to explicit, orderly rules. If the initial observer-reports, or "measurements," are clear, and if the hypothesis to be documented is clear, then the observer-reports are obviously relevant to the hypothesis, as evidence. The example of the students' ages, in its humble way, exemplifies the research model.

We shall deal with this in more detail in Chapter 4. For the moment, let us turn to *dis*orderly and problematic collating. This sort of thing is more or less forced upon all of us. It is part of the fabric of our lives. Many generalizations cannot or have not been "tested" in the course of measurement-based research. In the absence of quantified data, we fall back on impressionistic evidence: "People in Georgia have southern accents." "Beautiful girls are more narcissistic than are homely girls." "A nation's international behavior is governed primarily by its own national self-interest."

Suppose Ego is asked to entertain such an hypothesis. Let us say that no research evidence is available. Rather than judging the hypothesis merely on the basis of faith, he may try to refer it to some observations. Perhaps he made some observations himself which he deems relevant. He has been to Georgia. Maybe he remembers others' accounts of observations which seem to "fit." Perhaps it is dimmer than this: he has the feeling he has heard or read various things in the past which indicate that others have made the relevant observations. This sort of mental "collating" is, of course, a jumbled mess. The steps of the process are generally so shrouded in mists that Ego himself has little idea of what happened. How many cases were observed? What cases? How were cases classified? How was each case classified with respect to the variable in question? What did the collating process consist of? When the presumed observer-reports were "pulled together," how did they "add up"?

Is such "impressionistic evidence" really evidence at all? Since the collating process—the link between observer-reports and hypothesis—is so obscure, this is a real question. In practice, such evidence can often inspire great conviction ("Rats have whiskers"). Perhaps the relevance problem is a bit less serious if Ego himself has made some of the observations. It also helps if the required observations are fairly "easy" to make, to report to one's self clearly, and to remember ("This rat has whiskers" as opposed to "That boy is experiencing a crisis of identity"). It likewise helps if the hypothesis itself is clear.

In other words, the orderliness of the collating process is one of three factors to consider when judging the relevance-fit between hypothesis and presumed observations. When the collating involves dredging one's memory and groping for impressionistic evidence, the dubiousness of any such "evidence" depends on the other two factors also. Reasonably clear observer-reports, clear hypothesis—these help. Thus Ego has some right to believe that rats have whiskers.

Let us now consider the other two factors. For simplicity's sake, we will keep to the example of the students' ages. In this instance, both the hypothesis and the supporting observer-reports are clear enough so that there is no doubt about the fit or relevance of the observer-reports ("I am 18," "I am 20," etc.) to the hypothesis ("Most of you are under 21"). The variable is age, in years. There should be unanimous agreement as to what the term "age" means, and as to what sort of answer the question "How old are you?" calls for. Surely, the question was interpreted in the same way by all the students. We, who are presented the evidence, are likewise in agreement as to what each point on the age scale means, and as to what a particular observer-report ("I am 24") means. Also, this agreement is fairly explicit. There is no doubt about what each scale point and each answer represents, or about the difference (in age) between 18 years old and 19 years old, or about what a case should "have" to be classified "19 years old." In giving the observer-reports, the students classified themselves with an *explicit sorting criterion.* Also, the sorting criterion must have been invariant: meaning the same thing to each student (and to us), classifying each case according to the same rule, or convention, or definition of the scale points.

For the hypothesis "Most of you are under 21," the variable is still age. The variable about which the hypothesis talks can be defined explicitly, and it is the same variable which was cited in the supporting observer-reports. Combine this with orderly collating, and you have an obvious, nonproblematic fit between observer-reports and hypothesis.

Now let us change this a bit, so that it is not so clear whether evidence is available or not. From the data in the table, the teacher concludes: "Most of you are immature." He takes the observations noted in the table, the reports of age, as indices or signs of an inferred variable, degree of maturity. He assumes that people "high" on the age variable, 21 or over, are mature, "high" on the maturity variable. In other words, he takes relatively advanced age (21 or over) as a sign of maturity, and relatively tender age (under 21) as a sign of immaturity. Since most of them are under 21, he concludes that most of them are immature.

This inferred-variable hypothesis, of course, raises a source of doubt. The "real relationship"—whatever it is—between age and maturity is unknown. There is a validity problem: Did his signs indicate rightly? In addition to this, the relevance problem has also come to the fore. What *is* "maturity"? According to the conventional meaning of the word, it means . . . what? Each of us, no doubt, has the feeling that he "knows what it means." But I doubt if anyone could say, explicitly, what one observes about a person in order to rate him at some point on a degree-of-maturity scale—either "mature" or "immature" or at some point in between.[10] The term "maturity" does not refer to the classification of cases according to clear rules, as does the term "age."

If an hypothesis cites a variable which is not clearly defined, then it is always problematic whether the hypothesis can be related to evidence. If we don't know, explicitly, what the term "maturity" means, then how do we know what sorts of observer-reports would be relevant, as evidence, for such hypotheses as "Most of you are immature" or "He is very mature"? In practice, many such unclear hypotheses are "tested" by research, and "related" to evidence. Yet in all such instances, the fit or relevance of any observations to the hypothesis is never obvious and

[10] Short of an unconventional definition, such as "Degree of maturity is how many years a person has lived."

"given," as it is with "Most of you are under 21." To say that such an hypothesis is supported by evidence requires "special allowances," a lapse of rigor, or something of the sort.

In Chapter 3 we will get further into questions of clarity. In Chapter 5 more will be said about the clarity-of-the-hypothesis problem, as it is posed by inferred-variable hypotheses. Now, let us briefly consider the "other end" of the clarity/relevance issue: the clarity of the observer-reports.

Suppose that the teacher gathered his "evidence" for the conclusion "Most of you are immature" in a different fashion. Since he knows his students fairly well, he considers each student's character, and then *rates* each either "mature" or "immature." Now the observer-reports are the designations "mature" and "immature" applied to each of these students, on the basis of these global judgments about each student's character.

These ratings were based on an inexplicit sorting criterion. I doubt that the teacher could tell us what behavior and mannerisms he observed in each student which made him designate the student "mature" or "immature." The teacher might object and say he *can* describe what led to each judgment; he might then cite one or several things he "observed about" each student. Even so, he could not tell us, clearly, what rule or standard he applied to each case in order to designate it "mature" or "immature." Suppose he tries to do this; he writes out for us his definition of maturity. Suppose further, for the sake of argument, that we have been in this classroom as long as he has; we have observed the same student-behavior that he has observed. We take his definition of maturity, apply it to each student, and thereby classify the students "mature" or "immature." If such a test of agreement were done, it would probably turn up some instances of disagreement—students classified "mature" by one observer and "immature" by another—due to the inexplicitness of the sorting criterion. Even though we all might feel that we "know what maturity means," that the definition is clear enough, when it gets down to the classification of individual cases, the sorting criterion is not really explicit. To apply it to a particular case, the observer must "add to it"—interpret, give subsidiary definitions. The more these interpretations differ from one observer to the next, the more, presumably, the disagreement.

The issue of the clarity of observer-reports and the explicitness of the sorting criterion is a difficult one. Judging clarity raises some controversial points; it is open to some differences of opinion. One possible approach to the clarity issue is presented in Chapters 3 and 5, and, as it relates to the observer-reports themselves, in Chapter 4.

For the moment, it is enough to say that if it is not clear what the observer-reports describe—if the sorting criterion is not made explicit—then any reported observations are not clearly relevant to a particular hypothesis, as evidence. One could cite more examples, where the nature of the sorting criterion might be even foggier than it is for the maturity rating. The teacher might have rated his students on egocentricity, or mental health, or impulsiveness, or sweetness, or expressiveness, or zepia, or other-directedness.

It might be mentioned in passing that measurement-based studies rate relatively high on the clarity of observer-reports and explicitness of sorting criteria. This is particularly true of research in the natural sciences. In the social sciences, monumental effort has been expended in trying to make the classifying rules, or measures, clear. But the nature of the subject matter resists this effort; the results have been spotty.

To sum up, one might think of the relating of evidence to an hypothesis as a three-step process: (1) statements of observations, (2) collating of these observer-reports, and (3) statement of the hypothesis itself. The observer-reports may be obviously related to the hypothesis, as with our well-worn example of the students' ages. Or at any point in the process, a shadow may fall: unclear observer-reports, slipshod collating, or unclear hypothesis. When this happens, the presence of evidence is no longer "a given." Whether or not one wishes to view the hypothesis as documented devolves on personal preference—whether one wishes to make special allowances.

The judgment of hypotheses (with their supporting "evidence") with respect to source-of-doubt G depends a great deal on personal preference. Whether this source of doubt even "exists," in a particular instance, is to some extent an arbitrary matter. In practice, there would be a good deal of disagreement about less "serious" cases, and perhaps fairly good agreement about the more serious instances. There are wide differences among individual observer-reports, and hypotheses,[11] as regards how clear or vague they are. Likewise, the collating process may present varying degrees of orderliness. Finally, the shadow may fall at only one point in the process, or at two points (as with the maturity ratings), or at all three ("Beautiful girls are more narcissistic than are homely girls").

## SOURCE-OF-DOUBT H: IS THE EVIDENCE SPURIOUSLY FAVORABLE?

This point has to do with observer-error. The question is not, "Was there any error?" Many an hypothesis can be well documented by flawed observer-reports. Rather, the question is, "Is the favorableness of any evidence due simply to observer-error?" Guessing about the seriousness of this source of doubt, for a particular hypothesis (with its accompanying evidence), raises a whole host of considerations. These could be conceptualized in various ways. Here, they are grouped under four points: the margin for error in the hypothesis; the presence or absence of consensual validation; the presence or absence of written records; and guesses about the magnitude and direction of error.

### *The Margin for Error*

The tolerance of error of hypotheses presents a broad continuum. Consider "I am between 5 feet 10 inches and 6 feet tall" as opposed to "I am between 5 feet 10 and 5 feet 10½ inches tall," "I am between 5 feet 10.1 and 5 feet 10.2 inches tall," and "I am exactly 5 feet 10.124 inches tall." As the margin for error dwindles, the hypothesis stands in greater and greater danger of

[11] The term "unclear hypothesis" is being used here to designate an hypothesis which cites a variable that cannot be clearly defined. This will be better explained in Chapter 3.

being untrue, because of a deviation in measurement. Likewise for generalizations: "X will win the election," as opposed to "He will receive over 55 percent of the vote," "He will receive between 56 and 58 percent of the vote," and "He will receive 57.2 percent of the vote."

If first the hypothesis is stated, and then data are gathered in order to test it, the margin for error is one determinant of the likelihood that the evidence will be *favorable*. This is illustrated by the election prediction. Even after the data are in, the margin for error must be weighed when judging the persuasiveness or strength of the evidence. The conclusion "He got 57.2 percent of the vote" might very well be wrong because of errors and hanky-panky during vote tabulation. A less precise conclusion, "He got over 55 percent of the vote," is in less danger of being spuriously documented; it leaves a margin for error.

Once the evidence is in, the margin for error does not depend solely on what the hypothesis says. Rather, it is the "play" or "distance" between the hypothesis and reported findings. "Over 55 percent of the voters voted for X" is more likely true if the vote tabulations credit him with 60 percent of the vote than it is if he is credited with 56 percent of the vote.

Statements of frequency may permit no margin for error: something "never" happens, or "always" happens, or happens "57.2 percent of the time." Or they may leave a small margin for error: something "rarely" happens, or "nearly always" happens, or happens "over 90 percent of the time," or "happens between 20 and 25 percent of the time." Or they may leave a really large margin for error: something happens "usually," "seldom," or "sometimes." Such statements may specify the limits of error ("happens over 75 percent of the time") or leave the margin for error unspecified and vague ("happens seldom").

An hypothesis which states a non-necessary-cause-effect relationship ("Broken homes are a cause for delinquency") or merely states a correlation ("Delinquents tend to come from broken homes") allows a large margin for error. It does not say how strong such a relationship is; it merely says that it exists. If we did a study to test such an hypothesis, any sort of positive correlation, even a weak one, would constitute favorable evidence. Of course, the stronger the correlation that emerged from the data, the less we need worry about the margin for error. With a strong correlation, there is more "leeway" between what the hypothesis states and what the data indicate; other things being equal, there is less chance of spuriously favorable evidence.

This is the usual sort of hypothesis that is stated and tested in social science—which is one of the major points of contrast between the *modus operandi* of social scientists and natural scientists. The hard scientist's hypothesis is ordinarily quite precise; margin for error is minimal. The same is true for the fabric of hypotheses which makes up modern technology ("This shaft will rotate properly within this bushing if the clearance is between .01 and .03 inches").

The virtue of the large-margin-for-error hypothesis is that it gives one some chance to be right, even in the face of considerable error. Most social scientists deal routinely with hypotheses of this sort for a very good reason: with the tools at their disposal, they would be foolhardy to do otherwise.

Some of these error-lenient hypotheses are of tremendous significance. They are well worth the trouble of testing. However they do lack a power of a special sort which does reside in the precise, error-intolerant hypotheses. These latter permit one to build systems which "work." An example is the previous one of shaft and bushing: a necessary-cause generalization,[12] with narrow tolerance limits. These, in combination, are the stuff of blueprints, designs, inventions. Once more: the conflict between significance and likelihood of truth.

## *Consensual Validation*

This term refers to a familiar commonsense notion: Two (or more) observers are better than one, especially if there is some reason for doubting the accuracy of the single observer's report. Thus in a court trial it is good to "have witnesses." The reasoning is that two or more observers are less likely to lie, hallucinate, or

[12] In a sense, any necessary-cause generalization permits no margin for error: any exception, and it is untrue.

otherwise distort than is a single observer; and even if they all do, it is unlikely that their reports will all agree with each other. Thus if several observers observe the same instance (or case), and if their ensuing observer-reports correspond with one other, the likelihood of observer-error is felt to be less than it would be if the observer-reports disagree, or if there is only one observer reporting. It also helps if precautions have been taken against collusion. The strongest consensual validation occurs when the observers give their reports before they discuss, among themselves, what they saw or heard.

In practice, consensual validation (of a sort) can occur at various points in the assembly of evidence. It need not be confined to the observer-reports or "raw data." The replication of a study is a sort of overall consensual validation of the study's statement of findings.[13] When raw data are then coded, several coders are customarily used and a test for agreement is done. This is, at least superficially, a kind of consensual validation, although actually the concern here is with the invariance or "reliability" of the coding rules, rather than with the accuracy of observation.

Sometimes the original observer-reports are subjected to consensual validation. This is rather uncommon in scientific research, I think; at least within the social sciences. In laboratory research, multiple observers (observing the same event) would be feasible, but ordinarily this is not deemed worth the trouble. Outside the laboratory, consensual validation of observer-reports is sometimes very difficult to arrange, often clearly impossible. Consensual validation—when it would be good to have, when it is impossible—will receive a bit more attention in Chapter 4.

### *Written Records*

Memory distortion is one source of error in the observer's report. If the observer immediately writes down how he classified a particular case, he obviates this source of error. Some things are easy to remember: for example, one's age, or that rat *X* had

[13] If the findings of two studies are at odds, this may be because of sample differences. Or it may be because of peculiarities or failings in one (or both) of the studies—in other words, because of "error."

whiskers. Other things are hard to remember: for instance, how many times one was spanked as a child, whether or not patient *X* was late for his appointment last September 12. With these latter sorts of observer-reports, written records—or the lack of them—become important.

When many observer-reports are drawn together in order to document a generalization, the collating process may be based on written records or it may rely entirely on memory. As was mentioned previously, memory collating raises source-of-doubt G: Is there any evidence? It also evokes source-of-doubt H: Is any "favorable evidence" which is dredged up simply the result of mistaken remembering? For example, the psychiatrist may have noted, "Whenever we talk about the fee, patient *X* tends to be late for the following session." This correlation—between talking about the psychiatrist's fee and subsequent tardiness by the patient—may be purely an artifact of biased remembering: exceptional instances forgotten, other instances misclassified as following the supposed trend. If there were full records of the therapy sessions to which the psychiatrist could refer, this particular doubt might be laid to rest.

Probably we all have certain misguided notions which appear to be "demonstrated by experience" but are actually the artifacts of biased remembering. The particular danger is that one's memory will "cheat," so as to present favorable evidence for hypotheses one wants to believe and produce unfavorable evidence for other statements which one would rather not believe. I would guess that such an hypothesis as "Strict parents tend to have better-behaved children" would tend to be "demonstrated by experience" for persons who view themselves as strict parents, but would tend to be "refuted by experience" for other persons who view themselves as lenient parents. As mentioned before: with research, the collating process is solely a matter of manipulating written records; memory does not enter in.[14] This is one source of the power of measurement-based research.

[14] In some research, the original observer-reports are based on memory. But the researcher, in collating these, never has to remember individual cases and cases' scores; these are written down.

### *Guesses about the Magnitude and Direction of Error*

Ordinarily observer-error is something that can only be guessed about. One rarely knows which cases were classified wrong, or how many cases, or—for that matter—whether the observer-reports bear any correspondence to reality at all. In practice, one guesses about whether or not the observer was able to report fairly accurately. So in survey research, for example, some questions are freely asked and the respondents' answers to them are accepted: "Are you male or female?" "How old are you?" "Are you married or single?" "Whom will you vote for?" Other possible questions never find their way into questionnaires; accurate answers to them would be too much to expect: "How often have you dreamed of falling?" "Are you a homosexual?" "Have you ever wished for the death of your parent/spouse/child?"

When one relates the findings of a piece of research to an hypothesis, he may likewise make a guess about the magnitude of observer-error, in estimating how strongly the research documents the hypothesis. For example, how seriously one takes the Kinsey studies, as testimony to the prevalence of extracurricular sexual activity in present-day America, hangs (in part) on whether one thinks Kinsey's respondents were exaggerating.[15]

One can also guess about the direction of error. Error may "help" an hypothesis; that is, the hypothesis may agree more closely with the observer-reports than it does (or would) with the reality which the reports presume to describe. Or, error may "hurt" an hypothesis; an hypothesis may (if we only knew) agree less closely with the observer-reports than it does with the reality "described" by them. Likewise, when one is testing a generalization beyond known cases, sampling error may "help" or "hurt" the hypothesis.

One might be impressed by Kinsey's evidence for the high rate of extramarital sexual liaisons. One may decide that observer-error was, on balance, negative. Respondents were more likely to have "held back" than they were to have exaggerated the exten-

[15] Other sources of doubt enter in too, of course. In this example, one wonders about the generalizability of the sample findings.

siveness of their sex experience; if the real facts were known, the rate was even higher (in Kinsey's samples, at least) than reported.

Suppose a researcher documents a cause-effect hypothesis by finding in a sample a positive correlation between the presumed cause-variable and effect-variable. The impressiveness of the evidence will depend, in part, on the strength of the correlation. If the study returns a pronounced trend with few exceptions, this leaves much leeway between what the hypothesis says ("There is a relationship") and what the data indicate. In other words, the margin for error is large. It also depends, in part, on a guess about the direction of error: whether observer-error acted to make the correlation weaker than it would have been if the variables could have been measured error-free, or whether "systematic bias" entered in, of such a nature as to exaggerate (or spuriously produce) the presumed relationship between the two variables. Systematic bias and guesses about the direction of error will receive more attention in Chapter 5.

## An Index of Likelihood of Truth

The "scheme for judging evidence"—or epistemological checklist, or whatever one wishes to call it—has now been presented in full. The crux of the scheme is eight "sources of doubt": special reasons why an hypothesis might be untrue even though supported by favorable evidence. Six of these sources of doubt concern the form in which the hypothesis is worded, what it says. The last two concern the nature of any supporting evidence. Under each source of doubt were listed subsidiary points, having to do with what is required in order partly to "answer" or "overcome" the sources of doubt. They might be termed "sources of strength." For the sources of doubt arising from the form of the hypothesis—A, B, C, D, E, and F—the sources of strength are special sorts of evidence which the sources of doubt "ask for." Thus, a generalization beyond known cases "asks for" evidence for a representative sample or, failing that, replications; a cause-effect statement asks for before-after conditions and, optimally, an experiment; and so forth. For the sources of doubt concerning the evidence itself—G and H—corresponding sources of strength come, in part, from the form of the hypothesis: Is it clear? Does it permit a large margin for error? They also come from assessments, or guesses about, the evidence itself: Was there any consensual validation? Was collating orderly, with written records?—and so on.

Nearly all of these points—the sources of doubt and the "answering" sources of strength—will be developed more fully as we proceed through the remainder of the book. But they have all been presented now, if in rather condensed and incomplete version.

Using this scheme to judge an hypothesis for likelihood of truth comes down to counting points. How many sources of doubt are present? To what extent have these been dispelled by corresponding sources of strength? Ideally, one could go down the entire sources-of-doubt checklist, add up points the hypothesis was "weak on," and arrive at an overall verdict. Evidence is very strong, moderate, weak, or absent. The hypothesis is almost certainly true, probably true, probably untrue; or there is no real evidence to indicate that it is true. In practice, though, such an adding-up would present a number of difficulties.

There are many points. The scheme is cumbersome. Applying it in a comprehensive way would be troublesome. When, in real life, we attempt to judge evidence in a rough-and-ready way, we probably consider a few of these points (or our own individual conceptualizations of them). But the scheme probably contains too many considerations to be held clearly in mind.

Although the scheme is an attempt to make the judging of evidence as rigorous and systematic as possible, there is a point beyond which rigor fails. If one did apply the entire scheme to a particular hypothesis in order to rate it for likelihood of truth, the final judgment would still depend, to some extent, on arbitrary decisions by the judge.

For one thing, many hypotheses are sufficiently vague so that before they can be judged, the judge must decide for himself what they mean. Whether or not they generalize beyond known cases, talk of cause and effect, or cite inferred variables, depends on how they are construed. This, as we shall see in Chapter 3, does not have to be a real problem. An hypothesis *construed in a specified way* can be rated for likelihood of truth. However, this can create a certain amount of confusion in any discourse about supporting evidence.

More serious is the question of the relative weights of the various points. How grave *is* a particular source of doubt for a given hypothesis? To what extent has it been answered by the evidence? Should source-of-doubt G be weighted more heavily than source-of-doubt B, C, or D? Such decisions must be made by the judge. In individual cases, there will certainly be marked differences of opinion.

Finally, there is the imprecision of the final verdict: "very strong evidence" or "moderately strong evidence" or "weak evidence." Unfortunately, the verdict cannot be phrased as a numerical probability statement: "Chances are 5 to 1 the hypothesis is true," or "The chances are .25 it is true." There is no way to justify this. So even if one goes through the rather arduous process entailed in a complete review of the sources of doubt, the final judgment must be rather vague: "Probably true." "Weak evidence; the probability of truth is not high." And given differences between individual judges in weighting the separate points, one judge can always rate a particular hypothesis as "strongly documented," while another judge might decide it is not strongly documented. Past a certain point, rigor fails.

One more difficulty should be mentioned. Occasionally it is possible to judge an hypothesis with the evidence fully in hand. The judge himself gathered the evidence. He was the observer, or the researcher. Or any write-up of the supporting evidence is so detailed that the reader can be said to "know" the evidence fully. Usually, though, any supporting evidence is merely alluded to, or presented in fragments, or at best summarized (leaving out some critical details). If one wishes to judge an hypothesis which is "documented" in this fashion, he must guess about the nature of any evidence. This makes an application of the scheme still more arbitrary and uncertain.

In practice, this is not such an obstacle as might first appear. Once the judge has decided for himself what the hypothesis means, he knows whether or not it presents sources-of-doubt A, B, C, D, E, or F. He can decide if it is clear enough to be actually related to evidence. And he knows something about the margin for error. If supporting evidence is summarized, as in the usual journal article, he also knows something about "sources of strength": sample characteristics, presence of an experiment, etc. Ignorance of the evidence is more limiting if the evidence is impressionistic (and comes to the judge secondhand), or if the supporting research is merely alluded to and not summarized in an accompanying research write-up.

If the scheme has virtue, perhaps this lies more in its general sensitizing value, rather than in its practical utility for judging particular hypotheses. That is, it can be viewed as a list of "things to consider" when thinking about research: an attempt to make these "considerations" as explicit as possible, to interrelate them in an orderly way, and to make them fully ranging, comprehensive. The scheme itself is, of course, arbitrary in one sense. "Epistemological considerations" could be conceptualized in alternative ways, given different names; "points" could be added or taken away, demarcated from each other and organized according to different systems. I imagine that if other social scientists were to formulate their own epistemological schemes, theirs would show a strong family resemblance to this one.[16] With any such schemes produced by natural scientists, the family resemblance might be less. And the epistemology of an historian, or a jurist, or an international-affairs expert would no doubt be *really* different.

Still, once one has gone to the trouble of making a formal list of epistemological considerations, one is tempted to go a bit further, formalize some more, and add numbers. The "index of likelihood of truth" to be presented below represents a yielding to

[16] Provided the schemes were for judging hypotheses, singly, for likelihood of truth.

this temptation. The "numbers" that come from this index are not numerical probability statements. These certainly could not be justified. Rather, they are scale scores, in the tradition of index making and rating scales. The variable we are interested in is an hypothesis' likelihood of truth, an unknown entity—in short, an inferred variable. Applying the index, one can score an hypothesis on likelihood of truth. If it scores well, then (we can infer) its likelihood of truth is high; the evidence is strong. If it scores badly, then (we might infer) its likelihood of truth is low; evidence is weak.

In other words, the index is a device for bringing a bit more order into the process, *if* one decides to apply the entire scheme to an hypothesis, in order to rate it for likelihood of truth or strength of supporting evidence. The index is only to be applied if evidence is *favorable*. If the judge knows—or guesses—that evidence is unfavorable, then the hypothesis can be judged "probably untrue" without further application of the index.

Likewise, the index should probably not be applied unless there is *some* evidence. If the judge decides there are no relevant observer-reports, he might reject the hypothesis immediately as "undocumented." Some hypotheses might be viewed as requiring certain minimal evidence before they can be said to be documented at all. For a generalization beyond known cases, this might be observation of a fair-sized sample. For a cause-effect statement, this might be an observed correlation between the presumed cause-variable and effect-variable. For an explanation of a single case, this might be evidence in support of the causal generalization or "law" which the explanation invokes. For a prediction, this might be observation of a past trend to which the predicted event rather clearly fits.

Scoring a particular hypothesis involves, of course, counting points. And, in order to tally the points so as to give an hypothesis an overall score, one must weight them. How much weight a particular point should be given is a matter of arbitrary decision. What follows is a general outline of a scoring-method, along with one possible way of weighing points. Any rules for weighting points might be changed at the reader's discretion.

In keeping with the generally negative approach inherent in

the sources-of-doubt notion, we might make 0 the highest score on the index. All hypotheses would receive a score lower than 0 (—2, —4, or whatever) depending on the number of sources of doubt.

Each source of doubt residing in the form of the hypothesis itself might be good for one point. If the judge decides the hypothesis is a prediction, one point off; if it is a generalization beyond known cases, another point; one point off for any inferred variable cited in the hypothesis; if it is a cause-effect hypothesis, another point; if it cites a necessary or a sufficient cause, another point; if it is a compound hypothesis, another point off.

Now we come to source-of-doubt G: Is there any evidence? Here, the judge may decide that there is no evidence because he has not really been given supporting observations, or because the relevance-fit between observer-reports and the hypothesis is so problematic. In this case, he can throw the hypothesis out, consider it undocumented. Or if observer-reports are given but are not clearly relevant as evidence for the hypothesis, he may decide to "make special allowances" and view the hypothesis as documented. In this event, he considers the three stages where the "shadow may fall" in the relating of observer-reports to any hypothesis. If he knows or guesses that the observer-reports are based on inexplicit sorting criteria, he can count a point off. If he decides the collating process was not orderly, he can subtract another point. And if, as he construes it, the hypothesis cites a variable which is not clearly defined, he can count a point off for that also.

On to source-of-doubt H. A point might be counted for the margin of error. If it is zero or minimal, subtract a point; if it seems ample, don't subtract a point. Finally, if the judge suspects that the evidence may be spuriously favorable because of observer-error, he might subtract a point for that.

The range of scores, then, might start at a point slightly less than 0 (for the "obvious truths" and "proven facts") and descend to something like —10, for the really doubt-riddled hypotheses.

Actually, one might usually want to subtract fractions of points, rather than full points. For sources-of-doubt A through F, how much is subtracted might depend on how well the judge decides the source of doubt has been answered or dispelled by special evidence. For example, if a generalization beyond known cases appears to be documented with a truly random sample, one might wish to subtract —.1 for that source of doubt, rather than —1. If, in any correlation in support of a cause-effect hypothesis, before-after conditions were present, one might wish to count —.8 or some other fraction for the causal inference, rather than the full point; if the causal statement is documented with an experiment, —.1 might be counted, rather than —1.

For the other points, fractions might be given too, at the judge's option. For example, scores of —1, —.5, or even —.05 might be given for the margin for error, depending on how ample it is. Likewise, the judge might represent his guess about the chance that favorable evidence is merely the artifact of observer-error by giving a score here which lies somewhere between 0 and —1; perhaps something, no matter how small, should always be subtracted here, to give obeisance to the assumptive gap between sense impressions and reality.

By way of illustration, the scoring system will be applied to two examples. The first one is a trivial hypothesis, which "says little" and hence makes rather small demands for evidence: "Rats have whiskers." Here, we will assume that the judge of the hypothesis has firsthand evidence—he has seen some rats.

It is a generalization beyond known cases (—1). There is no margin for error (—1). Finally, let us allow for the possibility of hallucination ( —.0001). The hypothesis scores —2.0001, which is very good. Its demands for evidence are modest, and clearly relevant observer-reports are available.

For the other illustration, let us take the hypothesis "Economic development promotes stable democratic government," as documented by Seymour Lipset (1960). It is a generalization beyond known cases (the case is a nation). There has been at least one replication of Lipset's study; also, the margin for error is such that the danger of sample bias seems very slight; [17] I shall count

[17] The reasoning behind this judgment is presented in Chapter 6, in the treatment of biased sample selection.

—.1 for this point. The hypothesis cites two inferred variables: degree of economic development, and presence or absence of stable democracy.[18] Lipset cites multiple indices for one of them, degree of economic development. These, for me, are quite persuasive; I shall count —.1 for this inferred variable. For the other, presence of stable democratic government, the index is less compelling; this will be scored —.4.

It is a cause-effect hypothesis, There was no experiment, or before-after conditions, so —1 will be counted here. The hypothesis will be construed as not citing a necessary cause; so nothing will be counted for that point. Neither is it a compound hypothesis.

As to source-of-doubt G, Lipset collates his evidence in an orderly manner, so that is all right. For one of the variables, degree of economic development, the indices are obviously explicit sorting criteria; however, for the other variable, presence of stable democracy, the sorting criterion is not quite so clear-cut. I shall count —.2 for that. Finally, as I construe the hypothesis, it does talk about variables that are not clearly defined: —1 for that.

The margin for error is maximal: no points off for that.

The likelihood that evidence is spuriously favorable seems very slight. The collating of data was based on written records, not on memory. There is a consensual validation of sorts, Cutright's (1963) replication. Only —.01 will be counted for source-of-doubt H.

In sum, the hypothesis scores —2.81 on likelihood of truth. According to this tally, the evidence is not much weaker than it was for the first example, "Rats have whiskers." This, again, points up the arbitrariness of any such scoring system. An experimental psychologist, for one, might have the firmest of convictions that the first hypothesis is true; yet he might entertain grave doubts about the Lipset hypothesis, which cites a cause-effect relationship, and yet is documented without benefit of an experiment. He would probably want to represent the "distance" between the

[18] Whether or not these are inferred variables is perhaps open to argument. The detailed definition of the term "inferred variable," from which this decision flows, is given in Chapter 5.

two hypotheses, on likelihood of truth, as much greater than 0.8099 points on a 10-point scale. In other words, he might wish to give greater weight to source-of-doubt D (the causal inference).

Also, of course, if one were a real purist, he could have thrown out all the research evidence, arguing that it could not be shown to be clearly relevant to the Lipset hypothesis, since the hypothesis cites inferred variables which are not clearly defined.

At any rate, if one wished to play this game further, he could score an entire series of hypotheses, thus placing them along a likelihood-of-truth continuum. The range might extend from "This rat has whiskers" (—.001, perhaps), to such hypotheses as "The popularity of existentialist philosophy reflects the identity crises of Modern Man" (—10 perhaps, if the judge decides such an hypothesis is documented at all).

## Evidence and Significance

There is a conflict between significance and likelihood of truth. The hypotheses which are more significant, more useful (if true), tend to present many sources of doubt. We gain power to manipulate events to our own liking—to build, to fix, to plan—by means of generalizations beyond known cases, predictions, inferred-variable hypotheses, cause-effect and especially necessary-cause statements, compound hypotheses, and precise hypotheses allowing minimal margin for error.

How has science been so successful in efforts toward prediction and control if its more useful hypotheses bristle with sources of doubt? The answer lies in the sources of strength. Many a "difficult" hypothesis, presenting many sources of doubt, has been well documented because favorable and strong evidence has been brought to bear, to answer the sources of doubt.

Actually, of course, a developing science confronts a mixed picture of opportunities and limitations. There are realistic limits to what can be done, what sorts of hypotheses can be adequately tested. With time, some of the limits may be pushed back; but, as we in the social sciences know all too well, their resistance is stubborn.

As mentioned before, the system-building and technological achievements of the natural sciences derive from precise hypotheses, allowing minimal margin for error, which ordinarily can be construed as necessary-cause generalizations. The evidence for these derives, in turn, from "controlled experiments": observational conditions where all significant and relevant variables can be controlled with some precision, thus producing relatively "pure" and exceptionless effects. In the study of human behavior, opportunity for such controlled conditions is limited. Thus, any real "behavioral technology" has yet to achieve take-off.

Another special limitation of the social sciences, residing in the nature of the subject matter, concerns inferred variables. Many of the more interesting questions we ask ourselves concern mental life: personality, attitudes, motives, cognitive styles. Mental-life variables are so important that they virtually demand study. Yet they can only be studied indirectly, and with "special allowances" at that, by means of indices and inferred-variable hypotheses. Even when one turns to human *behavior*, one's possible range for potentially useful hypotheses and important questions is very limited without resort to inferred variables and indices. We direct most of our energies to testing inferred-variable hypotheses; we have no choice.

Hedged about with limitations, we are left certain opportunities. For one thing, we can relate *some* evidence to important hypotheses, where previously there was none. If the sources-of-doubt orientation creates uncertainty about scientific findings, it can be applied with equal justification to the discourse of everyday life and to nonscientific writings; here the results are *really* devastating. One way or another, decisions must be made, policies must be formulated. All too often in human affairs, such a choice must be made with no real evidence at all; and frequently it turns out to be the wrong choice. We have some opportunity to relate some evidence to policy-relevant beliefs, thereby improving the batting averages of the decision makers. Also, of course, research can stimulate new hypotheses, provide new—and documented—policy-relevant beliefs. Even though we have produced no behavioral technology, the practical pay-off from social science research is already quite formidable. The flowering of new teaching methods in the past fifteen years—along with evidence for their efficacy, from evaluation studies—is a case in point. Another is the achievements of actuarial studies. Still another is the applications of behavioral psychology, especially the Skinnerian brand, to teaching, psychotherapy, and work on mental retardation. Keynesian economic theory is yet another example. The list could, of course, be greatly extended.

Some evidence is better than none. Strong evidence is better than weak evidence. Any bona fide evidence, even though weak, if it can be related to a crucial point of decision, represents a gain.

## Selected References

Philosophy of science, general:

Quentin Gibson, *The Logic of Social Enquiry*. Pp. 120–143 give an alternative approach to the margin for error, and chapter 3 discusses the need for the more "ambitious" hypotheses, i.e., the ones that present serious sources of doubt.

Ernest Nagel, *The Structure of Science*. On pp. 447–502 Nagel compares the social sciences with the natural sciences and discusses the special problems that arise when one turns the scientific method upon the study of human behavior.

## *Chapter 3*

# DEFINITION AND EVIDENCE

> We in academic life owe understandable allegiance to erudition and elegance of expression, and all too often we take a definition to be adequate (in the sense of clarifying meaning) if it sounds well. More is required, of course. Clarification of meaning (whether couched in formal definitions or in illustrative examples) takes place only if the terms defined are actually geared to the experience of the people concerned.
>
> ANATOL RAPOPORT (1958)

This chapter will elaborate on two points that were introduced in the previous chapter. The first has to do with the term "construe," which has been used a number of times. The ordinary hypothesis, being couched in words, has a certain rubbery nature. It can be interpreted in alternative ways, stretched and twisted into various shapes, at the listener's discretion. At times it is perfectly clear, from the wording of the hypothesis or from its context, what the statement was meant to convey. More often, the listener is left some latitude for interpretation. If he wishes to judge the hypothesis for likelihood of truth, he must first make explicit, to himself, what the hypothesis *means to him.* When he does this, he must make choices. Some hypotheses can be construed in alternative ways, with respect to what variable(s) they cite and what the case is. If the judge decides to take an hypothesis as a generalization beyond known cases, then he may have to decide, for himself, about the parameters of the population which the hypothesis talks about. Depending on interpretation, some hypotheses may or may not cite inferred variables. Sometimes the author of the hypothesis clearly indicates his intent to state the causal inference, with terms like "because," "produces," "resulted in;" for other hypotheses the author's intent is not obvious, and they could be read as either causal or noncausal statements. Likewise, whether an hypothesis states a necessary or sufficient cause may be unclear, and hence left to the listener's choice. And the margin for error, too, can sometimes be construed in alternative ways.

Often hypotheses do not come to us singly. Rather, in a book or lecture or conversation or argument, they come in series. The speaker needs more than a single sentence to "develop his point"; he requires a paragraph or page or chapter, or even more space than this. Presented with such an utterance, the listener has several options. He can accept or reject the entire argument, on the criterion of "reasonableness"; this is our usual habit, I suspect. He can break the utterance down into its component statements and try to judge all single hypotheses within it on the evidence. In practice he would never do this: it is too much work. Many of the hypotheses in the series would be too trivial to warrant all this trouble. Besides, the hypotheses would be flying by at too rapid a rate. A final possibility is to focus simply on the "main point" or on several points and try to judge *these* on the evidence. If the listener does try to do this, his latitude for construing becomes even greater. First of all, he must decide for himself what the main point is; or rather, what point or points he will try to judge. This is an arbitrary judgment; different listeners would tend to choose differently. Second, he must state these for himself, and construe them so he can identify variables, case, and sources of doubt. If he construes a point as an hypothesis, rather than some other type of statement (such as a value judgment), he can then decide if any evidence is available. If he decides that there is, he can then go about rating the point for likelihood of truth.

If the listener does go through this process, he is not so much judging what the speaker said, as he is judging something *he* said to *himself* which was suggested by the speaker's utterance. Any ensuing "argument" or "disagreement" with the speaker becomes rather unreal and unfair, of course. It is perhaps unsettling that truth or likelihood of truth should hinge so much on arbitrary decisions as to meaning, which vary between individuals. At any rate, I suppose, the important thing (for the listener) is not what the speaker said, but what the listener decides to believe or disbelieve.

The need to construe presents a broad continuum. Sometimes what the speaker means is absolutely clear-cut, as with "Most of you are under 21." In a journal write-up of a piece of research, the intent of any hypothesis to be tested or statement of conclusions is usually fairly obvious too. Here, though, there is sometimes room for alternative interpretation. The author may exhibit a certain coyness about generalizing beyond his sample, or about drawing a causal inference, so that what the study "shows" can be interpreted in several ways. When one turns to speculative writings, latitude for alternative constructions is enormous. Often the speaker's intent is so slippery, so nebulous, that one cannot squeeze it into one or several hypotheses without doing considerable violence to it. What one comes up with is clearly not Parsons, or Goffman, or Sartre, or Riesman, or Freud any more, but rather one's distant association to the original text—one which, no doubt, the author would view with some horror, feeling that the "essence of the idea" had been lost or greatly distorted.

And he would probably be right. The great speculative writers, operating on the frontiers of awareness, dealing with shadowy entities, interpreting "deeply," must struggle for expression as best they can. Many a complex idea can neither be stated clearly nor boiled down to one or several hypotheses without losing an important essence. For examples such as the one below, all efforts to construe—and, thereby, to relate to evidence—should probably be given up.

> We believe that civilization has been built up, under the pressure of the struggle for existence, by sacrifices in gratification of the primitive impulses, and that it is to a great extent forever being re-created, as each individual, successively joining the community, repeats the sacrifice of his instinctual pleasures for the common good. The sexual are among the most important

> of the instinctive forces thus utilized; they are in this way sublimated, that is to say, their energy is turned aside from its sexual goal and diverted toward other ends, no longer sexual and socially more valuable [Sigmund Freud, *A General Introduction to Psychoanalysis,* translated by Joan Riviere].

Statements that are framed, and offered, in such a form so that they can be related to evidence, we might term "empirical discourse" or "scientific discourse." Statements like the quotation above, which cannot be related to evidence if one does not first grossly change and even distort them, we might term "humanistic discourse." These are offered with some sort of feeling of conviction. But the conviction does not stem from supporting evidence; at least, not "evidence" as the term is being used here. If such humanistic discourse is not summarily thrown out as "undocumented" it must be evaluated in the light of some other epistemological criterion—faith, or "reasonableness," or something of the sort.

In practice, I suspect, humanistic discourse looms very large, in our communications with each other and in our private beliefs. The more important, basic, and orientation-giving the issue is, the more our thinking takes the form of humanistic discourse: a negative correlation, perhaps, between the significance of belief and the orderliness of human thought processes. Does one need a shave? One consults the evidence in the mirror. Should one enter a monastery? One "thinks it through," instead.

To sum up: before evidence can be brought to bear on some assertion, the statement must usually be "construed." If the statement is a long one, one or several main points can be decided upon, and then framed in hypothesis form. What an hypothesis requires in the way of evidence, and how strong any such evidence is, depends on what the hypothesis means. In many instances, any judge of the hypothesis must explicate its meaning for himself: variable(s) cited, case, and sources of doubt. It is only then that he is able to decide if any evidence is available and, if so, how strong the evidence appears to be.

The second and last point to be elaborated on in this chapter concerns clarity: in the definition of variables in an hypothesis and in the classification of cases (with respect to variables) in observer-reports. We turn to this point now.

## Definitions: Clear and Vague

Under source-of-doubt G, the "relevance-fit" between an hypothesis and any supposed evidence was discussed. It was said that if any variables in an hypothesis are not defined clearly, then any observations are not clearly relevant to the hypothesis, as evidence. The example was the data on the students' ages, used as evidence for the conclusion "Most of you are immature." Since "maturity" was not clearly defined, it is an open question what sorts of observations are necessary to document the hypothesis "Most of you are immature." Therefore, it is problematic whether or not the data on the students' ages should be accepted as documenting a statement about their maturity. An uncertainty has crept in, a "shadow falls," between the point of observation and the point of drawing a conclusion. This was contrasted with "Most of you are under 21"; here the variable, age, is clearly defined, and the students' reports on their ages are obviously relevant, as evidence.

Likewise, with any observer-report, the rule or convention which was used to classify a case (with respect to a variable) may be clear and explicit, or it may be vague, fuzzy, undetermined. The example was "I am 20 years old" as opposed to "You are immature."

If a variable has a "clear meaning" or if it is "clearly defined," this means that the rule or convention which was used (or could be used) to classify cases—with respect to "how much of" the variable they "possess"—is clear. *The sorting criterion is explicit.* We know what must be observed about the case in order to classify it at one scale point rather than at another. Observer-reports (or hypotheses) on the order of "I am 25 yeas old" (the variable is age, in years), "I made $10,000 last year" (the variable is annual income, in dollars), and "My grade-point average is

3.25" cite clearly defined variables. Sometimes this clear definition comes by way of mechanical devices: "The temperature is 87 degrees," "I weigh 170 pounds."

The explicitness of the sorting criterion can be indicated indirectly by a test of agreement. If it is clear, several observers should be able to sort the same cases with it, and agree on the cases' scores. For example, Ego might mount the scales, a number of observers might read the dial, and we could see if they all do read "170 pounds." [1]

A good many terms for physical objects have the nature of explicit sorting criteria. If several observers were presented with an assortment of objects, they would agree closely on which of them were rocks and which were not, which were bicycles and which were not, which were fish and which were not, and so forth. There might be a bit of disagreement over a few marginal cases—for example, is a little pebble a "rock"?—but these disagreements would no doubt be few.

When they turned to the properties of objects, the observers would still agree in those instances where they had standardized measuring-devices in hand: on weight, length, hardness, density, speed, and so on. If beauty, cuteness, symmetry, and such were to be judged, the observers would have to fall back on their own personalized and vague criteria, and major disagreements would arise.

When one wishes to describe humans—human behavior, the human mind—terms are generally vague. A few are not: thus age, income, population density, running speed. These clear terms ordinarily refer to a *count* of explicitly agreed-upon units (years, dollars, bodies, yards per second). But most are vague: maturity, honesty, cleverness, hunger, diligence, deference, status seeking, humility, activity level, ad infinitum.

When they came on the scene, the social sciences inherited a glossary of vague terms. Conceivably, they might have set up some sort of Bureau of Standards, agreeing on standard measures and meanings of commonly used variables. Curiously, this did not

[1] As these examples suggest, sometimes a test for agreement is not possible.

happen. There is nothing in the *Dictionary of Sociology*, say, that corresponds with ergs, watts, amperes, decibels, the meter scale, the Fahrenheit scale, grams, or pounds. Technical languages developed, to be sure; but they are, in general, just as vague as their folk-language forebears. Instead of clear terms we have "concepts": drive, reinforcement, extinction, discrimination, cathexis, aggression, nAffiliation, nAchievement, social stratification, cultural complexity; not to mention society, culture, institution, status, role, personality, and group.

A defense of these concepts is that they are on a high level of generality; any one of them is inclusive in nature, "pulling together" many observations in disparate settings; each is multifaceted. Hence they can be said to have a synthesizing, summarizing function, directing our attention to the "big picture," allowing us to penetrate beyond the facade and interpret. They are orientation-giving. They set the frame of reference from which hypotheses issue; they themselves are not the stuff of hypotheses. There is some truth to this. Some of these concepts never become variables in hypotheses that social scientists try to test. Others do, however. In the absence of any board of standards or anything like watts and ergs, we spend much of our energy testing hypotheses which cite such variables as need-Affiliation and social-class position.

If one were to pore through any fair-sized university library, he should be able to find at least two dozen separate definitions for any of the above-mentioned concepts. This goes, too, for other concepts which were not mentioned, such as defense, adaptation, value, social integration, power, authority, norm, family, socialization, social control, social cohesiveness, bureaucratization.

The multiplicity of definitions and meanings is perhaps not a serious problem: confusing, yes; still, definition is a mere matter of convention. In the absence of any agreed-upon convention, such as one issuing from the Bureau of Standards or our common understanding of what the term "sky" means, there is nothing to prevent each new personality theorist from giving his own definition of "personality." Further, he can define the term "personality integration" in his own way; and for the scope of his study, or article, or book, that is what personality integration *is*, no matter how other writers have defined it. Since the labeling process is arbitrary, a definition cannot be true or false, right or wrong.

We have been able to get along, more or less, with multiple definitions of key terms. The more serious problem, I think, is that so few of these definitions are clear. Kroeber and Kluckhohn (1952) devoted an entire monograph to a compilation of definitions of the concept "culture"; one looks in vain throughout this monograph for one clear definition. The same would be true, I think, for any compiled definitions of role, authority, group, organization, culture trait, society, many other of our "key concepts." Up to a point, perhaps, this does not matter. But it does matter when one of these shadowy concepts enters an hypothesis as a variable and the hypothesis is "tested." Any such testing takes on a slightly unreal quality, since it is not obvious that any "evidence" that was gathered is actually relevant to the hypothesis, as evidence. This is the familiar business of "the shadow falls," discussed in Chapter 2 under source-of-doubt G and again alluded to early in this chapter.

It is now time to review some individual definitions, and to begin to consider what makes a particular definition clear, what makes another one vague. We shall start with Robert M. MacIver's definition of the term "authority":

> By authority we mean the power attached to office, involving the respect, the submission, or the reverence accorded to those who represent the office or are invested with its rights [1937:336].

Can you imagine taking this definition, applying it to a collection of persons, groups, offices, or social positions, and thereby classifying each case as either "having authority" or "not having authority"? One could perform such an operation, of course; no doubt one does, in the course of life, in a more or less conscious way. Still, how one classified a particular case would have little to do with MacIver's definition. The definition really does not tell you what you must "see" in a particular case in order to classify it one way or another. It does not tell you what the "cutting point" or "boundary line" is, between having authority and not having authority. The definition relates authority to equally nebulous and ill-defined terms: respect, submission, power, reverence, rights.

Definitions of this sort will be termed *connotative definitions.* They are not really meant as devices for sorting cases. Rather, they are meant to suggest, to call up associations. It is as if MacIver had said, "When I think of authority, I think of power, and the rights of office, and receiving respect and submission and reverence. The term 'authority' is associated, in my mind, with these other terms." Once the reader or listener is notified of such-and-such connotations, the "defined" term can then be used in discussion, and communication—of a sort—can proceed.

Our important concepts are generally defined in this way. This is true not only for social-science concepts, but also everyday terms for the "important things in life": happiness, security, love, self-realization, and the like. In a sense, such a "definition" is no definition at all, and usually need not even be given. Even if one has never heard the term before, he can go on reading and, from the contexts in which the word is used, piece together a definition which is just as adequate as the one which was formally stated.

Now we turn to a second example. In this one, the authors seem to have the classifying function of definition somewhat in mind:

> *Small group.* By this term is meant an aggregate of people, from two up to an unspecified but not too large number, who associate together in face-to-face relations over an extended period of time, who differentiate themselves in some regard from others around them, who are mutually aware of their membership in the group, and whose personal relations are taken as an end in itself [Berelson and Steiner 1964:325].

This might sound very good. It comes from a great book by two distinguished authors. It seems very inclusive, and it "says what they mean" very clearly, one might think. One might ask, though: What *is* a small group? Not what is it in the abstract, but how do you know one when you see it? When is an aggregate of people a small group, when is it not? It is a small group, the definition says, if (1) it is not too large (?); (2) if the members associate, face-to-face, over an extended (?) period of time, (3) differentiate (?) themselves from others, (4) are mutually aware (?) of their group membership, and (5) take their personal relations as an end in itself (?). So what is a small group? This family? That clique? The students in *X* seminar? *Y* friendship?

The definition does not say what a small group *is*. It refers you back to various vague and undefined subsidiary terms within the definition: not too large, extended association, differentiated from others, mutual awareness of membership, group relations taken as an end in itself. If one were to use the definition to sort aggregates of people into small groups versus non-small groups, he would have to give the definition considerable "help," in the form of his own private definitions of these vague (but key) subsidiary terms. Say a person tried to do this: his own definitions for the key subsidiary terms remain private, known only to himself; also, no doubt, some of them will be quite vague. He counts the total of small groups in Dormitory *X* and comes up with a total of 57. This count—and subsequent report—is essentially meaningless. We do not know what he observed to reach such a count. More important, we do not know what standard or rule he applied to the dormitory cliques in order to designate some of them "small group." Also, another inmate of the dormitory might apply the definition and get a much different tally: 34 perhaps, instead of 57. Since private subsidiary definitions enter into any application of the definition, the range of disagreement would doubtless be great.

We are now ready to take up a bona fide clear definition. First, however, a word of apology to MacIver, Berelson and Steiner: I think their definitions are as good as any other. That is, I have yet to see a clear definition of "authority" or "group" or "small group." These terms could be defined clearly, but only by resort to very unconventional, idiosyncratic definitions—ones which would stand scant chance of ever enjoying wide usage. More of this later.

The clear definition—which, as a matter of fact, is a bit tainted also, not absolutely crystal clear—was authored by someone in the U.S. Census Bureau. It is a definition for the term "family": "The family . . . is a group of two persons or more related by blood, marriage or adoption and residing together . . ." (Bureau of the Census, "Households and Families, by Type: 1947 to 1955," *Current Population Reports: Population Characteristics*, Series P-20, 59 [August 12, 1955], p. 2). This definition refers back to three subsidiary terms or phrases:

A. "group of two or more persons." The meaning of "two," "more," and "persons" must be explicitly agreed upon among speakers of the English language.
B. "related by blood, marriage or adoption." There should also be fair agreement as to what this means.
C. "residing together." This, in practice, might be ambiguous enough to turn up a few instances of disagreement. If two census takers were to canvass a block, they might disagree as to whether the household of a truck driver, or a soldier, or a travelling salesman "contained a family." A subsidiary definition might be added here: "sleeping under the same roof at least half the time," or something of the sort.

If such a block canvassing takes place and the enumerator subsequently announces, "There are 23 families in this block," this is a meaningful statement, in the sense in which "There are 57 groups in this dormitory" was not. We know what rule the census taker applied to each case (each household or "dwelling unit") in order to classify it as "containing a family" or "not containing a family." His observer-reports, which might be in the form of a filled-in questionnaire for each dwelling unit, are clearly relevant as evidence for his conclusion "23 families."

A clear definition, then, is made up of terms which (1) are clear with respect to their meaning and (2) either have universal meanings (within a given language) or have their meanings specified in the definition. In other words, if the definition cites a term which admits to alternative meanings, then that subsidiary term must also be clearly defined.

The question "How clear is clear enough?" of course comes up here. This, unfortunately, may not be answered in a really emphatic (i.e., "clear") way. Some leeway exists for individual differences of opinion: for example, as to whether the slightly flawed Census Bureau definition of "family" is clear enough to be taken as an explicit sorting criterion, giving obviously relevant evidence to the conclusion "23 families in this block."

Ideally, the explicit sorting criterion—which might be a clear term, or a clear definition for a term, or a measuring device of some sort—classifies cases "all by itself," without any "help" from the human agent. No individualized judgment or opinion or interpretation need be made by a person who applies such a standard. He need do nothing that is the slightest bit creative. He merely allows the sorting device to "act through him." Thus, when Ego gets on the scales, the scales do all the work. All any observer must do to classify Ego with respect to the weight-variable is to read the dial and report: "170 pounds." Actually, especially when the sorting device is verbal rather than mechanical, something in the way of "common understandings" must be invoked in order to classify a case. The "rule" may not be completely contained in the written definition. Thus the definition of "family" refers back to "common understandings" of the meaning of "related by blood," "related by marriage," "persons," and so on. Thus, too, my temporizing in the face of the question "How clear is clear enough?"

The best that can be said, perhaps, is that if a variable is defined clearly, then there is good agreement about what a particular case must "have" or exhibit in order to be classified with respect to the variable: containing a family versus not containing a family; possessing authority versus not possessing authority; constituting a small group versus not constituting a small group; weighing 124 pounds, 160, 170, or 234. This is what is meant by a clearly defined variable. Some observer-reports cite clearly defined variables; others do not. Likewise for all hypotheses. Only when both observer-report and any hypothesis to be documented cite clearly defined variables are the observer-reports obviously relevant to the hypothesis, as evidence. The example—yea, again—is the students' ages.

Some terms for variables are clear to begin with: age, height, weight, race, typing speed, income, and so forth. Other terms can be made clear, within the context of a particular article or discussion, by invoking a special clear definition: "family," for example. The following is another example of this sort.

A psychologist is working on the general problem of the relation of drive-level to performance. Since he is an experimental psychologist, drive-level narrows down to hunger, thirst, and pain, since these can be most easily manipulated in the laboratory. In this particular experiment, he relates hunger to speed of learning a particular maze. He divides his rats into two groups. The control-group rats get food up to the time they run the maze. The experimental-group rats are deprived of food for twenty-four hours before they run the maze. At the end of the maze, the reward—reinforcement, pot of gold, or what have you—is a food pellet. He hypothesizes that his hungry rats will learn the correct turns in the maze more quickly then the others since they are more highly motivated—for food.

"Hungry" is a common term. We "know what it means." Yet it is not a clear term, in the sense of fixing cutting points. In its everyday usage, it does not tell one when someone should be designated "hungry" or "not hungry"; or "very hungry," "moderately hungry," "not especially hungry," or "satiated." One can ask, of course. Even then, the answer "I'm fairly hungry" does not clearly indicate a point on a scale, in the manner of "I'm twenty years old." The psychologist, in his experiment, can do a little better than this. For him, "hungry" is being without food for twenty-four hours up to the time of running the maze. "Not hungry" means having food in the cage up to the time of running the maze. He gives some rats food, keeps other rats away from food, and in this manner neatly divides them into "highs" and "lows" on the hunger scale. In his subsequent discussion of the experiment in a journal article, he is careful to define hunger as twenty-four hours without food.

Theoretically at least, we could take almost any of our familiar, vague terms, and supply them with this sort of clear, operational definition. "School ability" or "academic achievement" can be defined as simply—and nothing more than—grade-point average. Creativity can be defined as score on the Remote Associates Test.

Social-class position can be defined as annual income, nothing more. Marital adjustment can be defined as not getting a divorce. Honesty can be defined as having no police record.

Such clear if truncated definitions tend to offend sensibilities. The listener is apt to feel that they are "not right," "not what the word *really* means." It may be hard for the operationalist to keep the listener's attention. After the communication has ended, the listener is likely to remember it in terms of "real" hunger, not twenty-four hours without food.

The general drift of social science is strongly in the direction of inferred-variable hypotheses. The ordinary hypothesis which is tested or stated does cite one or more variables which are only defined connotatively—that is, not really defined at all. Social scientists speak of "operationalizing our concepts," but this seldom comes down to a clear—if uncommon—definition to a familiar term. The Remote Associates Test is used to study creativity: not creativity as defined as score on the Remote Associates Test, but creativity in the conventional (and unclear) meaning of the term. Perhaps this is a good thing, perhaps not. The issue has its pros and cons. A price is paid for this, of course. With the introduction of such terms into an hypothesis, likelihood of truth declines. Also, we are vexed by the relevance question: if we can't clearly say what we mean by the concept "creativity," it is problematic whether the Remote Associates Test—or any other test or observation—can furnish relevant evidence for any hypothesis about creativity.

"Operationalizing our concepts" generally means supplying a clear index of the concept. Cases are first classified with respect to a variable which can be observed, according to clear rules. In the case of the Remote Associates Test, these rules consist of a list of test questions, a list of the "right answer" to each, and a scoring convention that tells one how to add these up to give a person an overall score on the test. The rules for categorizing a person with respect to his score are absolutely clear. Any observer-report on the nature of "He scored 18" is clear also. The case has been classified with an explicit sorting criterion; at any rate, it is explicit once one sees the test questions and knows the scoring convention. Then after this point is reached, the test score can be used as an index or sign of the inferred, unclear variable, creativity.

In discussing the relating of observer-reports to an hypothesis in order to muster evidence, I mentioned three points where the shadow might fall: unclear observer-reports, disorderly collating, unclear variable in the hypothesis. We in the social sciences feel bound to go on testing unclear hypotheses; hence we often labor in an aura of uncertainty regarding the relevance of what we are doing in our research. However, the situation could be much worse. That is to say, we have improved on prescientific attempts to bring evidence to bear on questions of the human mind and human behavior. In our research, the collating of observer-reports is orderly. And in our measurements, we have done much to make observer-reports clear and sorting criteria explicit.

## *Selected References*

Labeling and definition—general:

Roger Brown, *Words and Things.*

S. I. Hayakawa, *Language in Thought and Action.*

Multiple definitions and meanings for social science concepts:

Melvin Marx, "Intervening Variable or Hypothetical Construct?" *Psychological Review,* Vol. 58 (1951), pp. 235–247.

Unstated "common understandings" that underly even the "clearest" definitions; the impossibility of getting fully explicit verbal sorting devices:

Aaron Cicourel, *Method and Measurement in Sociology,* especially pp. 22–24.

# *Chapter 4*

# MEASUREMENT-BASED STUDIES

## Measurement

The term "measurement" refers, of course, to giving cases numerical scale scores with respect to some variable. Thus Torgerson: "Measurement . . . concerns the assignment of numbers to objects to represent amounts or degrees of a property possessed by all the objects" [1958:19]. And Torgerson again: ". . . measurement pertains to the *properties* of objects, and not to the objects themselves. Thus, a stick is not measurable in our use of the term, although its *length*, *diameter*, and *hardness* might well be . . ." [1958:14].

One measures by applying a measuring instrument: a rule, standard, or convention of some kind. Thus S. S. Stevens' popular definition: "Measurement is the assignment of numerals to objects or events according to rules" [1951:22].

In measuring the properties of objects, the measuring instrument is customarily a mechanical device of some sort (accompanied by an agreed-upon convention as to how to apply it and read it). Temperature is measured with a thermometer, length or height by a tape measure, weight by the bathroom scales. In measuring human-behavior variables, the measuring instrument is usually verbal: coding rules, scaling conventions, tests (with their accompanying scoring conventions), rating scales, even single questionnaire items ("How old are you?").

Someone must apply the measuring instrument to the case. That is, an observer must observe the case, with the measuring instrument in hand or in mind, and thereby classify the case with respect to whatever variable is being measured. The results of measurement can then be given or noted in an observer-report: "His temperature is 98.6 degrees." "He is 6 feet 3 inches tall." "He weighs 206 pounds." "He says he is 19 years old." "He scores 23 on the Incomplete Sentences Test, 97 on the Weschler-Bellevue IQ Test, and 96 to his opponent's 94 in the just-completed ten-round fight."

The magnitude or "degree of" a variable possessed or exhibited by a particular case is represented by a scale score. The measuring instrument offers a scale with an ascending series of scale points. Each scale point is a category in which a case may be put; and, at whatever point the case is classified, that is its scale score. Generally, the numbers go up as magnitude of the variable increases: 190 pounds is heavier than 170 pounds. There are a few exceptions, such as scores on speed.

The minimum number of scale points is 2, in which case one has a yes/no, high/low, so-called nominal scale: "Male? (yes/no.)" "Is the family polygynous? (yes/no.)" "Did this marriage end in divorce? (yes/no.)" "Is this voter a Republican? (yes/no.)" "How did he do on the driving test? (pass/fail.)" Some writers would consider such 2-point scales as "measures," others would not (Coombs 1953:473; Underwood 1957:20; Torgerson 1957:17; Riley 1963:328). When these are used, scale scores are usually represented by words rather than by numbers. Of course, numbers can be used whenever one wishes, assigning "high" or "yes" or "pass" a score of 1 and giving "low," "no," or "fail" a score of 0. Here, we will include sorting devices yielding 2-point scales under the rubric "measuring instrument." [1]

[1] Many-point scales are termed ordinal scales, interval scales, and ratio scales, depending on whether an absolute zero and the magnitude of scale intervals are presumed to be known. Scales for most indices would be

The scale score gives a rather precise indication of the relative magnitude of the variable possessed by a case, more than do the vaguer terms of ordinary speech. ("He weighs a lot." "He's tall." "He's not very smart." "It was a fairly close fight.") The architect of a measuring instrument values this precision. So that this precise statement be meaningful, he also wants to make the instrument invariant, even-handed, fair, classifying cases according to an unchanging standard. Ideally a yardstick should not shrink, expand, or stretch. Attention is given to "reliability." If the instrument is repeatedly applied to the same case, the scale score should be the same (or almost the same) at each reading. If several observers apply the measure to a particular case, they should agree on its scale score. In the social sciences, at least, measures are frequently subjected to tests of agreement.

The general drift of measurement is in the direction of clear observer-reports, explicit sorting criteria. In part, this may be merely because of the sharpening effect that numbers have on language ("He's 6 feet 3" rather than "He's tall"). In part, this may stem from the concern with reliability, leading researchers to search for number-assigning conventions which would stand up well under a test of agreement. In general, I think, a sorting device can be invariant, permitting different observers to concur on what score to give a particular case, when the rule for sorting cases is explicit. For agreement to take place, it must be clear what is to be observed about a case in order to give it a particular scale score. In other words, if the measuring rule is explicit, this permits it to be invariant. Therefore, measurement tends to yield explicit sorting criteria, clear observer-reports.

---

classified as ordinal, the "weakest" type; zero point of the inferred variable is unknown, as are the "distances" between scale points. For example, we do not know what sort of performance on an IQ test shows zero intelligence; nor do we know that an IQ of 160 signifies twice the intelligence of an IQ of 80. The scale merely "tells" us that the person scoring 160 is more intelligent. With an interval scale, the magnitude of scale intervals is known, although absolute zero is presumed to be unknown. An example would be the Fahrenheit thermometer: the scale intervals—the degrees of temperature—are equal to each other. A scale which merely represents a count exemplifies the ratio scale. When counting people, seconds, number of right answers to a test, etc., zero is known and scale intervals are all equal to each other.

In practice there are some exceptions to this. An explicit sorting rule can yield low agreement in a particular instance because of "mistakes" by one of the observers. The reverse can happen: a sorting convention which seems extremely vague to the outsider can bring about remarkably good agreement, because of extensive but unstated "common understandings" between the observers, which stem from "special training." [2] Admitting these exceptions, it is still my guess that there is a strong correlation between the explicitness of the sorting convention and its invariance. In order for observers to agree on how to score a case, they must agree rather explicitly on what to observe about a case in order to give it a certain score.

This was discussed a bit in the previous chapter, in the treatment of clear definitions and clear terms. In fact, the measuring instruments of the social sciences, being verbal in nature, can be construed as nothing more than clear definitions and clear terms. That is, they are verbal rules which say what particular scale scores "mean" in terms of observations: what must be observed about some case in order to give it a particular score on some variable. For example, the Remote Associates Test is a standard list of written problems accompanied by a scoring key, which designates "right answers" to the problems and tells one how to add these up in order to give a person a score on the Remote Associates Test. What was observed in order to give him this score can be made perfectly clear: the tester can provide the list of problems, the person's answers to them, and the written scoring key. In a sense, this is an elaborate definition of what the scale score means and of what scores on the Remote Associates Test generally mean in terms of observed behavior. One more example: measurement by means of a single term with an explicitly agreed-upon meaning. A questionnaire includes the item "Num-

[2] "The reader who is unfamiliar with draft-horse judging will be aware that there are hardly any instructions which anyone could follow and come to the same judgments; the rules work only where there is a common body of understanding as to what is meant by the various terms and what represents good and bad characteristics. Nonetheless, the adoption of this segmentation results in agreement within one or two points between experienced raters using the full hundred-point scale" (Lazarsfeld and Barton 1951:167).

ber of children?" The respondent applies this standard to himself, and answers "none" or "two" or the number of children he happens to have. Anyone who "knows the family" would no doubt agree with his answer (i.e., with the score he gave himself on the variable "number of children").

A measuring instrument, like any definition, is an arbitrary rule for classifying cases. There is nothing in nature that dictates that a centimeter must be a certain length; this was an arbitrary decision, made by a group of men. How the variable is to be defined, how many points the scale will have, the cutting points or lines of division between points on the scale, the nature of any standard situation in which a measuring instrument is to be applied—all of these, likewise, are arbitrary decisions. However, once the convention has been agreed upon, cases are classified by merely following the rules. Arbitrary departures from the rules on the part of the observer, individualized interpretations of how the measure is to be applied—these do not enter in. Hence the observer-report which gives the results of measurement is a clear one. This is the ideal, at any rate. As we shall see, some variables strongly resist measurement by clear rules; scale scores may be assigned, but what the numbers mean in terms of observations is not optimally clear.

## Collating in Research

In a measurement-based study, data are first gathered; then they are processed in a series of steps. Data gathering consists of pulling together the original observer-reports: how a rat ran on a particular trial; the kin relations in a given household; how a person answered a particular test question; how long a group member talked in a certain small-group session; answers to questionnaires; responses to interviews; and so on. Each of these observer-reports is a written description (sometimes numerical or graphic) of a case; it characterizes the case with respect to a variable. We shall term these original observer-reports the raw data.

Sometimes the raw data are reports of measurement: "I'm 33 years old." "The rat made the correct turn in the T-maze." "Member *X* talked for 4 minutes and 38 seconds." Sometimes they are not; a second step, termed coding, is required to give the cases scores. To illustrate coding, we might turn to an example from the previous chapter: the census taker with his definition of "family." He goes to a dwelling unit and questions the lady of the house, asking who lives there and what the kin relationships are. The original observer-reports are given by the lady of the house and are entered on the census taker's form. Then, if the census taker or someone wishes to classify the dwelling unit as to whether or not it contains a family, he must scan the census form and apply the census' definition: ". . . two persons or more, related by blood, marriage or adoption, and residing together." Thereby, the household is classified or scored with respect to the variable "containing a family," yes or no. The definition is the measuring instrument: a coding rule. In other words, coding rules are definitions of scale points; by coding (i.e., applying coding rules), previously recorded observations can be assigned scale scores and rendered into numbers.

A further step in the processing of data, which sometimes enters in and sometimes does not, is scaling. This step always involves measurement; in a sense, it is secondary measurement. After cases have been given scores—either in the original observer-reports or in subsequent coding—these scores may be combined to give summary scores. For example, a test scorer might score a person's answer to a particular test question "right" or "wrong" (the original observer-report). After he has done this for all the test items, he can give the person an overall score on the test. The overall score comes by way of scaling convention, a rule which says how answers to all the questions should be combined in order to arrive at a test score. The rule may be very simple, on the order of "You count each right answer worth one point, and then add up all the right answers." Scaling, being summarizing, changes the nature of the case and the variable. In this example, for the original observer-report the case was a person's answer to a particular test question; the variable was whether the answer was right or wrong. After scaling, the case was the person's performance over the entire test; the variable was how well he performed.

Often scaling is merely a count, as in the above example. Or it may be some variant of a count, as with speed scores or population density (number of persons per square mile). Sometimes the combining of items, units, or discrete "small" variables to give summary scores involves more than simply counting—as with, for example, the Guttman scale.

Past the point of scaling (if scaling is required), the data are further summarized in tables, charts, graphs, percentages, or statistics, and thus brought to bear as evidence for (or against) some hypothesis. Nearly always the hypothesis to be tested is a generalization; hence the need for many observer-reports, many cases. Ordinarily it is a correlation statement. This means that the cases have been classified and then "processed" with respect to more than one variable—at least two. Often the researcher wants to test a number of hypotheses in the same study, so his sample of cases may be measured with respect to perhaps a dozen variables, sometimes more.

With this ultimate summary of data—in table, chart, or statis-

TABLE IV

RELATION OF EDUCATION TO FAMILIARITY WITH ISSUES, 1956

| Familiarity with issues | From no formal schooling to completion of 8 grades (543 cases) | High school, some or completion (890 cases) | College, some or degree (331 cases) |
|---|---|---|---|
| High | 21% | 31% | 50% |
| Medium | 37% | 47% | 44% |
| Low | 42% | 22% | 6% |
| | 100% | 100% | 100% |

*Source: Campbell, Converse, Miller, and Stokes 1964:102*

tics—hypothesis and evidence can be said to "meet." That is, at this point evidence can be related to the hypothesis. In Table IV is an example, drawn from *The American Voter*, in which a correlation is given between level of education and degree of familiarity with the issues in the 1956 Presidential election campaign.

The data in Table IV can be used to document such an hypothesis as "Education makes one more likely to attend to campaign issues," or "There is a positive correlation between level of education and familiarity with Presidential campaign issues." 1,764 cases, respondents to a questionnaire, were measured for two variables: level of education and familiarity with the issues. For level of education, the respondent merely said how many years of school he had completed; no coding or scaling was required. For the other variable, each respondent was asked a number of questions about campaign issues. His answers were then coded, using some set of coding rules; he was given a score on extensiveness and/or accuracy of information. Probably coding was done separately on answers to several questions, and then scores on all questions were combined into an overall score on "familiarity with the issues" by means of some scaling convention. The table says that college-educated people tended to score high on familiarity with the issues; ill-educated people tended to score low. The table summarizes all cases' scores on both the variables, representing the variables with three-point scales.

As was mentioned before, the great virtue of research is that collating is orderly. When observer-reports are "pulled together" and then "processed," everything is written down. Memory distortion is avoided. The rules by which scaling is accomplished and by which trends are summarized in tables and statistics are standardized and clear. Compare the quantified data in Table IV with any impressionistic evidence on the order of "It has been my experience that well-educated people know more about politics," or "From my experience, ill-educated people don't know what the campaigns are all about." For the latter, the number of cases observed, the standard for classifying cases, the classification of each case—all are unknown. The "voice of experience" cannot actually remember having gathered this so-called evidence; he merely has the vague impression that it was gathered.

By contrast, Campbell and his colleagues can cite sample size, questionnaire items, coding rules, scaling convention, tabulating convention; and, if pressed, they can say how each case scored at each point in the processing of data.

For documenting generalizations, especially those that cite non-obvious and imperfect trends, the quantified data of research are to be preferred to the impressionistic evidence of "experience." For one thing, remembered evidence—when many cases must be kept in mind—stands in danger of being spuriously favorable, because of "memory cheating" (source-of-doubt H). Also, the orderly collating in research minimizes the relevance problem (source-of-doubt G). To go back to "the shadow falls" notion: whether or not any supposed observations actually *are* evidence for some hypothesis depends on the clarity of any observer-reports, the orderliness of the collating process, and whether or not the hypothesis cites clearly defined variables. Of course, the research process does not affect the clarity of the hypothesis being tested. When we test an inferred-variable hypothesis, some residue of the relevance problem stays with us. Sometimes the effort to measure produces clear observer-reports, occasionally not; with quantified data, the shadow may fall at this point too. But at least collating is orderly; the shadow does not fall at this point. So when quantified data are related to an hypothesis, as in Table IV, their relevance to the hypothesis, as evidence, tends to be less problematic than is so-called impressionistic evidence, dredged up from memory.

## Sources of Raw Data

In this section a bit will be said about the gathering of the original observer-reports by means of (a) self-reports, (b) tests, (c) standardized behavior observations, (d) written texts, which may be subjected to coding or content analysis, and (e) ratings (in that order). The focus of attention will be on the clarity of observer-reports, the explicitness of criteria by which cases are classified. In other words, now we turn to the first point where the shadow may fall.

As was mentioned before: our language gives us vague terms for describing human behavior. Research people have struggled mightily to make verbal measuring devices explicit. The subject matter resists. Scaling conventions which enable secondary measurement are always explicit; there is no problem there. The difficulty resides in the original classification of cases: in the first observer-reports or in coding. We do our best to make these clear. When this is impossible, we sometimes settle for an inexplicit sorting criterion such as a rating rule or an unclear questionnaire item.

## *Self-Report Data*

With self-report data, the observer is also the case; he "observes" and reports on himself. The variables he describes are his own traits: something that happened to him, something he did, what he thinks or feels, how he stands with respect to such variables as age, sex, place of birth, political-party affiliation, tastes in food, and so forth. Self-report data may come from an interview, in which an interviewer asks the self-reporter a standard list of questions and then records the answers. Or it may come from a questionnaire, to which the respondent writes out the answers himself. Or self-report data may be gathered in a less standardized manner. An example would be stated beliefs about ghosts, given to an anthropologist by a number of tribal informants, which the anthropologist eventually summarizes in an ethnography.

Sometimes measurement occurs in the original observer-report, that is, in the self-report. An example is the questionnaire item "Age?" to which the respondent replies, "19." At other times measurement waits on subsequent coding, as with long-answer or open-end interview questions, or as with the ghosts example. (This and many other ethnographies might eventually be the raw material for a cross-cultural study, in which tribes are coded for fear of ghosts.)

When measurement waits on coding, the measuring instrument is of course the coding rule. When measurement occurs at the point of self-report, the measuring instrument is the questionnaire item itself.

In a self-report, the respondent characterizes himself with respect to some variable: whether or not he has it, or how much of it he has. In order to categorize himself, he applies to himself some kind of standard. The standard is verbal. It is represented by one or several key terms, in the questionnaire item, or the interview question, or the self-report itself. The simplest of questionnaire items are questions like "Age?" "Sex?" "Number of dependents?" which present a single-term classifying convention, with which the respondent scores himself: "42," "Female," "3." At other times the standard is not neatly summarized in a single term, as with this question from an interview with a mother:

> All babies cry, of course. Some mothers feel that if you pick up a baby every time it cries, you will spoil it. Others think you should never let a baby cry for very long. How do you feel about this? [Sears, Maccoby and Levin 1957:491]

This question invites the mother to give an opinion concerning how one should respond to a crying baby. The standard she must apply to herself is something on the order of "my opinion about how to respond to a crying baby." (Whatever answer she gives is recorded by the interviewer, later coded for "warmth," and eventually combined with answers to other questions in a "warmth scale.")

The explicitness of the self-report depends on the explicitness of this standard which the respondent applies to himself, on the extent to which it has a clear and universal meaning in a given language. If the respondent is in doubt as to how to apply the standard to himself, if it is subject to different interpretations by different respondents, then the classifying device is not explicit, and the resulting self-report is not clear. If we were deeply concerned about the explicitness of observer-reports, our use of self-report data would be very limited. Questionnaire respondents would only be asked about variables like age, sex, income, marital status, number of children, grade-point average, years of schooling, and the like; in general, they would only be asked to count explicitly agreed-upon units. Unfortunately, information about many of the variables in which we are interested is only accessible through self-reports.[3] In practice, our questioning is not limited to the more prosaic demographic variables; we also ask for opinions, preferences, beliefs, attitudinal variables. Thus we extend our range of inquiry. We do what we can in the phrasing of questions to make the sorting criteria which the respondents must apply to themselves less nebulous, more nearly standardized and clear. However, most such self-reports are not, strictly speaking, explicit; they leave some doubt about just what the respondent "observed" in himself in order to categorize himself in a particular way; they rely on "standards" that are certainly not as explicit and invariant as "age," "income last year," and "grade-point average."

Perhaps this judgment is too harsh. The question "How clear is clear enough?" admits to differences of opinion. Some questionnaire items are just faintly ambiguous with respect to what standard the respondent classified himself with, and whether the standard was the same for all respondents; in practice, these might be clear enough to satisfy most persons. Examples might be: "During the past month, how often did your child receive a spanking?" (What is a "spanking"?) "During the past week, how many dates did you have?" (What is a "date"? Did the term mean the same for all the girls that were asked this question?)

Other possible questionnaire items are manifestly vague, and leave considerable doubt as to what the respondent "observed" in himself in order to classify himself in a particular way. For example, "Since you have been in college, has your faith in God gotten stronger, or gotten weaker, or stayed about the same?"

The problem of the clarity of observer-reports is sometimes avoided—on a semantic level, at least—by construing answers to questionnaires not as self-reports, but as "bits of behavior" in themselves; that is, as responses to test items. This gambit raises characteristic problems of its own; it will be discussed soon.

In addition to the clarity problem, there is also the problem of

[3] Thus the dictum attributed to Samuel Stouffer: "If you want to know, ask."

observer-error, of course. Consensual validation of self-reports is rarely possible; they cannot be checked against other reports by outside observers. No one can climb inside the informant's head to check on his true memories, beliefs, attitudes, thoughts, or feelings. It is a matter of guesswork whether, and to what extent, self-report data are true. In practice, such easy questions as "Age?" "Marital status?" and "Whom will you vote for?" are freely asked and the answers generally believed. More difficult questions are either not asked, or the answers are taken with suspicion and hopes for the best. By a difficult question, I mean (1) one which requires a difficult feat of memory ("How old were you when you got your last spanking?") or (2) one which asks for a difficult generalization ("When you were 10, how often were you spanked?") or (3) one which asks for a fine discrimination ("Do you prefer Budweiser or Busch Bavarian Beer?") or (4) one which asks some respondents to fight a tendency to give an untruthful but less embarrassing response ("Do you masturbate?"). As a variant to point 4, questions are avoided to which the respondent may give a sincere answer after lying to himself; i.e., questions calling forth rationalizations and perceptual distortions ("Are you prejudiced against Negroes?").

Once the questionnaire is given and the self-reports are gathered in, one can only guess about the direction and magnitude of error. Guesses about *how much* error occurred would devolve on an estimate as to the difficulty and clarity of the questionnaire item. With really difficult and/or vague questions, the answers may bear no correspondence to reality at all (and ordinarily, such questions are not asked in the first place; when they are, the answers are taken as responses to test items, not as self-reports). Guessing about the *direction* of error usually hinges on guesses about what Douglas Crowne and David Marlowe term the social-desirability factor (1960). One can ask himself: Is the question value-loaded? And if he decides it is, what is the "proper" or socially desirable answer? Thus, if a survey reports that "94 percent of our respondents feel all citizens should have the right of free speech," one may decide that this is an exaggeration of the actual percentage, due to the workings of the social-desirability factor. "Proper" answers to value-loaded questions will receive more attention later, when we take up the subject of systematic bias.

### *Tests*

The term "test" has varying meanings. Generally, it refers to a standardized problem situation or cue—usually a series of these —to which the test subject responds. The responses are then scored with a scoring key; then they are summed up to give the subject an overall score on the test, by means of a scaling convention. Most tests used in research bear some resemblance to the "objective tests," multiple-choice or true-false, used in school. The "standardized cues" are questionnaire items. The scoring key resembles the teacher's list of "right answers" to his tests. Scaling involves simply adding the number of "right answers," i.e., answers contributing to a score on whatever is being measured. With some tests it is more complicated than this. Elaborate rules may be required to score the responses. At times, scaling involves more than a count. Also with some tests the standardized cues are not questionnaire items; the subject might have to draw pictures, or give his associations to a standardized series of pictures, or "respond" in some other way.

Generally, tests get around the problem of the clarity of observer-reports. As mentioned earlier, even if a test is questionnaire-based, the answers to the questions are not construed as self-reports, but rather as "behavior." The observer who classifies is not the test subject; the observer is the test scorer. What a given test score means can be made explicit, in terms of observed behavior. One merely needs to view the list of test items, the subject's recorded responses to them, the scoring key, and the scaling convention.

However, tests as they are used in research seldom get around the relevance problem. They are usually used as indices for inferred variables. Thus we have intelligence tests, special aptitude tests (mechanical, mathematical, verbal, etc.), various attitude tests, and tests that purport to "measure" certain personality traits. Test scores may be subject to explicit definition, but the inferred variables seldom are.

Depending on how one construes a test score, the problem of

validity may be slight, or it may be rather grave. Observer-error narrows down simply to mistakes by the test scorer; one would suppose that errors rarely occur. If an IQ of 122 is construed as merely a report that a person scored 122 on a particular IQ test, then this report is no doubt true. But if it is taken as evidence that the person stands at a particular level with respect to general intelligence, then the validity problem is quite real. Tests used as indices, and the validity problem, will receive more attention in the next chapter.

### *Standardized Behavior Observations*

If one wishes to classify behavior with respect to some variable, there are several options. Self-reports can be used at times. A second option is a test. The test, with its standardized items, cues, or response situation, tends to shape and predetermine whatever behavior is observed. What response will be given is not predetermined; but the range of possible responses is considerably narrowed: "yes/no," "agree/disagree," or whatever, to a standardized item or question. A third possiblity is simply to observe and record running behavior in a situation that is less contrived, where possible responses have not been so shaped and narrowed. One can observe a group of children at play or a psychiatric patient in a therapy session or some other person or group, and record by means of shorthand, tape recorder, or movie camera all that happened, all that was said. Then, if one wishes to score the case (whatever it or he may be) on some variable, the record of running behavior can be coded, applying some coding rule.

A fourth option is standardized behavior observations. An observer can score cases on variables as he observes the running behavior; in other words, subsequent coding is not required. Research on groups has relied heavily on this sort of measurement. An observer can observe a group in session, perhaps through a one-way mirror, and score such variables as talking time (for each person in the group, with the aid of a stopwatch), how often each person spoke, how many questions were asked, how many laughs, and so forth. The observations may be noted on a time chart, which at the end of the group session will show the sequence of questions, answers, jokes, laughs, etc., with who-did-what specified.

In order to measure the variables that the researcher deems of interest, the observer must usually make inferences about intent and feeling-tone. He scores acts as "asks for help," "expresses aggression," "offers support," and the like. Thus Freed Bales' (1950) early scoring system directs the observer to note each time a group member "shows solidarity," "shows tension release," "gives a suggestion," "gives an opinion," "agrees," "asks for an opinion," "disagrees," "shows antagonism." Scoring rules are provided, i.e., definitions of all such variables which must be noted. When the observer must note more than simple "behavior"—when his scoring decisions involve guesses about the intent or import of observed acts—then, in a sense, his notations represent inferred-variable hypotheses. This is another arguable point. The dividing line between inferences and simple reports of "what happened" is not absolutely clear-cut and could be moved back and forth somewhat, depending on individual opinion. At any rate, standardized behavior observation presents the same dilemma as do self-reports. As soon as one reaches beyond the basic (and dull) facts—age, income, marital status; talking time, questions asked, laughs—and tries to penetrate to a wider range of variables, the explicitness of the sorting criterion becomes a problem. When the observer must gauge intent, as with "shows solidarity" and "shows antagonism," the standard by which cases are classified is less explicit than it is with mere talking time. Also with self-reports: for some variables the ambiguity is very faint, and would not bother many persons.

A variation of standardized behavior observation is the specification of *treatments,* which can be made in an experiment. Here, one need not catch variables that flow out of running behavior. Rather, one merely notes what was done to the subject. Thus the experimental psychologist can divide his rats into two groups: those who get food in their cages up to the time they run the maze, and those who get no food for twenty-four hours prior to running the maze. This treatment—what was done to the animals—can be clearly described. Some got food, others didn't;

some can be scored "high" on the hunger-variable, others can be scored low (the subsequent running of the maze could be construed as a "test").

### *Coding and Content Analysis*

As mentioned before, sometimes the original observer-reports, the raw data, are not reports of measurement. Rather, they are running narratives or descriptions, long answers to interview questions, ethnographies, or some other accounts which have yet to be rendered into numerical scale scores. Measurement is then accomplished by coding. Coding rules are drawn up; coders read the written accounts with the coding rules in hand, and thereby score cases. A tribe might be coded "present" or "absent" for the fear-of-ghosts variable (after the coders consult the ethnography which describes the tribal customs). Mothers' answers to the Sears-Maccoby-Levin interview question about how one should respond to a crying baby can be scored "high" or "low" for the warmth-variable. The census taker, after listening to the lady of the house and filling out his form, can code a household "yes" or "no" for the variable containing-a-family. A coding rule is, in a sense, a written definition of the variable. An effort is made to make the definition clear. One wants to make the cutting point dividing "high" from "low," "yes" from "no," as explicit as possible, so that the coding rule will stand up well in a subsequent test of agreement. (Two or more coders code the same material; afterward, one counts the percentage of cases that were given the identical score by all coders.) Some coding rules provide for more than a two-point, yes/no type of scale; the scale may have more than two categories, and hence more than one cutting point. In such cases, each point on the scale must receive a special definition of its own.

The term "content analysis," as it is customarily used, is more or less synonymous with coding. The operation is the same. Content analysis may be done on books, newspaper or magazine articles, speeches, myths, or art works such as films, paintings, or even music. If a distinction were to be made, it might be this: content analysis, essentially the coding operation, can be performed on textual material which is not a series of observer-reports; that is, it need not be a "secondary analysis" of observer-reports that have already been gathered in. When Alan Lomax scores an African song, or when Martha Wolfenstein scores a movie, *they* are the original observers; the results of their content analyses are the raw data.

Sometimes the scorer must count as well as code. A "recording unit" is fixed upon: this might be a fight, a kiss, an expression of anger, a reference (favorable or unfavorable) to a particular political candidate, public figure or ethnic group, a ceremonial, or whatever. The scorer notes the unit each time he decides it occurs in the text; after he finishes coding, he counts the number of times it has occurred.

As these examples suggest, with some coding tasks it is easy to achieve an explicit sorting criterion; with others this is difficult or impossible, and some less-than-explicit compromise solution may be settled for. Occasionally the task is so easy that no special rule or definition is required; classification is accomplished by a single clear term (kiss, paragraph, sex of characters, etc.). But as with self-reports and behavior observations, the researcher is tempted to reach beyond such clear-cut little units and variables and to code more interesting variables which resist clear definition.

### *Ratings*

A rating is a global judgment, a summary of some large and ill-specified chunk of reality. Informally, in everyday life, we rate parties for how much fun they are, people for how socially poised they are, girls for how pretty they are, children for how well-behaved they are, parents for strictness, traffic for congestion, music for various good and bad qualities, and so on. More formal rating occurs in competitions of many sorts, where the contestants are judged and given scores: dog shows, flower shows, film festivals, fights, diving competition, ski jumping, beauty contests, figure skating, etc.

The researcher may turn to rating as a last resort, when any more precise and explicit convention for scoring cases is either impossible or is deemed too much trouble. Thus in a study of juvenile delinquency, any assessment of family background variables may be possible only by way of rating. A social worker visits a boy's home and interviews, or one way or another "gets to know the family." Later she can rate the family on severity of discipline, on mother's and father's warmth (toward the boy), or perhaps on some sort of home-atmosphere variable (McCord, McCord, and Zola 1959:16). Certain characteristics of "natural groups" are only assessable through ratings. Thus a meeting might be rated for such variables as the following (Heyns and Zander 1953:386–387):

a. Understandability: to what extent were the participants getting the meaning of each other's statements?
b. Opportunity to communicate: to what extent did the participants have opportunity to talk?
c. Ego-involvement: how much did the members have at stake in any decisions or outcomes issuing from the meeting?
d. Urgency: how urgent did the participants consider any problems discussed in the meeting?
e. Formality: how formal was the meeting?
f. Group support: how supporting and accepting were the group members toward each other.
g. Atmosphere: how pleasant was the atmosphere of the meeting?

When he rates, the researcher is often concerned about reliability (i.e., the invariance of the classifying convention). Ordinarily he makes up rating rules. In so doing, he may be able to reduce somewhat the vagueness of raters' observer-reports. If the rating scale is one of more than two points, then each point in the scale is ordinarily ticketed with a special definition (or term) of its own. An example is a rating scale authored by Lippit and Zander (1943) for measuring tension in a Boy Scout meeting: (1) very relaxed (lowest point on the tension scale); (2) relaxed; (3) middleground; (4) restless; (5) keyed up (highest point on the tension scale).

For each scale point there is a paragraph-long rating rule, directing the rater as to what he should observe in order to rate a meeting at this point, rather than at an adjacent scale point.

Sometimes one can choose between rating and bona fide explicit measurement. For example, it is possible to rate books or articles, or passages within them, for how easy (or difficult) they are to read. If two raters were to score a collection of passages for reading ease, agreement would no doubt be low, because of the vagueness of rating rules. The alternative is to use one or several *indices* of reading ease. The readers, instead of trying to rate, can simply score the passages for average number of syllables per word (word length), or average sentence length (Flesch 1946). Now agreement should be perfect, barring mistakes. The scorer need merely count explicitly agreed-upon units. Choice of a Flesch reading-ease index reduces the relevance problem. It still exists; "reading ease" is an inferred variable, not clearly defined. But the relevance problem is only half as serious as it was with the rating. With the ratings, both the original observer-reports (giving scores to passages) and any eventual conclusion ("this passage was the hardest to read") cite unclear variables; with the Flesch index, only the conclusion (if it speaks of reading ease rather than sentence length) is unclear.

Occasionally, if one wishes to take the trouble, he can "break the variable down" into smaller, discrete units, thus substituting a clear coding rule or standardized behavior observation for rating. As another example of this, Heyns and Zander might have counted the number of laughs in a meeting, rather than trying to rate the meeting on "pleasantness of atmosphere."

Some "measurements" that issue from self-report data, from behavior observations, or from coding and content analysis are rather vague, global judgments, and hence could be construed as ratings: thus the Heyns-Zander and Lippit-Zander assessments of meetings, which came from observing running behavior and were characterized as ratings. Content analysis is, at times, simply a matter of rating: of novels, for various "themes" they might present; of newspaper articles, for favorableness or unfavorableness of news-slant with respect to some policy or group or public figure. Self-report items which ask the respondent to express opinions or attitudes could often be viewed as devices for self-rating. Attitudes on many subjects must be rather complicated, multi-faceted, and variable; the respondent, in answering, must sum these up as best he or she can: "Strongly agree," "Yes," or "Most of the time, a baby should be picked up when it starts to cry."

Heyns and Zander speak of the rater as "a human collating machine" (1953:397). That he is. The analogy could be made to collating with impressionistic evidence: many observations gathered together and then "weighed," in the memory or in the mind. The process is complex and obscure; the classification, storing, and summing-up of observations is not in accord with explicitly stated rules. Nevertheless, some variables are only assessable through rating. At times we must rate, or not do the study at all.

## Conclusion

Perhaps, after all this carping, it would be fitting to change direction here, and end the chapter on a positive note. For documenting generalizations, the measurement-based study represents a tremendous improvement over impressionistic evidence. If quantified data are at times a bit shaky with respect to sources-of-doubt G and H, the remembered "evidence from experience" is much more so. The difference is particularly great as regards collating (disregarding any special mental "collating" that must be done by raters)—the pulling-together of observations of many cases in order to document a generalization. With research, collating is impeccably orderly and explicit; with impressionistic evidence, collating is in the memory and is generally indescribable, and stands in considerable danger of memory cheating. With the original observer-reports, we do the best we can. Given the nature of the human subject matter and of words themselves, there are limits to what we can do. Perhaps it is best not to be too fussy. For many a variable that resists explicit and error-free classification, imprecise measurement is no doubt better than no measurement at all.

# *Selected References*

Self-report data:

Daniel Katz, "Three Criteria: Knowledge, Conviction, and Significance," in Bernard Berelson and Morris Janowitz, eds., *Reader in Public Opinion and Communication*, pp. 50–57.

Douglas Crowne and David Marlowe, *The Approval Motive.*

Herbert Hyman, *Survey Design and Analysis.*

Tests—their scope and variety:

Oskar Buros, *The Sixth Mental Measurements Yearbook.*

Anne Anastasi, *Psychological Testing.*

Coding:

Bernard Berelson, *Content Analysis in Communications Research.*

Dorwin Cartwright, "Analysis of Qualitative Material," in Leon Festinger and Daniel Katz, eds., *Research Methods in the Behavioral Sciences.*

Rating:

Paul Lazarsfeld and Allen Barton, "Qualitative Measurement in the Social Sciences," in Daniel Lerner and Harold Lasswell, eds., *The Policy Sciences: Recent Developments in Scope and Method.*

Roger Heyns and Alvin Zander, "Observation of Group Behavior," in Leon Festinger and Daniel Katz, eds., *Research Methods in the Behavioral Sciences.*

The research process—from beginning to end:

James Davis, "Great Books and Small Groups: An Informal History of a National Survey," and Charles R. Wright and Herbert Hyman, "The Evaluators," in Phillip E. Hammond, ed., *Sociologists at Work.*

*Chapter 5*

# INFERRED VARIABLES AND INDICES

The subject of this chapter is an especially crucial area, and it is one which seethes with controversies and ambiguities. It is with inferred variables especially that rigor fails. Much hangs on personal taste and prejudice. A number of the major issues, here, could be conceptualized in different ways; depending on one's starting point, one's discussion could end with very different conclusions. A case can be made that when one comes to inferred variables, evidence more or less ends and faith takes over. Or one can argue the opposite—inferred-variable hypotheses *can* be documented—and proceed to erect an elaborate technical superstructure toward this end. We have been able to avoid this Pandora's box for four chapters. Now we must take off the lid.

The necessary starting point is definition of the term "inferred variable." This, like any definition, must be arbitrary; and, being a point of departure, the definition will do much to shape the subsequent discussion. For one thing, it will determine what sorts and how many of the hypotheses that we state and test in research will be construed as inferred-variable hypotheses.

In Chapter 2, an inferred variable was defined, in a preliminary and incomplete way, as a variable that cannot be directly observed. One observes something—say, a person's score on an IQ test—and takes this as a sign or indicator of another variable: some characteristic of the person that "lies behind" the IQ score, is expressed by it, is reflected in it, or causes it. The inferred variable in this example would be general intelligence, or overall intellectual capacity, or "smartness," or "brains." The higher the IQ score, the greater the intellectual capacity (one infers). A person with an IQ of 165 is a genius. A person with an IQ of 60 is a moron.

All variables might be classified as either *inferred variables* or *observed variables*. Characteristics of cases that can be directly observed can be termed observed variables: the person's score on the IQ test. Presumed characteristics which cannot be observed fall into the residual category, inferred variable: the person's intelligence.

Now to develop this definition for our purposes here: an observed variable is one which can be observed, *and* one which can be explicitly defined in terms of observations. All others will be considered inferred variables: those that cannot (or were not) directly observed *and/or* those that are not explicitly defined in terms of observations.

By the definition, such variables as age, weight, height, grade-point average, years of schooling, talking time, and most test scores qualify as observed variables. They can be directly observed, and any observer-reports concerning them classify cases with explicit sorting criteria. Thus what a score of 112 on a particular IQ test means, in terms of observations, can be made clear: you need merely see the list of test questions, the person's answers to them, and the scoring key for the test.

Unobservable entities are inferred variables: intelligence, neuroticism, morale, idealism, conservatism, and so on.

Finally, variables that do not admit to clear definition will also be classed as inferred variables. Any reports of rating, for example, will be taken as inferred-variable hypotheses: how relaxed the Boy Scout meeting was, whether an editorial was favorable or unfavorable to the civil rights movement, a mother's warmth, which passage was the most difficult to read, who was the most beautiful girl in the beauty contest. The reasoning, here, is that because the rating rule (if there be any) does not explicitly fix cutoff points, it is ambiguous what a particular score on a rating scale means in terms of observation—hence, an inferred variable. With this proviso, then, many a variable which refers to observation of some sort, but is not explicitly defined, qualifies as an inferred variable: social-class position, poise, sociability, and so on.

If the dividing line between inferred variables and observed variables is set in this manner, then most of the variables we talk about—especially in discourse about human qualities and human behavior—become inferred variables. The dividing line could be moved back and forth somewhat, making the term "inferred variable" more or less inclusive, depending on one's personal opinion with respect to the question "How clear is clear enough?" In short, this definition of "inferred variable," itself, is less than ideally explicit. A thoroughgoing conservative might construe statements like "She had three dates last week" and "Our little boy got two spankings last week" as inferred-variable hypotheses, citing the faint ambiguity surrounding the terms "date" and "spanking." Or one could be more liberal, feel that the terms "date" and "spanking" are clear enough, and decide that the above statements are observed-variable hypotheses.

Ambiguity can also arise with respect to whether something is "directly observed" or merely "inferred." One might claim that *all* variables are inferred, on the ground that all observations require a certain amount of inference from past experience before mental images of shapes and colors and sounds can be ticketed, say, "flames," "tantrum," "talking time." This issue has its many fine points, and we shall pass over them. They have been well enough discussed by others (Mehlberg 1958: 144–146; Nagel 1961: 82–84; Kemeny 1959: 122–124). They would overload us here.

At any rate, the observed-variable/inferred-variable dichotomy is an inexplicit one, with some ambiguity as regards the precise cutting point. Some borderline instances will come up, where one judge might decide that a variable is "observed," while another person would decide it is an inferred variable. For variables near either end of the continuum, there should be little disagreement: thus, the inferred variables faith in God, societal complexity, Dionysian ethos; the observed variables IQ score, weight, blue eyes.

This distinction accords in a very general way, I think, with those made by other writers on the subject. Some past writers have focused on delimited varieties of inferred variables, and have given the animal numerous different names: inferred entity, intervening variable, latent trait, abstract concept, theoretical construct, hypothetical construct (Beck 1950; Kantor 1957:55–60; Spence 1944; McCorquodale and Meehl 1948; Marx 1951; Coombs 1953; Nagel 1961:86–87).

Most of the more important and interesting variables clearly qualify as inferred variables. First of all, there are the personality traits and characteristics of mental life: desires, opinions, attitudes, emotional states. All these, except the few that can be described in clear self-reports, may be construed as inferred variables.

The higher reaches of science—statements on a high level of generality, high-level laws and theories—are generally inferred-variable hypotheses. Theory in the physical sciences can be pictured as a sort of abstraction pyramid. At the pyramid's base are observed-variable hypotheses, directly tested, the so-called "fact-like statements" and "experimental laws." These are explained, brought together, at a higher level of abstraction by more general statements. These in turn are explained by still higher-level theories which are explained by still more high-level theory. Thus Kepler's laws, the law of free fall, and the law of the tides can all be explained—at a higher level of abstraction—by Newton's laws. Newton's laws, and the law of motion of light rays, are explained by the general theory of relativity. Relativity theory, along with similarly abstract statements such as in quantum mechanics and Maxwell's laws, may eventually prove to be explainable by Einstein's unified field theory (Kemeny 1959:124–140, 168). Such, at any rate, is my secondhand understanding of this rarified realm of science.

The high-level theories of the physical sciences take the form of mathematical models and formulae. The variables in them can be clearly defined—but only in terms of one another. That is, one abstract concept (represented by a mathematician's symbol) is equated with a certain combination of other abstract concepts; but the abstract concept is not defined in terms of something that can be observed. In order to make a bridge between it and the world of real observations, an assumption must be made, an index must be decided upon—and the shadow falls.[1] This is no problem if one decides not to judge the theory for likelihood of truth. Such high-level theories are customarily rated with respect to other criteria instead: usefulness, elegance, explanatory economy, or success at prediction.

Similarly, the verbal concepts of the social sciences, those on a high level of generality, can be considered as terms for inferred variables: authority, functional specificity, social cohesion, and the like. They, too, are not clearly defined in terms of observations. When one of these enters into an hypothesis, the result is frequently what will be termed here a high-level law. This will be discussed toward the end of the chapter.

## Indices

It is now time to make another dichotomy, one which parallels the inferred variable/observed variable distinction. All measures will be considered as either *direct measures* or *indices*. If an observed variable is being measured, then one has a direct measure. If one wishes to "measure" an inferred variable, then his measuring instrument is an index.

Which sort of variable it is sometimes devolves simply on definition. To return to the IQ test: if "IQ" is defined as merely score on this IQ test, then IQ is an observed variable, which is directly measured with the test. If, on the other hand, IQ is defined as intelligence, then it is an inferred variable, and the IQ test

[1] See especially Weaver 1961.

becomes an index. This is represented in the following little paradigm:

| IQ defined as score on the Stanford-Binet IQ Test | IQ defined as general intelligence |
|---|---|
| The test is a direct measure. | The test is an index. |
| IQ is operationally defined. | IQ is not operationally defined. |
| IQ is an observed variable. | IQ is an inferred variable. |

If one stays with operational definitions[2] of this sort, he can steer away from inferred variables and avoid the subsequent problems of validity and relevance. Usually this is not done, of course. The researcher is bold enough to say that what he is really interested in is intelligence, or mental health, or persistence, or prejudice, not simply scores on some measuring instrument. So his measure becomes an index, and his variable is an inferred variable.

Occasionally some study finding may be stated as either an inferred-variable or an observed-variable hypothesis, depending on one's choice. The "inductive example" in Chapter 2 mentioned the correlation between voting turnout and years of schooling; people who didn't go far in school are less inclined to vote. This is an observed-variable hypothesis; it has two variables, directly measured: years of schooling, and voted (yes/no) in *X* election. If one wished to read a bit more into this correlation, he might conclude that ignorant people are less likely to vote. Ignorance is an inferred variable; years of schooling has become its index.

A direct measure of one variable, then, can later be used as an index for another. An example is a ball player's batting average,

[2] "Operational definition," in the narrower usage of the term, means that a variable is defined as merely score on some specified measuring instrument. The term in its broader usage means definition in terms of specified observations, in other words, any reasonably clear definition (Hampel 1954:52, Plutchik 1963).

taken as an indicator of how good a batter he is. Economic indices are a further instance. For example, price-rise in a few selected industries or types of product may be interpreted as an indicator of a general price-rise throughout the economy (Zeisel 1957:92, 115–120). A test score may be used as a predictive index; for example, score on the Graduate Record Examination as a predictor of future success in graduate school.

An inferred variable may be "measured" by many indices—thus the many "intelligence tests." Indices for social-class position passed the two dozen mark some years ago (Kahl and Davis 1955); no doubt there are three dozen of them by this time. Some SEC scales sort persons into two classes, some three, some five, some six, some more than these. Income may figure in the index; occupation, house type, neighborhood, association groups, reputational ratings; these are mixed in various combinations, with differing cutting points and scaling rules, to produce the manifold indices of social-class position. An observed variable, by contrast, is measured only one way.

The natural sciences also have their inferred variables. However, it is my impression that there is an important difference of emphasis. Their abstraction pyramid is superimposed on a broad substratum of observed-variable hypotheses, and these are taken seriously in their own right. For one thing, they are the stuff of which the technology is made. The theories float above the "observed facts," and are viewed as useful devices for summarizing and collating the "facts"; but the "facts" are there, they have their uses, and they accumulate. In the social sciences, on the other hand, less emphasis is placed on gathering and ordering any such substratum of observed-variable hypotheses. When one does research, one generally sets out to "test" an inferred-variable hypothesis by the use of an index.

The strong trend in the social sciences in the direction of inferred-variable hypotheses appears to be firmly fixed. No doubt this is a good thing. Any marked counter-trend toward operational definition would signal a wholesale retreat from problems and a narrowing of interests. However, the price we pay for our "concepts" and our "constructs" is considerable. This price is at least threefold. First of all there is the oft-mentioned relevance issue: with rare exceptions, inferred variables are not clearly defind; most of them are essentially undefined. Second, there is the validity problem: one rarely knows what the relationship actually is between any index (an IQ test, say) and an inferred variable (such as intelligence) of which it is taken as a sign. Third: inferred variables with their vague definitions and their multiple indices bring disorder and ambiguity into any accumulation of research. The writer of a review article, who must sum up a tradition of research in some narrow problem area, finds himself talking about variables that were "measured" in different ways in different studies, and which were related to other variables, likewise "measured" in different ways in different studies. Often some of the findings of the studies contradict each other; the reviewer must rationalize this as best he can. An example is the clash between child-rearing studies as regards the effect of social class on parental strictness: several studies find lower-class parents to be relatively permissive and lenient; other studies show lower-class persons to be relatively harsh and strict parents. Why the contradiction? Sample differences? Slip-ups in a few of the studies? Bronfenbrenner (1958) explains it as a time shift: the middle class has mellowed in recent years (the more recent studies have generally been the ones to show the lower-class parent as relatively strict). Perhaps so. Still, the inferred variables social-class position and parental strictness are, in a sense, "something different" in each study; they are represented in each by different indices. Perhaps the contradictory findings are merely due to this, perhaps not; thus the ambiguity. If we were simply talking about annual income and frequency of spankings, rather than class position and parental strictness, one would imagine that the picture would be more clear.

## Evidence for Validity

In speaking of "measuring" inferred variables I have been putting "measuring" in quotation marks. This was meant as an acknowledgment that one does not actually measure an inferred variable.

Rather, one measures an observed variable; then, he assumes that this is a sign of an inferred variable. *X* IQ test measures performance on X IQ test, which is heralded by a test score; then one can take the test score as an index of intelligence. The term "IQ" does stand for "intelligence quotient"; tests of this sort are customarily labeled intelligence tests. Many of our indices are ticketed—rather brazenly, perhaps—as tests or measures of inferred variables. They are not, of course, measures of inferred variables in the sense that they tell you how cases stand with respect to them. An IQ test does not tell you what your intelligence is, nor does the Remote Associates Test tell you how creative you are, nor does the Incomplete Sentences Test tell you how mentally ill you are—not in the sense that you can tell your temperature with a thermometer, or that a person can tell you his age.

One *infers* from an index score the presence or magnitude of an inferred variable. The actual relationship between inferred variable and index scores is unknown. For a single case, an index score may signify an inferred variable rightly or wrongly. For a group of cases, the relationship between presence or magnitude of an inferred variable and index scores might be viewed as a correlation. One hopes it is a perfect positive correlation, a true isomorphism; but the correlation may be imperfect but strong, or it may be less than strong, or it can be nil. This correlation can be viewed as the index's degree of validity. If the correlation is perfect, we have a completely valid index; it actually measures what it purports to measure. If the correlation admits exceptions, but is still a strong one, then we still have a fairly valid index. If there is no positive correlation at all, the index is totally invalid.

The little examples in Chapter 2 mentioned the sight of flames as an index of heat, a tantrum as an index of anger, and driving a Cadillac as an index of wealth. With these, direct validity tests would be possible. One can directly observe and measure heat, wealth, and (through a self-report) anger. Flames, surely, would turn out to be a perfectly valid index of heat, or rather, it would be a perfectly valid "positive sign." The only exceptional cases, if the correlation were run, would be hot objects which were not emitting flames. Likewise, the correlation between throwing a tantrum and feeling angry should be very strong. Again, the tantrum is no doubt a perfectly valid positive sign of anger; the only exceptions to the correlation would be angry children who were not throwing tantrums. The correlation between wealth and Cadillac-ownership must be weaker, with exceptions in both directions: wealthy persons who do not drive Cadillacs and nonwealthy persons who do.

This sort of direct validity test is almost never possible in actual research, since the inferred variable cannot be directly observed and measured. If it could be, we would have no need of the index. Our only opportunities for bona fide validity tests come with predictive indices and actuarial prediction. Thus a language-aptitude test can be used to predict performance in an accelerated foreign language program. After a certain number of persons have actually taken the test and gone through the program, their scores on the language-aptitude test can be correlated with some criterion measure, which in this instance would probably be course grades. The resulting correlation coefficient is taken as a "validity coefficient." It represents how closely scores on the predictive index—the language-aptitude test—corresponded with scores on the criterion measure, course grades. In practice, of course, actuarial prediction is seldom this simple. An entire battery of measures is often used; the measures are weighted so as to give the highest possible validity coefficient. (The students might be subjected to a variety of measures. After they finish the foreign language course, their grades in the course are correlated with each of these. In this manner, those measures are selected that "discriminate"—between the students who did well in the course and those who did badly. In this manner, too, item weights are decided upon for a compositive predictive index. Then the predictive index can be used to select future candidates for the foreign language program.) Often the validity test is not really so direct, because of the fact that the "criterion" one wishes to predict cannot be directly measured. If one wishes to predict convicts' success during parole, or flight officer candidates' future success as Air Force pilots, or the success of a particular type of treatment for a certain category of psychiatric patient, or a student's success in or adjustment to some future occupation or profession, the assessment of "success" turns out to be a rather messy business, relying on ratings and indirect signs—i.e., indices. Even for the language-course example, if "success" is construed as "learning well" or "benefiting from the course" or anything more than course grade, then success itself is not measured directly, but merely represented by another index, course grade.

At any rate, actuarial prediction offers the best opportunity for direct validity tests. If one wishes to use a measure not as a predictive index, but as an index of a true inferred variable which cannot be directly measured, even in the future time, then any evidence for validity must necessarily be less direct, more roundabout; and, it is problematic whether any such "evidence for validity" is really evidence at all.

Index makers do show considerable concern about validity. The makers of psychological tests, especially, go to elaborate lengths to assure themselves that in its final form a test is at least a halfway valid measure—that the test scores bear some general correspondence to the magnitude of the underlying inferred variable. A good-sized segment of what is termed methodology, in the social sciences, has to do with the indirect "validation" of indices.[3] The sources of such assurances are varied. Here we shall skip over them rather lightly, starting with (a) correlating the index with other indices of the same inferred variable, then going on to (b) test-retest reliability checks, (c) demonstrations of the unidimensionality of the index items, (d) evidence for the propriety of the scaling convention, (e) construct validity, and (f) face validity.

### *Correlating the Index with Another Index*

The maker of a new test often follows the lead of actuarial studies. He gives the test to a "known group," correlates the test scores

[3] For a review of some alternative approaches to "validation," and alternative conceptualizations of the validity problem, see Cronbach and Meehl, 1955.

with a "criterion measure." A marital-adjustment test might be given to couples seeking divorce. If the test does reflect degree of marital adjustment, these couples should score low on it. A neuroticism test might be administered to a group of patients in psychotherapy; if the test scores do deflect degree of neuroticism, they should score high. Similarly, a racial-prejudice index might be administered to some racist demagogues; a mathematical-aptitude test can be correlated with grades in mathematics courses. If any such correlation is strong, it may engender considerable conviction that the index does, to an important extent, actually measure what it is supposed to measure.

Sometimes an index can be correlated with scores on one or several other tests, which also purport to measure the inferred variable in question. For example, if numerous tests of nAch (need to achieve) correlate strongly with each other, then they all serve to "validate" each other. If they do not intercorrelate strongly, then one may have doubts about them all.

Index scores probably reflect a variety of factors or variables. If an index is at all valid, then to some extent scores are determined by magnitude of the inferred variable which the index purports to measure; and, to some extent, cases' scores are influenced by other, extraneous factors. Correlations with other indices give more impressive evidence for validity if the indices are really different from each other; if we have some assurance that the correlations are not merely due to similarity between the indices with respect to extraneous factors (Campbell and Fiske 1959:84). For example, there are a number of masculinity-femininty tests which intercorrelate rather strongly. These are all questionnaire-based. Another femininity index, the Franck Drawing Completion Test, shows little relationship to these questionnaire-based tests (Shepler 1951). Either all these tests but Franck's are fairly valid, or perhaps none of them are; maybe the correlations between the questionnaire-based indices were due to the fact that they are all questionnaire-based, and hence are somehow all reflecting some common extraneous factor(s).

Following the assumption that an index is at best an impure reflection of its inferred variable, some researchers elect to measure inferred variables by means of *multiple* indices. If one wanted to measure femininity, he might use the Franck Drawing Completion Test (Franck and Rosen 1949), a questionnaire-based index of femininity of interests (in occupations, hobbies and recreations), and ratings of effemininacy. By a scaling convention, he might then combine scores on these three indices to get a composite index of femininity, in hopes that the different extraneous factors, contributing to scores on the three indices, would to some extent cancel each other out in the composite scores.

### *Test-Retest Reliability Checks*

The usual test does not purport to measure some unstable and fluctuating state, such as hunger, or degree of sexual arousal. Rather, it tries to measure a fairly stable trait: marital adjustment, mathematical aptitude, intelligence, effeminacy, neuroticism, or whatever. In other words, the inferred variables which, hopefully, are reflected in the test scores are viewed as stable enough so that persons can be classified as generally apt or inept in math, effeminate or manly, neurotic or "healthy," and so on. An IQ test is supposed to indicate how intelligent a person *is*, not merely how intelligent he was when he took the test. The test items are viewed as a sampling of the behaviors which reflect the inferred variable. And this sampling has its time dimension: if, in fact, a person scored 105 on an IQ test, then retook the test a month later and scored 150, his IQ would have more the appearance of an unstable state, rather than of a fairly stable trait. In other words, if the test purports to measure a trait, then instability of the tested behavior, over time, is a source of nonvalidity.

This is something that the test maker can often check out; he normally does so if this is at all possible. He might give 100 people his mathematical-aptitude test, wait a month, and then give them the test again. If he finds a strong positive correlation between test scores on the first and later testing sessions, then he has evidence that the tested behavior does stay fairly stable, over time.

### *Unidimensionality of Index Items*

When making a test, how should one choose test items? Face validity is one criterion: one selects or invents items that look as if they should reflect one's inferred variable. Ordinarily, the test maker is not satisfied with face validity alone. First he gathers a fairly large "pool" of possible items for his test. Then he selects some of these and discards the rest. This selection often rests on a test of unidimensionality. By one of a variety of treatments,[4] he can get evidence that some of the items do, to some extent, "measure the same thing" (and, hopefully, this "same thing" is the inferred variable which the test is designed to reflect). These are the items chosen to be included in the test.

### *The Scaling Convention*

For observed variables, scaling presents no problem. Either no scaling is required; or the variable is defined as frequency of something, and scaling consists of nothing more than a count or some variant of a count. For example, if population density is defined as number of people per square mile, one merely counts the number of persons living in a particular area and then divides by square miles of territory in the area. The scaling convention is a "given," specified in the definition of the observed variable. The same is true for IQ, defined as number of right answers to *X* IQ test; one merely counts the number of right answers, and that *is* the person's IQ score.

Some indices, likewise, present no scaling problem, since no "scaling" is required. The index consists of only a single item, one observer-report; items do not have to be combined to give cases summary scores. An example would be annual income, taken as an index of social-class position.

When an index does require scaling, however, problems arise. Suppose that a social-class index takes into account several fac-

[4] Discriminate function analysis (Rao 1952); cluster analysis (McQuitty 1957); factor analysis (Thurstone 1947); scalogram analysis or Guttman scaling (Guttman 1950, Lazarsfeld 1950, Coombs 1952, Green 1954, Torgerson 1957:298–359).

tors: income, type of occupation, "goodness" of neighborhood, and how expensive a person's house is. For a person to be scored on social-class position, he must first be scored on each of these four sub-variables; then the four scores must be combined to give him an overall score on social-class position. How will these scores be arrived at? What will be the relative weights of the sub-variables? Are income and neighborhood equally important, or should one be weighted more heavily than the other? A scaling convention must be decided upon; and choice of the convention will have an effect on cases' scores. It will also affect persons' relative positions on the social-class scale; whether person *A* will be ranked higher, lower, or the same as person *B*. If social-class position were operationally defined as so much of this and so much of that (that is, if it were defined in terms of the scaling convention) then there would be no problem; the scaling convention would, of course, be the proper one by definition. But if the variable social-class position is construed in the customary way—that is, not operationally defined—then one's scaling convention is *not* proper by definition.

Perhaps, if one only knew, some items in an index represent a greater magnitude of an inferred variable than do other items. These "heavier" items should be worth more points. Suppose, for example, we had an index of wealth based on 3 questionnaire items: "Do you own a bicycle?" "Do you own a telescope?" and "Do you own a yacht?" We might decide on a 20-point wealth scale; bicycle-ownership could be worth 1 point, telescope-ownership worth 4 points, and yacht-ownership worth 15 points. An alternative would be to weight the items equally; a "yes" answer to any of the 3 questions is worth 1 point; highest possible score on wealth is 3. If we did this, we might find a few yacht owners (who have no bicycles or telescopes) who score lower on wealth than do some bicycle owners (who had telescopes but no yachts).

Similarly in a mathematical-aptitude test: some test problems are probably more difficult than others; right answers to them represent a higher level of mathematical aptitude, and they should be worth more points than the easy questions. Other tests of aptitude, ability, or performance—in fact, multi-item indices in general—might be viewed in the same way.

In short, with indices one's scaling convention is open to question; it must be defended. The scaling problem can be dealt with in various ways. A test may be composed of a great many items; in scoring the test, one weights the items equally, hoping that any inequities with respect to true item weights will to some extent cancel each other out over the long series of test questions (Anastasi 1954:153). Or a scale may assign unequal weights to items on the basis of one of the treatments cited in the footnote on page 127 (see especially Torgerson, 1957). Each of these scaling treatments can be viewed as an attack on the validity problem: it is an attempt to minimize the disparity between scale scores and the true magnitude of the inferred variable which the index presumably measures.

### *Construct Validity*

After an index has been in use for a while, a network of correlations may gradually evolve which can act, to some extent, to confirm one's faith in the validity of the index. Some of the older intelligence tests are in this favorable position. Thus, one would imagine that individuals get more intelligent as they grow up; adults tend to perform better on IQ tests than children do. Brain damage should affect one's intelligence; brain-damaged people tend to score low on the tests. Eminent philosophers, scientists, and artists should have high intelligence; they score high on the IQ tests. High-IQ children should do well in school; in general they do (Anastasi 1958:379–408, 439). Each of these correlations can be viewed as: (a) evidence for reasonable hypothesis about what intelligence should be related to, and (b) evidence that the IQ scores do reflect general intelligence.

### *Face Validity*

This is easy to achieve. One merely points out that the index, on the face of it, "looks as if" it measures the inferred variable. Thus if a mathematical-aptitude test is composed of a series of mathematics problems, it seems reasonable that a person with high mathematical aptitude would be able to answer most of the test problems and a person with lower mathematical aptitude would be able to answer fewer of them; in other words, mathematical aptitude (the inferred variable) should actually be reflected to some extent in the test scores. Similarly for divorce as an index of marital adjustment; there must be at least some tendency for couples seeking divorce to have worse marital adjustment than other couples who are not seeking divorce. The same argument could be made for Angell's (1941) index of moral integration (a community's crime rate divided by community-chest contributions): a community's level of moral integration must have something to do with its crime rate and it must have something to do with how much people are willing to give to the local community chest.

No doubt every index that was ever invented has some modicum of face validity; the architect of the index, at the very least, believed that it "looks as if" it measures the intended inferred variable. From the viewpoint of the outside observer, reader, or critic, some indices can inspire considerable faith on grounds of face validity alone. The mathematical-aptitude test and divorce as an index of marital adjustment would be examples of these. Others, for example some of the more far-out indices of personality variables, may not appear to be "obviously" face-valid. In practice, when we must decide whether to accept or "believe" a particular index, the face-validity judgment probably carries more weight than anything else.

The face-validity judgment has nothing to do with evidence; it hinges on other epistemological criteria: faith and "reasonableness." In fact, the acceptance of any index, no matter how well "validated" it is, devolves in the last analysis on faith. The validity tests, to the extent that they offer real evidence, are essentially negative tests. They offer testimony that particular sources of nonvalidity are minimal. Thus a test-retest reliability check (if favorable) testifies that instability of measured behavior, over time, is not producing a gross measure of nonvalidity. A Guttman scale pattern can give assurance that an improper scaling convention is not producing gross nonvalidity. A demonstration of unidimensionality can testify that all items in the index are, to some extent, "measuring the same thing." The real question, though, must remain unanswered: What is the correlation between index scores and magnitude of the inferred variable? Direct, "positive" evidence of this sort is out of reach.

In a sense, direct measures must be accepted on faith too. One rarely knows for sure that a respondent is really 19 years old, or that a town's population numbers 3,264 souls, or that a test scorer made no mistakes. Observer-error is, ordinarily, something that can only be guessed about. So, in a sense, the real correlation between scores on a direct measure and the "real" or "proper" magnitudes of the observed variable is also unknown. In practice, some observed-variable hypotheses are accepted on faith, since one decides that the chances of observer-error are slim, as with reports of age. Others are viewed askance; the likelihood of *accurate* observer-reports appears to be slim. This was discussed a bit in Chapter 4, during the treatment of "difficult" questionnaire items.

Unknown observer-error creates an uncertainty, then, even with a direct measure of an observed variable. If one wishes to use this measure as an index for an inferred variable, he adds a second uncertainty. As an illustration of this, we turn to the following example.

## Nonvalidity and Spurious Findings

Karl Deutsch (1956) has gathered data on transaction flows—in particular, letters and telephone calls—and has made ingenious use of these, in order to make inferences about various political variables. One such political indicator is the ratio of foreign mail to domestic mail. If the people in a country send a relatively high proportion of their letters to foreign countries, this is taken as a sign that the country is internationalist and "outward-turning" in its orientation. If a country's percentage of foreign mail is very low, this indicates that the country is relatively nationalist and "inward-turning." Following this ratio of foreign to domestic mail over the years for a large sample of nations, Deutsch found that it increased during the 1880–1913 period, but has been declining ever since: one sign among many that nationalism is on the rise and nations are becoming less internationally oriented.

The observed variable here is ratio of foreign to domestic mail, computed for a given country in a given year. Needless to say, an enormous amount of recording and record keeping lies behind any score for any country during any year. Errors must have occurred somewhere. Perhaps they had a negligible effect on cases' scores; or perhaps, for a few cases, really sizeable errors occurred in record keeping, enough to make those cases' scores substantially higher or lower than they should have been. So that is the first uncertainty: the correspondence between scores and what the scores "should be"—would be in the absence of any observer-error. No doubt the correspondence is fairly close.

The second uncertainty is the relationship between these scores, used as indices of internationalism, and the "true" level of internationalism in the various countries. Perhaps the real relationship, if we only knew, looks something like the picture in Table V.

TABLE V

| | *Reported ratio of foreign to domestic mail* | |
|---|---|---|
| Level of internationalism | High | Low |
| High | 20 | 4 |
| Low | 8 | 18 |

The correlation is fairly pronounced. The foreign-mail ratio is a fair indicator of internationalism. It did, however, misclassify 12 countries: 4 internationalist countries with low reported rates of foreign mail, and 8 non-internationalist countries, with high reported rates of foreign mail. The source of the disparity between index scores and real magnitude of the inferred variable must have been twofold: (a) Observer-error, which might have been this:

TABLE VI

| Real ratio of foreign to domestic mail | *Reported ratio of foreign to domestic mail* High | Low |
|---|---|---|
| High | 27 | 2 |
| Low | 1 | 20 |

and (b) disparity between level of internationalism and the real ratio of foreign to domestic mail, which might have been this:

TABLE VII

| Level of internationalism | *Real ratio of foreign to domestic mail* High | Low |
|---|---|---|
| High | 21 | 3 |
| Low | 8 | 18 |

Suppose we wished to use this index to test hypotheses about sources of nationalism and internationalism. We might choose an economic interpretation: nations are bound to each other by foreign trade. A nation which is mutually dependent economically with other nations becomes more internationalist in outlook. One step in the direction of world community would be an intensification of commercial ties between nations. To test this, we might correlate Deutsch's internationalism index with some measure of importance of foreign trade; this might be the ratio of value of exports to gross national product. Again, the case would be a country during a given year. Suppose we found this for a sample of 50 countries in the year 1966:

TABLE VIII

| Importance of foreign trade: reported ratio of value of exports to GNP | *Internationalism index: reported ratio of foreign to domestic mail* | |
|---|---|---|
| | High | Low |
| High | 23 | 6 |
| Low | 5 | 16 |

Table VIII gives evidence favorable to the hypothesis that foreign trade promotes internationalism. The evidence is not especially strong, since our hypothesis presents the classic sources of doubt: it is a causal hypothesis, it cites an inferred variable, and it is a generalization beyond known cases. The hypothesis is an "easy" one in one respect: it allows a large margin for error. For it to be true, there merely need be a positive correlation between trade and internationalism: the correlation could be a weak one (trade might be a "weak cause") and still the hypothesis would be true. Table VIII shows a pronounced correlation. It leaves considerable leeway. Observer-error and nonvalidity might have exaggerated the strength of the true relationship between foreign trade and internationalist outlook; even so, the relationship might exist. Perhaps, if we only knew, the true correlation between the two variables is something like this:

TABLE IX

| Importance of foreign trade: true ratio of value of exports to GNP | *Level of internationalism* | |
|---|---|---|
| | High | Low |
| High | 24 | 3 |
| Low | 0 | 23 |

As a matter of fact, the opposite happened. Error variance—discrepancies between scores and "real values"—acted not to exaggerate the true relationship, but to make the correlation from the study findings weaker than the true relationship actually is. Error variance might be viewed here as having three sources: (a) discrepancies between scores and true values for the foreign trade variable; (b) discrepancies between scores and true values for the foreign-to-domestic-mail-ratio variable; (c) and discrepancies between true values of foreign-mail ratio and true level of internationalism. The "errors" of classification must have been fairly random in direction; their overall effect was to weaken the actual correlation.

Let us now forget about Table IX. It is, of course, the sort of table that one never is privileged to see; in practice, we only have access to data of the sort that are given in Table VIII. Let us focus on Table VIII, which documents the hypothesis "Foreign trade stimulates internationalist sentiments."

A correlation hypothesis of this nature is the usual sort of hypothesis we test in our research; and this is most prudent of us. Its margin of error is huge. If the correlation we find is at all pronounced, then the likelihood that the direction of the correlation is merely an artifact of error is very slim. From Table VIII: it must surely be true that, for this sample of 50 countries at any rate, there must be a real positive correlation between foreign trade and foreign mail. How could observer-error possibly have spuriously produced such a correlation? The only possibility is that errors were not only sizeable and frequent, but also positively correlated themselves: cases mistakenly classified "high" for importance of foreign trade also tended to be mistakenly scored "high" for ratio of foreign to domestic mail; countries mistakenly scored "low" on foreign trade tended also to be mistakenly scored "low" on percentage of mail to foreign countries. All other possibilites, with respect to the direction of error, would have acted to weaken the reported correlation, not spuriously strengthen it: error that was random in direction for both variables; error that was random in direction for one variable, systematic in direction for the other; or error that was *negatively* correlated (cases mistakenly scored "low" for one variable tending to be mistakenly scored "high" for the other). Therefore, if we "scaled down" our hypothesis, stripped it of its inferred variable and its causal inference and its generalizing inference, then surely it must be true. For this sample of 50 countries, there must be a real association between foreign trade and foreign mail; chances are slight that the evidence we have is spuriously favorable.

If we do insist on using the table as evidence for an inferred-variable hypothesis, then likelihood of truth declines, of course. It may be that the correlation in the table has nothing to do with the inferred variable cited in our hypothesis. Foreign trade might act to stimulate foreign mail, and the bulk of the mail might be purchase orders, requisitions, receipts, routine correspondence between business firms; yet it might have little if any effect on a nation's overall "international orientation."

When one weighs some research findings as evidence for an hypothesis, and guesses about the likelihood that evidence is spuriously favorable,[5] the margin for error is certainly an important consideration. Presence of an inferred variable in the hypothesis can also make quite a difference. One can also guess about the likelihood of systematic bias, that is, correlated error. On some occasions, as in the previous example, it is hard to imagine how systematic bias could have spuriously produced a correlation. For other correlations, systematic bias looks like a real possibility. As an illustration of this, let us return to the *Patterns of Child Rearing* study, which was based on interviews with mothers. The study produced a great number of interesting findings, one of which was a negative correlation between maternal warmth and children's disturbances. Mothers were scored for "warmth" on

[5] The term "spuriously favorable evidence," means evidence indicating that a certain hypothesis is true when in fact, if one only knew, the hypothesis is not true. If one is persuaded by this evidence and accepts the false hypothesis, he is committing what the statisticians term a Type I error. The Type II error—rejecting a true hypothesis on the basis of evidence that is interpreted as unfavorable—would be likely in instances like the example above, where sizable and uncorrelated measurement error obliterates a true relationship.

the basis of their answers to a number of interview questions. One of these was cited in Chapter 4: how, in the mother's opinion, one should respond to a crying baby. Evidence of disturbance in her child was derived from further interview questions (asked of the mother), concerning such things as bed wetting, tantrums, feeding problems, and development of self-control. The correlation would seem to say that maternal warmth is a determinant of healthy development, or that "warm" mothers had "better" children (Sears, Maccoby, and Levin 1957:483). Or one might conclude that mothers who described themselves as particularly "warm" also tended to describe their children as particularly "good." In other words, systematic bias may be inflating this negative correlation between maternal warmth and children's disturbance. The same mothers who gave an exaggeratedly "warm" picture of themselves in their answers to the interview questions also tended to give a falsely "good" or undisturbed picture of their children. This correlation might be completely the artifact of systematic bias. Probably it is not, but on the face of it, it looks faintly suspicious.

Systematic bias, if it occurred here, stemmed from "the social-desirability factor." The correlation is based on self-report data. The direction of the correlation is in accord with value-loadings in the questions: "good" or socially desirable answers (maternal warmth) are correlated with other "good" answers (undisturbed children). No doubt some mothers were more frank (both with themselves and to the interviewer) than were others. The danger is that the less candid mothers systematically gave what they considered to be "good" or "proper" answers throughout their interviews and that this alone produced the correlation. Sears, Maccoby, and Levin were attuned to this danger; they did what they could, in their wording of interview questions, to avoid it.[6] Generally, though, when a correlation derives from self-report data, and the correlation is in the direction of social desirability, the danger of systematic bias becomes more serious.

[6] "All babies cry, of course. Some mothers feel that if you pick up a baby every time it cries, you will spoil it. Others think you should never let a baby cry for very long. How do you feel about this?" (Sears, Maccoby, and Levin 1957:491).

One may also suspect systematic bias in correlations between certain indices. Such a correlation may stem from a common extraneous factor, which is affecting scores on both indices. Or, both indices, no matter how they are labeled, may be to some extent "measuring the same thing." For example the F Scale, the popular index of authoritarianism, correlates negatively with scores on IQ tests. Does this mean that authoritarians are stupid, that authoritarian attitudes are incompatible with great intellect? Or does it simply mean that the F Scale is, to an important extent, really a (negative) measure of intelligence rather than a measure of authoritarianism? Or, whatever determines scores on the F Scale and whatever determines scores on IQ tests, does it mean that some common factor—literate skills, or whatever—is an important determinant of scores on both measures? (Cohn 1957: 211–212)

To sum up: any evidence for an inferred-variable hypothesis must come by way of an index. Judging this evidence starts with an act of faith: one must decide whether or not to "believe" the index. Faith in an index means an assumption that index scores correspond—not perfectly, but to a moderate degree—with true magnitudes of the inferred variable. Then one can guess about the likelihood that systematic bias has produced spuriously favorable evidence. If one is judging a correlation hypothesis, no doubt one will usually decide that the danger of this is slight; errors of classification—and this takes in the partial nonvalidity of the index—are probably acting to weaken the correlation, rather than to strengthen it.

If we could only stop here, we might be rather lenient in our assessments of inferred-variable hypotheses. More is involved, of course. The hypothesis may pose other sources of doubt. Also, if we were to continue testing an inferred-variable hypothesis, using a wide assortment of indices, sooner or later we would be bound to find some *un*favorable evidence. At least, we would come up with findings that could be construed as unfavorable evidence.

# Inferred Variables and Indeterminacy

An observed variable can be measured in only one way. It is operationally defined as score on a particular measuring instrument [7] or in terms of a particular convention for classifying cases ("age," "sex," "score on *X* test," etc.). An inferred variable, not clearly defined in terms of observations, leaves the choice of measures open. It may be represented by a variety of indices.

Let us return to the hypothesis about foreign trade and internationalism: if a country trades extensively with other countries, this tends to make it more outward-turning and internationalist in orientation. The make-believe evidence for this was given in Table VIII, in which foreign mail stood as an index for degree of internationalism. If we wished to test this hypothesis further, we could dream up more indices of internationalism and correlate each of these with importance of foreign trade. As a starter, assuming we had the wherewithal to gather the necessary data, we might use these ten indices:

1. Ratio of international to domestic news (derived from a content analysis of news media in each nation in our sample).
2. Total foreign aid expenditures (for a given year) perhaps divided by GNP.
3. Support (in dollars) given to the United Nations, perhaps divided by GNP.
4. Percentage of the population who can speak a foreign language (if this could somehow be assessed, perhaps on a sample basis for each nation).
5. Percentage of citizens who are studying in foreign universities.
6. Percentage of the country's university students who are citizens of other countries.
7. Foreign travel—percentage of citizens who crossed the nation's border during the past year.

[7] More precisely: as score on a particular measuring instrument, provided the measure was applied accurately. Thus, weight can be defined as where the needle points when one gets on the scales, assuming the scales are in good working order.

8. Influx of foreigners—number of foreigners who entered the country during the past year perhaps divided by the nation's population.

Finally, each country might be rated for: 9. The liberality of its immigration laws; and 10. The liberality of its customs regulations.

If each of these indices were correlated with foreign trade, it is highly unlikely that all ten correlations would be positive. In the improbable event that they all were, we need merely go out and find some more indices. Sooner or later, we would turn up some unfavorable evidence. I think this is true for any inferred-variable hypothesis: unfavorable evidence is there waiting; if the first index succeeds, try, try again.

Once such a messy situation has been created, the matter can be set straight again by further acts of faith. Any indices that bear bad tidings can be dismissed as irrelevant, not true indices (of the inferred variable in question) at all. Suppose, for example, that foreign trade correlated positively with seven of the internationalism indices, but showed zero or negative correlations with the other four; these might be indices 1, 2, 3, and 6. One could decide that these indices are totally invalid; thereby, one could write off these four correlations with foreign trade as irrelevant to the hypothesis. An alternative would be to hold all the presumed evidence in mind and to conclude that, though the evidence is flawed, there looks as if there may be something there. A third alternative would be to accept indices 1, 2, 3, and 6 and reject the rest; then one has "consistent evidence" that foreign trade is *not* conducive to internationalism.

In other words, since an inferred variable leaves the choice of measures open, it is undetermined just what sorts of observations are actually relevant as evidence for a particular inferred-variable hypothesis and what sorts are not. When an inferred-variable hypothesis enjoys solely favorable evidence, this is, I suspect, only because "testing" did not proceed very far.

Some inferred variables are, I think, much more open-ended than are others. The indeterminacy problem is worst with high-level abstractions, variables such as stress, social cohesiveness, and positive reinforcement. Inferred variables of this sort will be termed *abstract variables*; an hypothesis that cites such a variable will be termed a *high-level law.* In order to distinguish this type of inferred variable, let us take a step backward.

Earlier, an index's validity was conceptualized as the correlation between index scores and magnitudes of the inferred variable which, presumably, the index scores reflect. The stronger this correlation, the more valid the index. The correlation could be stated in hypothesis form; for example, "Score on the Stanford-Binet IQ Test reflects level of intelligence." Such an hypothesis might be termed a *linking statement.* It links an inferred variable (intelligence) to an observed variable (IQ score), thus telling us what observations can be interpreted as a "sign" of the inferred variable.

Linking statements, sometimes termed "rules of interpretation" (Kemeny 1959:124–130), appear to be of two general types. Some are true hypotheses, statements of covariance or correlation, like the one just given above. Ordinarily, these are also cause-effect hypotheses. The linking statement may say or imply that the inferred variable causes the index score. This is the case with "Stanford-Binet score reflects level of intelligence." Occasionally, it states the reverse: the phenomenon measured by the index is a cause for the inferred variable. This would be true for age used as an index of maturity. Implicit in the linking statement is an assertion that the correlation is fairly strong; otherwise, the index would be grossly invalid.

Other linking statements are not true hypotheses. For want of a better term, I shall call them pseudo-analytic statements. These say that the index represents a special type, a subcategory, of the inferred variable. Thus a variety of things have been termed, in the literature of psychology, "rewards" or "positive reinforcement": rat pellets, cessation of shock, praise (to a child), success at a task or problem (for a student at a teaching machine), smiles, M & M's, and so on. Positive reinforcement is an abstract variable; it subsumes a great range of such observed variables, each of which is viewed as a special type of positive reinforcement. The limits of this class of observed variables—positive reinforcements—are not clearly drawn. As with other abstract concepts, people share some "general understanding" as to what the term means, but no definition is provided which tells one, clearly, what is a positive reinforcement and what is not. Perhaps "positive reinforcement" is a bit atypical of abstract concepts, in that its meaning is less vague than most. As long as psychologists keep to cut-and-dried laboratory situations, they would probably agree as to what is a positive reinforcement; but if they were to code running accounts of human interaction for incidents of positive reinforcement, I am confident the disagreement would be considerable.

An abstract variable, then, is on a high level of generality; it subsumes an array of lower-order, more particular, observed variables. It is a term that stands for a class of observed variables. And the parameters of the class are not clearly specified. What is or is not an instance of reward, or of stress, or of social cohesiveness is undetermined; it is left to individual judgment.

When an abstract variable enters an hypothesis, the resulting high-level law is a summary of many lower-level hypotheses. Thus a statement on the order of "Positive reinforcement produces faster learning than does negative reinforcement" summarizes a good-sized experimental literature, in which performance on a variety of learning tasks is related to type of reinforcement: rats, pigeons, dogs, college sophomores; on mazes, bar pressing, button pressing, verbal learning; with food, shock, head-nods; and so on. In practice, special footnotes or qualifiers may be appended to the law, citing limiting conditions, special circumstances in which the law seems not to work.

As mentioned previously, in the natural sciences such laws are customarily judged for their usefulness. And useful they are, in their summarizing economy and in their suggestive power. They are the most prestigeful of hypotheses, the upper-upper class of hypotheses. On an official level, at any rate, they are not judged for likelihood of truth. This would seem to be a wise choice. To illustrate how arbitrary any such judgment would be, how messy any process of "weighing the evidence," we turn to the following example.

# Stimulation in Infancy

This particular law summarizes a series of dramatic experiments. In each experiment, a sample of infants is sorted into an experimental group and a control group. The antecedent variable is stimulation of some sort during infancy. The type of stimulation varies from one study to the next. It might be simply handling or "gentling." In a good many of the experiments, the stimulation was rather violent: rough handling of various sorts, frightening loud noises, even mild electric shock. The experimental-group infants receive some type of "stimulation"; the control-group infants do not get this type of treatment. Then the study must take a pause, while the infants grow to maturity. When they mature, various assessments are made to determine the effects of stimulation in infancy.

The effects of such stimulation seem to be generally benign. The experimental-group rats tend to be healthier, larger, calmer, longer-lived; they mature sooner and are more adept at the little problem-solving tasks posed to them by the psychologists (Denenberg 1963; Denenberg and Karas 1959; Levine 1960; Levine, Chevalier, and Korchin 1956; Bovard 1958).

These findings might be summed up in a law: *stimulation in infancy produces more robust individuals.* The law cites two abstract variables: stimulation in infancy, and robustness, each of which has its retinue of lower-order variables. For "stimulation in infancy," these include what was actually done to the experimental-group rat pups during the various experiments: a number of styles of handling ("gentling" and "roughing"); mild shock by methods varying in intensity, duration, and frequency; loud noises; bright lights. For the other abstract variable, "robustness," these include: mortality rate; weight (at different ages); exploring behavior versus "freezing" in an open field situation; speed in learning various laboratory problems; age at sexual maturity. All of this is represented in the paradigm on page 144.

| ABSTRACT VARIABLES | *Stimulation* | *Robustness* |
|---|---|---|
| Lower-order variables | S = 1. gentling<br>S = 2. roughing<br>S = 3. shock (condition A)<br>S = 4. shock (condition B)<br>S = 5. bright light<br>S = 6. loud noise | R = 1. mortality rate<br>R = 2. weight<br>R = 3. open field behavior<br>R = 4. learning speed (condition A)<br>R = 5. learning speed (condition B)<br>R = 6. age at sexual maturity |

The experimental evidence consists of correlations between observed variables in the left-hand column and observed variables in the right-hand column (Actually this is oversimplified; there are more observed variables than these): S-1 with R-1 and R-2. S-2 with R-1, R-2, and R-3. S-4 with R-1, R-2, R-4 and R-6, etc. Each correlation can be stated as an observed-variable hypothesis; and for each such hypothesis the evidence is fairly strong, likelihood of truth is reasonably good.

In no study was each of the six indices or types of stimulation related to each of the indices of robustness. We do not, in fact, have evidence that each of the stimulation variables is positively correlated with each of the robustness variables. Yet the high-level law "Stimulation in infancy produces more robust individuals" would appear to imply that this is true. Difficulty number one.

Difficulty number two: Assuming that all the evidence is favorable, what is the law's likelihood of truth? Is its truth value contingent on the truth values of the 36 hypotheses that state causal relations between the 12 lower-order variables? If so, then by the principle of multiple contingency alone, its likelihood of truth must be extremely low; at the very least, it rests on 36 subsidiary hypotheses. Perhaps this is too severe. If so, what *is* the proper manner of weighing sources of doubt in the lower-order hypotheses, in order to assign a truth value to the law?

Difficulty number three: As experimenters continue to explore the area, try out new types of "stimulation," and relate them to other adulthood variables (which might be construed as indices of robustness), surely some "unfavorable" evidence will emerge, which would further complicate any such judgment. Undoubtedly this has already happened.

Therefore, the high-level law is a handy summarizing device, and useful for suggesting new lines of inquiry, but it is nothing to be believed. It defies assessment for likelihood of truth.

The momentous question that can be asked here is: Might this also be the case for *all* inferred-variable hypotheses, including those that are not high-level laws? Should we not apply a truth epistemology to any of these, but instead judge them as the high-level physicial laws and theories are judged, for "usefulness" or for "success at prediction"? I don't know. There has been much talk about prediction, but to my knowledge we have nothing approaching a workable scheme for judging lower-level hypotheses for success at prediction. Perhaps the least unsatisfactory alternative is to go on judging them for likelihood of truth. Feasible or not, this is probably what we shall continue to do, in practice; it appears to be the "natural" and human way to proceed.

Such a judgment must hinge partly on faith or "reasonableness": in one's selection or rejection of indices and of possible evidence that comes by way of different indices. But it need not be solely a faith judgment—far from it. An inferred-variable hypothesis can be scanned for other sources of doubt. Evidence by way of indices can be strong or weak with respect to sampling, likelihood of observer-error, evidence for direction of causation, clarity of observer-reports, and order in collating.

## *Selected References*

Indices:

Hans Zeisel, *Say It with Figures*, chap. 4.

Paul Lazarsfeld and Morris Rosenberg, *The Language of Social Research*, sec. 1.

Actuarial prediction and validity coefficients:

Harrison Gough, "Clinical versus Actuarial Prediction in Psychology," in Leo Postman, ed., *Psychology in the Making.*

Paul Meehl, *Clinical versus Statistical Prediction.*

Evidence for validity:

L. J. Cronbach and Paul Meehl, "Construct Validity in Psychological Tests." *Psychological Bulletin,* Vol. 52 (1955), pp. 281–302.

Scaling:

Allen Edwards, *Techniques for Attitude Scale Construction.*

Bert Green, "Attitude Measurement," in Gardner Lindzey, ed., *Handbook of Social Psychology.*

Paul Secord and Carl Backman, *Social Psychology,* pp. 97–107.

Warren S. Torgerson, *Theory and Methods of Scaling.*

Joining theory to observation in the natural sciences—the shadow falls:

W. Weaver, "The Imperfections of Science," *American Scientist,* Vol. 49 (1961), pp. 99–113.

The suggestive power of high-level laws—a specimen:

George Homans, *Social Behavior: Its Elementary Forms.*

## *Chapter 6*

# SAMPLING

Having emerged from the murky depths, we can now deal with a relatively simple and straightforward problem. In its mathematical elaborations, sampling can get complicated, to be sure. However, on the non-mathematical level in which it will be treated here, it is a fairly easy area to handle.

The sampling problem arises when one generalizes beyond known cases (Source-of-doubt B). One observes a sample of cases, and then states a generalization about the class or population to which those cases are said to belong. In research on human behavior, the case is usually a person. The researcher studies a sample of people in order to test a generalization about humans. Occasionally the case is some collectivity of people: a group, family, organization, community, even society; and the generalization is about groups, families, organizations, communities, or societies. At times the boundaries of the population are not clearly drawn; it is not clear whether the researcher wishes to generalize about people, or merely about people in this day and age, or people in the United States. In any event, the generalization is about some large population, and the study sample includes just a small fraction of its members.

The researcher measures his sample of cases with respect to one or a number of variables. He runs 30 rats through a maze, or interviews 50 families, or codes the folktales of 40 societies, or gives a questionnaire to 2,000 respondents, or tests 500 subjects, or whatever. The sample is the collection of cases—the experimenter's 30 rats, the pollster's 2,000 respondents—which is subjected to measurement.

After the study is done, the researcher may merely generalize about the cases in his sample, thus avoiding source-of-doubt B. The experimenter might conclude, "The hungry rats in my sample tended to learn the maze more quickly than my satiated rats did." Occasionally, such a cautious statement of findings is all that is offered in a research report. In itself, it is a trivial statement. In order to invest the study with any significance, someone must relate the study findings, as evidence, to some more sweeping generalization. For this example, the generalization beyond known cases might be: "Hungry rats learn this type of task more quickly than satiated rats do." Now the generalization extends beyond the 30 experimental rats and applies to all rats. (In this particular example, in fact, the generalization must be more sweeping than this to achieve any kind of importance. It would probably have to be a high-level law, having to do with the relation of drive level to speed of learning, and applying to some huge class of cases such as "organisms" or "vertebrates" or "mammals.")

The doubt raised by a generalization beyond known cases is, of course: the trend reported in the study might very well hold for the sample that was observed; yet it might not hold for the entire population that is being generalized about. Perhaps if *all* rats were to be run through the maze, the hungry ones would *not* tend to learn more quickly.

Suppose that a pre-election poll, in which a sample of the voters is canvassed, comes up with the prediction that 55 percent of the voters will vote for candidate *X*. The election then takes place, and *X* gets 47 percent of the vote. This disparity of 8 percentage points might be viewed as "error." This error has two possible sources: first, observer-error, disparities between what the sampled voters said they were going to do and what they actually did in the polling booths. Some of these people might have said they were going to vote for *X* but then voted for the other candidate. The other possible source of error is sampling error. Perhaps when the poll was taken, only 47 percent of the electorate intended to vote for *X;* but the sample selection was such that pro-*X* respondents were over-represented in the poll. Either observer-error or sampling error, or both combined, made this pre-election poll go wrong.

Sampling error, in its turn, will be viewed here as having two possible sources: (1) chance variability and (2) a biased selection method. To put this another way: in order to avoid (or minimize) sampling error, a sample must have two characteristics. (1) It must not deviate from the true population value as a result of chance variability, a real possibility when the sample is very small. (2) It must not deviate from the true population value as a result of a biased method of sample selection. The selection method, whatever it is, must be totally unrelated to any factor which affects or helps determine cases' scores. Each of these will be discussed in turn, starting with chance variability. First, a brief illustration of these two sources of sampling error, using the example of the pre-election poll.

For *chance variability*. Suppose only 20 voters were polled. By the luck of the draw, 11 persons in this little group were favorable to candidate *X*. Thus the foolhardy prediction: *X* will get 55 percent of the vote.

For *biased selection.* Suppose *X* is a Democrat. The sample is drawn from only one precinct district. The district happens to be a heavily Democratic one; most of the voters in it are going to vote Democrat. When a sample is drawn from this district, 55 percent of the respondents say they will vote for *X*.

## Chance Variability and Sample Size

Probability theory tells us that the instability of sample values depends on sample size.[1] Returning to the pre-election poll: suppose that there was an unbiased method of selection. Suppose fur-

[1] It also depends, of course, on population variability.

ther that 10 samples of voters were polled. For each sample, N was 20. Since the samples are small, the range of sample findings should be fairly wide: one sample might have 55 percent pro-X respondents; another 70 percent; another 15 percent; another 40 percent; and so on. If, on the other hand, the samples were larger—each, say, with 100 people in it instead of 20—the sample values would be more alike. They should be bunched around 47 percent; few if any would be below 40 percent, or above 55 percent. Differences between sample values—deriving from chance, the luck of the draw—decline as sample size increases.

Similarly, a sample value should get nearer and nearer the true population value, as sample size increases—assuming an unbiased selection method. Suppose one starts to flip a coin, recording the incidence of "heads" and "tails." By the luck of the draw, one may get at first a run of heads. The first 3 flips may come up 100 percent heads. The first 10 flips may yield 70 percent heads. By 100 flips, one will be coming fairly close to 50 percent heads, assuming there is nothing peculiar about the coin. As the sample gets larger and larger, the odds get stronger and stronger that one will come closer and closer. With 100 flips of a true coin, the odds are .16 that one will get as many as 55 heads; the odds for as many as 60 heads are .03; and one has virtually no chance of getting as many as 65 heads. As the sample continues to increase, this range—odds for chance deviations of given amounts—continues to narrow. One reaches a point of diminishing returns rather soon: one is *so* likely to be *so* close to the true population value, that there is little reason to continue gathering cases. To put this another way: the curve representing odds-for-$x$-deviation tends to flatten out near the 0 point, as sample size increases. With 200 flips, one is fairly sure to have about 50 percent heads, and he might as well stop flipping. After this point, even a spectacular run of heads will have scant effect on this percentage.[2]

How large should a sample be? This depends, first of all, on what level of certainty is desired—that chance variation is within a given range. It also depends on the range itself; that is, on the

[2] For a higher-level discussion of this, see Stephan and McCarthy (1958), p. 192 ff.

margin for error. Suppose a pollster predicts, "Candidate *X* will win the election." If he bases this prediction on a poll which showed 51 percent of the respondents favoring *X*, then his sample must be relatively large. Chance deviation of his sample finding from the true population value of anything over 1 percent in a negative direction, would mean an inaccurate prediction. If, on the other hand, his poll showed 55 percent of the respondents favoring *X*, then a prediction on the same level of confidence could be made, based on a much smaller sample.

(In practice, of course, if the poll showed only 51 percent favoring *X*, the polling agency would only predict that the election would be close. Observer-error can also throw the poll finding off, and no amount of inflating of the sample can ameliorate this.)

For single-variable hypotheses, sample size depends on how much one is willing to pay in order to stop worrying about chance variation. One can be extravagant, gather a large sample,[3] and be 99 percent sure that the sample value does not deviate from the population value by more than 2 percentage points—as a result of chance variability alone. Or one can pay less for the survey, gather fewer cases, and be 90 percent sure that chance variability is less than 5 percent; or 95 percent sure that chance variability is less than 8 percent. For two-variable hypotheses (statements that simply say that there is a correlation, positive or negative, between a pair of variables), the sample can be much smaller. A sample of 30 will often do well enough. Sometimes the sample can be considerably smaller than this. The necessary sample size depends, in part, on characteristics of the scales that are used; this we will not consider here. It also depends very much on the margin for error, which depends, in turn, on the strength of the correlation which emerges from the sample findings.

To illustrate this, let us suppose we found a positive correlation

[3] For nationwide surveys, optimal sample size is about 3,500. Ordinarily it is half this (Parten 1950:291). For the problem of chance variability alone, N need not be even this large, but the polling agency's notions of a proper stratification method may push N to this size.

between cigarette smoking and lung cancer, which came from a sample of 96 medical case histories (Table X). The correlation is

TABLE X

| Cigarette smoker? | *Had lung cancer?* Yes | No |
|---|---|---|
| Yes | 34 | 15 |
| No | 14 | 33 |
| | | $P < .01$ |

fairly pronounced: about two thirds of the smokers contracted lung cancer, as opposed to about one third of the non-smokers. With a sample this large (96 cases), there is less than 1 chance in 100 that a trend this strong could be simply a coincidence (using a Chi Square test). In other words, the likelihood that the *direction* of the trend—a positive correlation—is solely due to chance variation is less than .01. To put this one more way: the likelihood that the evidence is spuriously favorable, that smokers are more prone to lung cancer, simply as a result of chance variation, is less than .01.[4]

As the trend gets weaker, and/or as sample size diminishes, the P value rises. This is illustrated in Table XI. Here, N has shrunk to 41. The trend is a bit less pronounced also. There is about 1

TABLE XI

| Cigarette smoker? | *Had lung cancer?* Yes | No |
|---|---|---|
| Yes | 13 | 6 |
| No | 10 | 12 |
| | | $P = .25$ |

[4] A formality which is adhered to in some circles is to state one's hypothesis first in the negative: "Cigarette smokers are *not* more prone to get lung cancer." Data are then gathered, a test of significance is applied, and this negative form of the hypothesis—the so-called null hypothesis—is rejected if the P value falls below some previously agreed-upon level (which is usually .05).

chance in 4 that a trend this strong, with a sample of this size, could be positive in direction simply due to coincidence, chance variation.

Similarly, if the correlation were to maintain its original strength, but if sample size diminished, the P value would rise. With correlations like this:

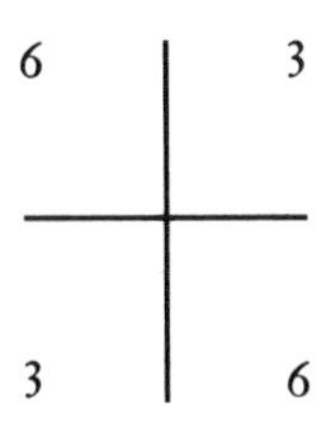


or this:

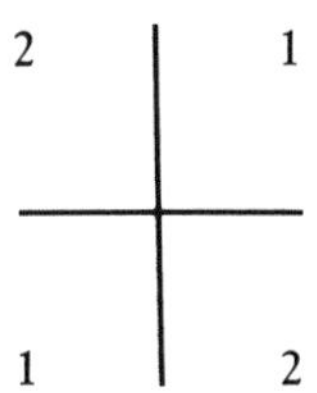


likelihood of coincidence is quite high; that is to say, the chances are fairly good that the direction of the correlation is merely a coincidence.

The usual hypothesis we test in our research is a cause-effect statement, which says that variable *A* is a cause for variable *B* (smoking is a cause for cancer). It is a tendency statement, admitting exceptions (smokers who don't get cancer; non-smokers who do). The minimal favorable evidence required by such an hypothesis is a positive correlation between the presumed causal variable and effect variable. If smoking is a cause for cancer, then smokers should be more prone than non-smokers to get cancer. The correlation might be a weak one (other and more powerful causes might outweigh smoking), but it should be positive, if the cause-effect statement is true.

The cause-effect statement is necessarily a generalization beyond known cases. Smoking causes cancer; and this tendency holds not merely for the people we are going to study, but for humans generally. Any evidence comes from a sample, as in the example above. Even if the evidence is favorable, it is in jeopardy with respect to source-of-doubt B; if *all* humans could be studied, perhaps we would find *no* positive correlation between smoking and cancer. In other words, it is possible that the favorable evidence is an artifact of sampling error. Sampling error, as mentioned earlier, can be viewed as having two possible sources: chance variability and biased selection. A good-sized sample is fair insurance against one of these, chance variability. How big the sample needs to be depends on the strength of the correlation that emerged from the sample. If the observed correlation were perfect, with no exceptions, then an N of 10 would yield a respectably low P value (Finney 1948). If the observed correlation is weak, several hundred cases may be required to lay the spectre of chance variability to rest.

Compared with the epistemological problems we have been considering in previous chapters, chance variability is a welcome relief. It is one that we can very definitely do something about, so we zealously run our tests of significance and spatter our research reports with P values. True, the statistical test does not give absolute assurance. With a P of .05, there is still 1 chance in 20 that the direction of trend was coincidental. Also, controversies do arise as to what sorts of statistical treatments are justified for certain types of data. Still, significance tests give relatively unambiguous answers, as compared with validity tests. They do provide numerical probability statements, and the reasoning that lies behind them is lucid and minimally controversial; in guessing about some other possible sources of doubt, we have no such clear benchmarks.

In most research, the problem of chance variability is well handled. A fair-sized sample is studied, not just one or a few cases. Findings are only construed as favorable evidence—for generalizations beyond known cases—if the P value is reasonably low. The conventional "confidence limit" is .05.

Problems occasionally arise, with respect to chance variability, in situations where a true sample is innaccessible or impossibly expensive. When the case is not a single individual but a *collectivity*—a community, group, or organization—the researcher often confines his study to a single case, or perhaps to several; and often he generalizes from his findings. An example is Sherif's (1958) oft-quoted boys'-camp study, which "demonstrated" that antagonistic groups can be made friendly, if they can be persuaded to combine their efforts toward common goals—on a sample of one case.

Once in a while ambiguity enters in, with respect to what the case *is*. Construed in one way, a study is based on many cases, and chance variability is well handled. Construed in another way, the study findings are based on just one or several cases; there is no real sample at all. As an illustration of this, let us take an imaginary town, Sugarville, which acquires a nearby army base in the year 1960. Soon after the soldiers move in, people notice a proliferation of prostitutes. Perhaps the Chief of Police has figures to prove it: 1959, few prostitutes; 1961, many prostitutes. The army base attracted prostitutes to Sugarville. What is the case here? Sugarville? A year in Sugarville? A whore? Depending on one's choice, one may or may not have bona fide evidence for the explanation of whores in Sugarville.

Outside the confines of research, of course, we blithely generalize "from personal experience," often without benefit of a sample. A person who is presented the research evidence that very early marriages stand a relatively poor chance of success is likely to retort that he "knew that already" he himself was married early in life, and it ended in divorce. His second marriage has been much better. He is generalizing from two cases; yet these may inspire stronger subjective conviction than the marital adjustment study, based on a proper sample.

Likewise, speculative writers feel considerable freedom to generalize without benefit of an observed sample. If any evidence is offered, it may be in the form of an example—one case.[5]

Impressionistic evidence for generalizations is frequently not

[5] I.e., an example used as evidence, not an example used solely for illustrative purposes.

true evidence at all, because of sample deficiencies. With respect to sampling, the superiority of the quantified data from research is especially marked. For one thing, with research findings it is usually clear what the sample is: how many cases, what cases. Also, the sample is usually large enough to handle the chance-variability problem.

## Biased Selection

As a simple approach to the topic of biased and unbiased sample selection, let us start with the following exercise. Consider University *Y:* 43 percent of its students are females. We could draw a number of samples from the student body, by a variety of selection methods, and see how closely each sample value approaches the true population value—43 percent girls. Let us make each sample large enough so that chance variability should have scant effect: at least 100 students in each sample.

The first sample is drawn from a particular dormitory: it yields 0 percent females. The second sample is drawn from another dormitory: 100 percent females. The third sample is drawn from participants in intramural sports: 2 percent females. The fourth is drawn from the College of Science: 8 percent female. The fifth is from the College of Education: 76 percent female. The sixth is drawn from students studying in the library at a particular time: 53 percent female. The seventh is taken by stopping students as they walk in from the university parking lot: 33 percent female. The eighth is drawn by walking around campus and picking out students "at random": 51 percent female. The ninth is taken by going to the Student Directory, an alphabetized list of all students' names, going down the list and drawing out every hundredth name: 43 percent females, the true population value.

The first sample was drawn from one subgroup of the population: one dormitory. To be included in the sample, a student had to live in that dormitory. It was a men's dormitory. The selection criterion—residing in *x* dormitory—was causally related to the variable being measured, sex. Likewise (in reverse) for the second sample, drawn from a girls' dormitory. Similarly, in less extreme form, for subsequent samples: Men are more likely than women to participate in intramural sports, to enroll in the College of Science, to have cars on campus. Girls are more likely than men to enroll in the College of Education. Various causal factors must determine who studies in the library, at what times. Perhaps girls generally are more likely to be in the library. Or perhaps the causal influence was less direct: it was term-paper time, or cramming-for-test time, in one or several large education courses, or something of this sort. Likewise for the sample chosen "at random." What classes are letting out or are about to convene, at a particular location on campus, at a particular time, can determine the sex ratio of such a man-on-the-street sample.

The ninth sample was a truly random one.[6] It was not drawn from one subgroup of the student population, but from the entire population. No sex-linked characteristic of the students could possibly affect who was chosen to be included in the sample.

This selection method—variously termed random sampling, a representative sample, proportional sampling, probability sampling—is the ideal (Chein 1959:514; Parten 1950:219; Stephan and McCarthy 1958:33–34). With random selection, one is assured of coming reasonably close to the true population value—assuming that the sample is large enough to take care of chance variability, and in the absence of sizeable measurement error. We have considerable evidence that this is so. A case in point is the precision of pre-election polls, in the face of measurement error and despite the fact that only a tiny fraction of the electorate is sampled.

If *all* cases in the population are accessible for study and if all can be put on a list (or some variant of a list), then the sample can be drawn from the list, using some selection criterion which could not possibly be causally related to the variable(s) under study: every hundredth name, every tenth name, the flip of a

[6] Strictly speaking, sampling people would term this a "systematic sample."

coin, the toss of a die, drawing names out of a hat, using a table of random numbers, or whatever.

In a minority of studies this ideal sampling method can be used, because the researcher is only interested in generalizing about a fairly small and circumscribed population: American voters in one election, American professors in a particular field, personnel in a single business organization, men in some branch of the armed services, Congressmen.[7]

Usually this ideal is beyond reach. In much research, the case is a single person, the sample is a collection of persons drawn from some locality, and the study is done to test a generalization about *people*. Only people in one tiny subgroup of the population have a chance to be included in the sample. Subgroup samples are especially the stuff of basic research, in both the social and the natural sciences. A generalization about human perception, or colloids, or cues to mating behavior in ducks, or whatever, can be documented only with a localized sample. The researcher does not know whether his sample value is representative of the true population value or not. For all he knows, he sampled from a very unusual subgroup; the effect he found in his sample might not show up if the entire population could have been studied. An analogy is the first eight samples of students in University *Y*. All were drawn from subgroups of sorts, some of which were more nearly typical of the population than were others.

Practically all basic research, then, cannot be conducted on "good" or "random" samples. Theoretically at least, biased selection is an ever-present danger. The population to be generalized to is so huge that a sample can only be drawn from a localized segment of it; and that segment may or may not be unusual with respect to the variables under study. When random selection is impossible, replications can serve at times to ameliorate (to some extent) the sampling problem. If when a study is replicated, the finding from the first sample emerges again from a sample drawn

[7] In practice, the only source of sampling error that remains resides in the "refusals" and the "inaccessibles." A fraction of the sample may refuse to be studied. This is a possible (and ordinarily a small) source of bias. The willingness-to-participate variable might be causally related to the variables under study.

from a different localized subgroup, this can give some assurance that the original study findings were not an artifact of a fluky sample. If more replications are done, sampling from still other segments of the population, and if they continue to agree with the original study, then the assurance gets stronger. Suppose, for example, that we wish to test the hypothesis that students in University *Y* are predominantly male. We sample the student body by observing one classroom: mostly males here, but quite possibly a biased sample. We sample another classroom: also predominantly males. If the students in University *Y* were *not* mostly male, then if we continued to sample classrooms we should run into a predominantly female class rather soon. If replications continue and this does not happen, we have some right to believe that this school *is* mainly for boys. Somewhat in this fashion, experiments may be replicated in various parts of the country (or of the world), sampling varied segments of the human race (or the rat race); if all turns out well, this is a second-best solution to the sampling problem, when truly random sampling is impossible.

At times such a series of replications is performed; often it is not. From the viewpoint of the sampling problem alone, it usually is probably not worth the trouble.

The gravity of the biased-selection problem depends very much, I think, on the margin for error provided by the hypothesis. In particular, it depends on whether the hypothesis cites one variable or two. A single-variable statement, such as "Candidate *X* will win the election" or "43 percent of the students in University *Y* are girls," is in real jeopardy. Numerous causal influences must be at work, which determine incidence of the single variable. Anything short of the optimally "good" selection procedure is likely to weight some of these influences too heavily in a single sample, weight others too lightly. This was exemplified by the samples from University *Y*. Another example is election predictions. We have evidence as to what some of the influences are which tilt voters in a Democrat or Republican direction: income level, education level, locality, occupation, religion, ethnicity. A forecast of a national election based on a poll which sampled from only one locality is about as likely to be wrong as it is to be right. If the subgroup sampled from is markedly different from the population with respect to religion or social class position or ethnic-group membership, the election prediction likewise stands a good chance of being wrong. If such an hypothesis admits a margin for error—"Most of the students are boys" rather than "43 percent are girls"; "Lyndon Johnson will win the election," not "He will get 65 percent of the vote"—then it stands a better chance of being right. But it might still be wrong.

With a correlation hypothesis, on the other hand, the problem is less severe. In fact, a case can be made that with correlation hypotheses which state non-necessary causal relationships, the problem of biased selection disappears entirely.

This, if true, is very fortunate, since this is the standard sort of hypothesis we test. It says that variable *A* is a cause for variable *B*. Occasionally it is stated more timidly: variables *A* and *B* are "related," causally connected in some way. Favorable evidence is in the form of a correlation, ordinarily positive, between *A* and *B*, drawn from a sample. Customarily the P value must be quite low before the study findings are construed as favorable evidence; so the problem of chance variability is well taken care of. To return to Table X: it is surely no coincidence that in this little localized sample, the smokers were more likely to get lung cancer. This evidence, by itself, demonstrates to my satisfaction a causal connection between cigarette smoking and lung cancer. One might object that this is a wildly unusual subgroup: half the people had lung cancer. This would not bother me. The hypothesis says nothing about the *rate* of cancer in the population (which is all humans); it merely says cigarette smoking is a cause for it. One might object again: we still don't know whether such a correlation exists within the population as a whole; maybe if all humans could be studied, we would find no correlation between smoking and cancer. Theoretically this is so. However, I cannot imagine how such a correlation could be purely an artifact of biased selection. This could only occur, I think, as a result of cheating: keeping or remembering cases that fit the trend; rejecting, losing, or forgetting the exceptions. This is probably a fairly routine operation, with impressionistic evidence culled from everyday experience, but one hopes it happens rarely in formal research.

Returning to Table X: suppose this study were replicated, on a number of other little samples. Suppose further that the replications are generally unfavorable. Perhaps one or several of these show a zero correlation between smoking and cancer. Even this would not shake my faith that smoking was a cause for cancer.[8] That is to say, unless the correlation in Table X is purely the result of dishonest sample selection or observer-error (i.e., systematic bias) or chance variability (the odds are .01 for this), then there must be a causal connection between smoking and cancer. The subsequent unfavorable replications I would construe as signs of limiting conditions: smoking must act as a cause for cancer only in the presence of some other causal agent(s). For the sample in Table X, this (or these) was present in sufficient degree to "show up" the causal connection; in the samples on which the unfavorable replications were based, this apparently was not the case.

Others, I am sure, do not take such a sanguine view of the problem of biased selection. When a researcher finds a correlation in a subgroup sample, it is true that he does not *know* that this correlation would hold up if his entire population could be studied. Neither do we know how many of these correlations would "wash out" if the entire population could have been measured. It is only my guess that incidence of this would be very low.

Biased selection, I suspect, is much more likely to produce mistakes of the opposite type: a weak or zero correlation leading to the conclusion that variables *A* and *B* are not causally related, when in fact—if we only knew—*A* and *B* *are* causally related. Again, my argument is in terms of limiting conditions. As an illustration of this: Caston (unpublished) studied the effect of bulletin board notices on the concert-going behavior of a group of

[8] This is a bit overstated. There must be a causal relationship between smoking and cancer. However, this particular study does not demonstrate the *direction* of the causal relationship. Direction of causation will be discussed in the next chapter.

junior high school students. Her sample was drawn from two junior high schools, both of which were located in a town with a University concert series. In one school, she plastered the halls with notices announcing coming concerts. In the other school, the concerts received no such advertising. She found that the advertisements had no effect on concert going: The students simply did not go. This was as true for the school with bulletin board notices as for the school without them. This no-cause conclusion is no doubt true for this limited situation. But surely, if these findings were used to document a broader generalization, something on the order of "Bulletin board notices have no effect on concert attendance," or perhaps "Advertising does not stimulate attendance," this conclusion would not be true. In certain contexts—certain types of people, certain types of performances —advertising, even bulletin board notices, must surely make a difference. Caston's study indicates that under some conditions this "law" does not hold. But under other conditions it must hold. Likewise, I suspect, biased selection or subgroup sampling more often leads us to reject true correlation hypotheses, rather than to believe untrue ones.

Perhaps it is frequently true that variable *A* produces *B* only under particular conditions, only in the presence of some needed interactive variable(s). When you pull the trigger the gun fires —if the gun is loaded, and if the gun is in proper working order. Sometimes the necessary conditions are present in the sample studied, and therefore the causal relation between *A* and *B* "shows up," as in the example of cigarette smoking and lung cancer. Sometimes the necessary conditions are not present—as appears to be the case in Caston's sample—and therefore the causal relation does not show up. Even if one's causal generalization is true—that, for example, bulletin board notices promote attendance—the practical issue is: how common is this effect? Is it statistically rare, occurring only under rather unusual conditions? If this were so, the hypothesis, even though true, would be of little use in understanding how to promote concerts, unless the needed interactive variables can themselves be discovered. Perhaps it is not rare. Maybe if a wide assortment of samples, age groups, concert series, were studied, we would find that bulletin board advertising usually helps attendance. Caston's sample might have been unusual.

Replications of such studies as smoking–cancer and Caston's bulletin boards, on a variety of subgroup samples, can serve to give some indication of the *generalizability* of causal hypotheses. They would seem to be needed not so much to answer the question "Is the hypothesis true?" Rather, they answer the practical question "Does the cause 'work' in most situations, or in relatively few?" Thereby, they help indicate the chances that the causal law will hold for new and untried situations and groups; and, presumably, they offer better guidance to decision makers.

## From Mice to Men

Having discussed the two classic sources of sampling error, biased selection and chance variability, we now turn to further ramifications of the sampling problem. These have to do especially with experiments. Many an experimental finding, when related to some generalization about "real-life phenomena," should probably not be construed as evidence at all, but rather as a sort of suggestive analogy to "real life." This is because the generalization must be stated as a high-level law. Also, experiments with animal subjects give the sampling problem a peculiar twist, since they tempt one to generalize from one species to another.

Often we are not interested so much in generalizing to an entire population as in generalizing from one subgroup of that population to another subgroup. This is the situation posed by animal studies done by experimental psychologists. If an hypothesis states a cause-effect relationship, then really good evidence requires an experiment. Quite often the hypothesis is such that, because of ethical and practical limitations, the necessary experimental manipulations cannot be performed on humans. But it may be that the experiment can be performed on some lower animal. So the study is done not with human subjects, but with rats, mice, pigeons, monkeys, dogs, hamsters, or some other creatures. When the study is finished and the findings are in, the experimenter comes to the usual choice point with regard to the generality of his conclusion. He may not generalize beyond his sample, hence divesting his study of any significance. Or the population he generalizes to may be merely the species he sampled from—albino rats, or whatever. Again, this robs the study of any value, unless one has an intrinsic interest in albino rats. Or he (or someone else) may take the leap and apply the findings to an hypothesis about humans. Thereby, the mice-to-men sampling problem has been created: the generalization may be true for albino rats but it might not be true for humans. This is somewhat analogous to testing an hypothesis on a sample of University of Colorado students, then applying the hypothesis to University of Indiana students and citing the data gathered at the University of Colorado as supporting evidence, on grounds that both groups are subgroups of a larger population, American college students. Beyond a point the analogy breaks down, of course; there are known structural differences between rats and men.

To illustrate this further, let us return to the cancer studies. The positive correlation between cigarette smoking and lung cancer is well documented (from real, not make-believe, studies). But the evidence for human subjects comes from surveys, not from experiments. It is conceivable that the correlation derives not from the fact that smoking is a cause for cancer, but from some third factor which is causing both variables, so as to make them covary. This might be a genetic predisposition of some kind, which makes certain people more prone to (1) yearn for cigarettes and (2) develop lung cancer. In other words, even if smoking and cancer are causally related, the relationship may be a remote one, and it may *not* be true that smoking, in itself, causes cancer. The only way to rule out such a possibility is with an experiment. Experiments have been done, but not on people. A biologist shaves a mouse's back, applies the tars from cigarettes, and waits; quite often, the skin so treated developes a malignant tumor (Brecher and Brecher 1963). This is a dramatic effect, and it converges nicely with the surveys done on humans. The evidence is about as strong as evidence can be that cigarettes are a cause for lung cancer. Still the apologists for cigarettes have a loophole. A mouse's back is not a man's lung. To generalize from the mouse experiments to cigarette smokers, the population would have to be "animal tissues" or "mammalian tissues." Findings from one subgroup of the population, mouse skin, must be generalized to another subgroup, human lungs.

In this particular example, the mouse experiments do provide bona fide evidence. The generalization which must be stated in order to make the bridge between the mouse and the cigarette smoker need not be a high-level law (It might be "Tobacco tars produce cancer in mammalian tissues," or "Cigarettes contain carcinogens"). In other instances, however, the findings from experiments must be related to high-level laws. The researcher has no in-between option. He can either state his conclusion as a conservative statement of findings, confined to his one experiment with its special experimental conditions and limited solely to his experimental subjects. Or he can view his findings as "evidence" for some high-level law. If he does take this second option, and construes his experiment as "saying something about" discrimination processes, or secondary reinforcement, or balance theory, or the effect of drive level on performance, or some other abstract concept(s), then his experiment could hardly be construed as "giving evidence," in the sense of bearing on the high-level law's likelihood of truth. (This frequently holds, I think, even when the experiment is done on human subjects. The variables may be operationally defined in terms of the special experimental situation. If this is done, the conclusion is limited to the one experimental situation, and it is trivial. The alternative is to construe the experimental variables as indices or "special types" of abstract variables; hence the high-level law.)

The literature of experimental psychology is organized around various theories or explicitly stated abstract systems. Under each such theory, or under a single high-level law, experimental findings can be given. These might be viewed as an elaborate series of footnotes, indicating where the law seems to "work" and under what conditions it seems not to work. In other words, these could be viewed as pointing to the "boundaries" of the law or theory or, if you will, citing limiting conditions. Reviewing such a high-level law, with its empirical footnotes, calls for a rather unnatural mental juggling act. The law itself can be viewed as a heuristic device for summarizing evidence in a particular area and pointing directions for further research. However, this "evidence" cannot really be related to the law in order to judge it for likelihood of truth, for reasons that were discussed at the end of the last chapter. Neither can the entire statement—law-plus-footnotes, general principle with limiting conditions—be judged for likelihood of truth. This is a situation in which no truth-epistemology, such as the one in use here, can be applied. The law must be judged with reference to some other epistemological criterion instead.

To close the chapter with an ambiguity: sometimes it is unclear, a matter of arbitrary choice, a matter of "construing," whether or not a generalization is a high-level law. Construed in one way, such a statement is no doubt true, resting on good evidence. Construed in an alternative fashion, it is a high-level law and cannot be judged for likelihood of truth. If one were to leaf through Berelson's and Steiner's *Human Behavior: An Inventory of Scientific Findings* (1964), he would no doubt decide that some of their 1,024 generalizations are not high-level laws and, in the light of the evidence, are probably true. Others are clearly high-level laws. Still others are in a twilight zone. Depending on a slight shift of emphasis in the reader's construing, they either are or are not "documented" by research findings. Here is one example from Berelson and Steiner (p. 166), cited earlier: "Meaningful material is easier to memorize than nonmeaningful material; and once learned, is retained longer."

Ambiguities, ambiguities.

## *Selected References*

Mathematical rationale for sampling—a simple introduction:

Celeste McCullough and Loche Van Atta, *Statistical Concepts*, chaps. 2, 5, and 13.

Significance tests and P values:

Celeste McCullough and Loche Van Atta, *Statistical Concepts*, chaps. 5 and 7.

Sampling—a higher-level treatment:

Frederick Stephan and Philip J. McCarthy, *Sampling Opinions.*

Sampling error stemming from chance variability—how to estimate its magnitude; how this calculation affects determination of sample size:

Isidor Chein, "An Introduction to Sampling," App. B in Claire Selltiz *et al.*, ed., *Research Methods in Social Relations*, pp. 509–545.

# *Chapter 7*

# CAUSE AND EFFECT

Numerous books and articles offer causal explanations of social phenomena. Some deal with social movements—the rise of fascism, the ebb and flow of democracy, the growth of some new cult, economic or religious. Some deal with social trends—urbanization, the tempo of technological exploitation, the changing phases of the "economic cycle," the decline of the birth-rate. Some deal with socio-pathological problems, explaining the relative frequency of crime, delinquency, pauperism, divorce, political corruption, and so forth. The incessant impact of social change in its myriad aspects is the perpetual challenge to which these responses are made. Not only our scientific interest but also the imperative demands of public policy here give weight and urgency to the investigation of causes.

ROBERT M. MAC IVER (1942)

Finally, as well as enabling us to discover and explain social facts, general statements are held to be required if we are to put out social knowledge into practice. Social enquiries are frequently carried on not for their own sake, but in order to help us to decide what to *do*. We have practical ends to achieve such as making profits or preventing wars, and we wish to know how to achieve them. For this we must know what will happen *if* we perform certain actions at particular times and places in the future. And in order to establish such conditional statements, the defender of scientific procedure will maintain, we require general statements about the consequences of various possible kinds of action in various possible kinds of circumstance.

QUENTIN GIBSON (1960)

By the verb *to cause*, I mean *to help make happen.* A cause is a variable which helps another variable happen. An effect is a consequence. By "*A* is a cause for *B*," I mean that variable *A* helped make variable *B* happen, that variable *B* is a partial consequence of *A*, that—in part—it resulted from *A*.

As we go through our daily rounds of activities, we are constantly making cause-effect statements to ourselves: out loud, implicitly, sometimes unconsciously. One turns the water faucet counterclockwise because that causes water to come out. He likewise turns his key in the lock, because that is the way to get through the door. He puts on his coat because that keeps him from getting quite so cold. We do most of the things we do because we expect certain consequences. The expectation of consequences frames and determines our acts. If cause-effect hypotheses were to be outlawed, life would freeze into immobility; we could do nothing. This is a ludicrous possibility, of course; we are cause-calculating animals.

There has been much discussion among philosophers about how *cause* might best be conceptualized (Ayer 1956:192; Bunge 1961; Feigl 1953; Kaplan 1964:118; Nagel 1961). Some would even like to outlaw the concept, as just defined, from scientific discourse, preferring to talk instead of mathematical functions or prediction (Russell 1929:180). Perhaps in response to the controversies among philosophers, causation has been handled in social science in a rather gingerly fashion. Some writers approach the subject with considerable circumspection, using various circumlocutions and euphemisms. They may speak only of "relationships" or "predictors" or "independent and dependent variables" or "antecedent and consequent conditions." Others do, of course, talk forthrightly about cause and effect (Underwood 1957:33; Campbell and Katona 1953; MacIver 1942).

It is true that some physical systems—the arc of a pendulum, the paths of the planets—can be adequately explained mathematically, without recourse to cause-effect statements. However, it would seem that we are bound to the notion of causation when we start talking about people. Most hypotheses of any import have to do with the consequences of human actions. It is impossible for me to imagine how we could proceed in our human, cause-calculating, decision-making style without routine use of the commonsense notion of cause. This goes for high policy, as well as for daily decisions about water faucets and keys. To put this another way: our decision making rests on the selection of some cause-effect hypotheses, to the exclusion of other possible ones. To be of practical use, any body of knowledge must provide criteria—evidence, if you will—for the acceptance of some cause-effect statements and the rejection of others. Whether it is "justified" or "legitimate" to speak of cause and effect—some philosophers claim it is not [1]—makes no difference. Willy-nilly, we must do it. The practical issue is: Are some cause-effect hypotheses better than others, more likely to enable the right decision?

The choice of terms does not matter. If one prefers to speak of "antecedents and consequents" or "dependent and independent variables" rather than "causes" and "effects," this makes no difference. To speak merely of "predictors," though, is not enough. Daylight is a predictor of night a few hours hence, but it is not a cause for it. Neither does "relationships" suffice, unless the direction of the relationship—what causes what—is specified. In other words, to guide ordinary decision making, an hypothesis must say more than that one event presages some other one, or that one factor is related to another; it must state a *consequence* (effect) of some *action* (cause) by the decision maker.

In practice, of course, cause-effect hypotheses are not limited to consequences of human actions. What makes the rain fall, what makes the grass grow, what makes rocks decompose, what makes the heart pump, what causes winter: all questions such as these are requests for causal explanations. Even in discourse about human behavior, many a causal hypothesis is not geared to the practical dilemma of some decision maker. In fact, in our quest for understanding and in our theory building, we have wandered rather far afield from the needs of policy makers. Some causal hypotheses have practical uses; others do not; some day, in some way, some of them (it is hoped) might. (The federal grant giver holds a loose rein.)

Causation can always be construed as occurring between a pair of variables: one variable is a cause for the other. In other words,

[1] Kemeny 1959:49–51.

a cause-effect statement is a correlation hypothesis of a special type. It says that two variables covary because of the fact (partly or solely) that one is causing the other. The pair of variables joined in a cause-effect relationship can be viewed as being linked with innumerable other variables in a ramified causal system, in such a manner that the "cause-variable" is itself an effect of other variables, the "effect-variable" is also an effect of other variables, and in its turn (along with the "cause-variable") is a cause for still other variables. Furthermore, both "cause-variable" and "effect-variable" are linked to still more "distant" variables in the causal system, both as "cause" and "effect." Although any two-variable causal relationship may be imbedded in such a vast system, it is still possible to isolate it out, and speak of one of the variables as "acting as a cause for" the other. Single cause-effect hypotheses are two-variable statements. A more complicated explanation can be broken down into a number of two-variable statements.

If "cause" and "effect" are construed as variables, they should, properly, be talked about in language befitting variables. The statement "The cause helps make the effect happen" should be reworded: "Variation in the intensity or magnitude of the cause-variable tends to cause variation in the intensity or magnitude of the effect-variable," or "Magnitude of the effect-variable is to some degree contingent on magnitude of the cause-variable." "Fever is caused by illness" means, then, that the fever variable possessed in some degree by a case (the patient may have zero fever, or fever of 1° F., or 3° F., or whatever) is partly the result of magnitude of the severity-of-illness variable possessed by that same case. (The patient may not be ill at all, or he may be slightly ill, moderately ill, seriously ill, desperately ill.) If we were to find, for a sample of patients, a positive correlation between amount of fever and severity of illness, we could explain this as due to the fact that amount of fever is contingent, to some extent, on severity of illness.

Sometimes, when an hypothesis is stated, the speaker signifies the causal inference with such a key term as "causes," "reason for," "determinant of," "makes," "produces," "eventuates in"; or "effect of," "consequence," "results from," or "develops out of." Other correlation hypotheses are not given such an obvious causal ticket; the reader or listener can choose whether or not he wishes to construe them as stating causal relations. For example, "Married students are better students" may or may not be taken to mean that getting married helps to make one a better student. "The hungry rats learned faster" might be construed as a cause-effect hypothesis ("Hunger caused the rats to learn faster") or as a noncausal correlation statement meaning, simply, that the hungry rats learned faster.

Causal statements could be broken down into types according to a variety of typologies. The one chosen for use here was given in Chapter 2.

1. Necessary-cause statements, which were divided into two subtypes: (a) the necessary-cause generalization, which says that *B* cannot happen unless *A* is present ("To fire the gun, you must pull the trigger"); and (b) the explanation for a single case ("The gun would not have fired just then if you had not first pulled the trigger").
2. The sufficient-cause statement, the mirror image of the necessary-cause, which says that *A* always eventuates in *B* ("A gun always fires when the trigger is pulled").
3. The necessary-and-sufficient-cause statement ("Always, and only when, the trigger is pulled, the gun will fire").

These are all relatively difficult and stringent causal hypotheses, in that they are particularly vulnerable to unfavorable evidence. All except the single-case explanation say that exceptions of certain types never occur: a gun never fires when the trigger isn't pulled (necessary-cause generalization); it never does *not* fire when the trigger *is* pulled (sufficient cause); there is a perfect, exceptionless correlation between trigger pulling and gun firing (necessary-and-sufficient cause). These require, for evidence, a search for such exceptions: what was termed, in Chapter 2, a test for negative cases.

4. The fourth type of causal statement is more modest. It does admit exceptions in both directions, instances of trigger pulling when the gun didn't fire and instances of gun firing

without any trigger pulling. "Pulling the trigger tends to make the gun fire," or "Pulling the trigger is a cause for gun firing." Ordinarily, it is this type of causal hypothesis that we test. It was labeled a "non-necessary-cause-effect statement." This is a rather ungainly title. In subsequent discussion, the term "causal hypotheses" will indicate a non-necessary-cause-effect statement.

5. Theoretically, there is room left for a fifth type of cause-effect statement, the *single-cause hypothesis: A* is *the* cause for *B* ("Gun firing depends solely on trigger pulling"). The structure of the gun, firing pin, ammunition, etc.—all are irrelevant. Pulling the trigger is all that matters. All such statements will be summarily dismissed here as untrue. Rather, if an hypothesis is worded, as it often is, in such a form as ". . . *the* reason that . . ." or ". . . *the* result of . . ." or ". . . *the* cause of . . . ," I would do the hypothesis the kindness of translating it into such a form as: ". . . *one* reason that . . .", or ". . . *a* result of . . . ," or ". . . *a* cause for. . . ." Any single-cause statement can be demolished by argument: thus Stouffer's (1958) Parable of the Dead Duck. A hunter shoots a duck in a Michigan marsh. Why did the duck die? Because the hunter shot him. Oh?

> Well, there is a physiological explanation. The duck died because of a hemorrhage, which left the heart no blood to pump. And there is a psychological explanation. The duck died because the hunter was the kind of person he was—if he had had different frustrations in his youth, he might not have become a bird killer. We might take a psychoanalytic dive into this one, but let's skip it. And there is an ideological explanation. If the culture of Michigan were like that of parts of India, the killing of a duck—or of any other animal, for that matter—would be reprehensible. And there is a geographical explanation. Note that the duck died in a marsh. No hunter probably would have been waiting for him on top of the hill. Finally, consider a technological explanation, the gun that killed him, a product of technical progress in the manufacture of lethal hardware.

Even the necessary-and-sufficient hypothesis, as ambitious as it is, does not preempt all other causes. Alfred Lindesmith (1948) appears to view his explanation for opiate addiction in necessary-

and-sufficient terms. Addiction (the effect) is due to experiencing withdrawal symptoms, taking the drug and experiencing relief of the withdrawal symptoms, and realizing that the drug brought one the relief (all this is the cause). Whenever this happens, the user becomes an addict, "hooked" on the drug. Unless and until this happens, the user is not addicted. Lindesmith apparently believes there is a perfect, exceptionless correlation between the cause, knowingly getting relief from drug, and the effect, addiction. Yet he surely would be the first to admit the contribution of other causes. Before the user reaches the point of experiencing withdrawal symptoms, he had to start taking the drug in the first place. Why did he start? Also, *why* does Lindesmith's cause, knowingly getting relief from drug, lead to addiction? What is the mechanism? At the very least, some sort of chain reaction must operate: the reason the drug was first taken, then Lindesmith's cause, then perhaps a psychological mechanism of some sort, then addiction.

## The Causal Skein

If one were to give his imagination free rein, it would be possible to draw pictures of possible causal systems. Each cause for a particular variable or event might be represented by a line or vector. One could start with a certain "effect," think of contributing causes, then of causes for the causes, then of causes for these, and so on, until he grew tired. The end product, the resulting vector field, might resemble a segment of a very large and elaborate spider web. One could then assign terms to typical combinations of strands within the web.

### *Historical Chain Reactions*

One thing is a cause for another is a cause for another is a cause for another. Thus with the Lindesmith example: something (no doubt many things) causes some people to take up heroin in the first place; for various reasons, some of these people continue taking it until their bodies adjust to the drug to the point that the body complains if the drug is not forthcoming (and some sort of physiological mechanism must intervene here); then Lindesmith's cause (and another intervening psychological mechanism); then addiction. A simpler example is one given by Zeisel, cited in Chapter 2: women have fewer accidents because they drive less. Rate of miles driven is a cause for accident rate; sex is a cause for rate of miles driven.

### *Additive Effects*

Numerous causal influences may converge on a particular effect. Accident rate must depend on more than rate of miles driven. Age, drinking habits, locality, and many other variables, must make a difference. An aged, drunken New York taxi driver must be a worse risk than a middle-aged, sober Kansas taxi driver. As another example, McCord, McCord, and Zola (1959:115) isolated four family-background causes of delinquency: maternal rejection, paternal rejection, maternal deviance (crime, alcoholism, or promiscuity), paternal deviance. For their sample (boys in a slum neighborhood), boys that were judged to have one of these delinquency predictors in their home environments had a 29 percent rate of delinquency; of the boys with two of these, 51 percent were delinquent; boys with three were 67 percent delinquent; boys with all four were 81 percent delinquent.

### *Threshold Effects*

One variable may act as a cause for another, but only when it is present at a particular magnitude. For example, John Whiting (Department of Social Relations, Harvard University) has some data that lead him to believe that there is a curvilinear relationship between the age of a child when it is weaned and how upsetting weaning is to the child. When a child is weaned in infancy, *or* when he is weaned at a fairly advanced age, weaning tends not to be traumatic. But if he is weaned when he is between 1½ and 2½ years old, the weaning experience is much more upsetting. In other words, age is a cause of weaning disturbance only when age is within a particular range: 1½ to 2½.

### *Interaction Effects*

One variable may become effective as a cause for another only under particular conditions, that is to say, only in combination with one or several other causal variables. A gun will fire when the trigger is pulled, *if* the gun is loaded, and *if* the gun is in proper working order. This is the notion of limiting conditions. It can be used to explain exceptions: trigger pulling without subsequent gun firing; cigarette smokers who do not get cancer; boys from "bad" homes who do not turn to crime.

Occasionally, especially when working with relatively simple causal systems, one can achieve "pure effects." All significant causal variables but one can be "controlled," "held constant"; then each time the cause is introduced, the effect follows. An example is the gun-firing instance. This also goes for various controlled experiments and demonstrations in the natural sciences, such as those performed by the chemist in his laboratory. Such a controlled situation can enable the more stringent causal hypotheses: *A always* causes *B; B never* occurs without prior occurrence of *A*. It even, at times, enables precise statements of magnitude: just so much increment of *A* produces so much increment of, or change in, *B*. To such a statement one must, of course, append a footnote: under such-and-such conditions, with such-and-such other variables controlled.

If one correlates the cause-variable and effect-variable without benefit of such controls, one would expect to find exceptions: some cigarette smokers who do not get cancer because the other enabling cause(s), which must interact with smoking in order to produce cancer, is(are) not present; some cancer sufferers who have never smoked (because additional causes for cancer have not been "controlled out").

In social and behavioral research, opportunities for this order of control are practically nil. Even in our so-called controlled experiments, variables within the organism remain uncontrolled and reflect themselves in individual differences in performance. Hence our correlations are rarely perfect, our experimental effects rarely "pure." We are pretty much confined to testing non-necessary causal hypotheses, for which evidence can be favorable even when exceptions are found.

## Cause and Correlation

When does one have *any* evidence for a causal hypothesis? What is the minimal favorable evidence? Opinions would seem to differ. In everyday life, the causal inference is sometimes based on observation of co-occurrence of a presumed cause-variable and effect-variable, in a single case. Sometimes a causal conclusion is based on an observed co-occurrence within a group of cases. At the other end of the spectrum are certain purists who hold that nothing, short of an experiment in which the causal variable is under the control of the experimenter, gives any evidence for a cause-effect statement (Larrabee 1945:357, 402; Underwood 1957).

Probably the majority opinion, within the social sciences at least, lies somewhere in between. A single case is not enough, because co-occurrence then might very well have been a coincidence. Mere co-occurrence, even with a sample of cases, is not sufficient either. Experimental evidence is good to have; however, in its absence, an observed correlation between two variables can give minimal evidence that one of them is a cause for the other. This will be the position taken here.

The reasoning is: if *A* is a cause for *B*, then *A* and *B* should covary. If smoking is a cause for cancer, then smokers should be more likely than non-smokers to get cancer. If economic development is a determinant of success at democracy, then economically developed countries should be more likely than undeveloped ones to be democracies. If father absence is a determinant of delinquency, then boys living with their fathers, as compared with boys without fathers, should show a lower rate of crime.

If we find, in fact, that *A* and *B* are not so correlated, then this would be evidence that *A* is not a cause for *B*. It would not rule out the possibility,[2] but it would be evidence for a no-cause hypothesis: *A* is not a cause for *B*. If, on the other hand, we do a study and find that *A* and *B* are correlated, then this finding is consistent with the notion that *A* is a cause for *B*. It is favorable evidence.

The usual convention is to consider any such evidence as favorable only when the P value is fairly low, under .05. This gives some assurance that the found relationship between *A* and *B* was not simply a coincidence, a chance happening. The low P value requires that the correlation must have been observed to hold for a fair-sized sample. Hence the observation of just a single case, or only a few cases, is not sufficient.

Occasionally a co-occurrence is observed, for a group of cases, which is not a true correlation. Imagine, for example, a sunrise ceremony performed by a primitive tribe. Shortly before dawn each morning, a shaman performs a ceremony, utters certain incantations, and then a short time later—presto! The sun comes up. The people believe the sun rises because the shaman performs this ritual. From time immemorial, every day, the ceremony has always been performed. The sun has always come up. The relationship between presumed cause and effect might be pictured thus:

TABLE XII

EFFICACY OF THE SUNRISE CEREMONY

| | Days the sun came up | Days the sun didn't come up |
|---|---|---|
| Days sunrise ceremony was performed | many | 0 |
| Days sunrise ceremony was not performed | 0 | 0 |

Sometimes the sunrise ceremony model is used as a basis for a causal inference. Most of us, surely, would feel that the minimal

[2] Non-validity of the measures may have obliterated the real relationship. Also, an essential interactive variable might have been absent in the sample studied.

requirements for evidence have not been met (even though, in our everyday lives, we occasionally do this sort of thing ourselves). Before there is *any* evidence, there must be a correlation. Some cases must be observed that can be classified "low" or "absent" with respect to the causal variable. Some morning the shaman should not perform that ceremony and see what happened.

If a true correlation can be observed between variables *A* and *B*, and if the P value is reasonably low, this is, I think, strong evidence that there is some sort of causal relationship between *A* and *B*.[3] The question then is: What is the *direction* of the causal relationship? Is *A* causing *B?* Or is *B* causing *A?* Or is the relationship more remote: is something else causing both of them, in such a manner as to make them covary?

## Closing the Trap

To rule out the possibility that the reason *A* and *B* are correlated is simply that *B* (the presumed effect) is really causing *A*, we must show *before-after conditions*. In the common conception of causation, there is the notion that cause and effect operate through time: first the cause occurs, then the effect follows. A consequence follows after whatever caused it. The time gap may be years, or it may be a split second, but the cause always precedes the effect in time (for some philosophic hairsplitting on this point, see Ayer 1956:192). Therefore, if *A* precedes *B* in time, then the correlation cannot be due to the fact that *B* is a cause for *A*. One turns the water faucet and water comes out. The spurt of water did not cause the turning of the faucet; it was the other way around. One turns the doorknob and the door opens; the first event must have caused the second, because it happened first. Likewise with experiments: some rats are kept from food, other rats are fed; then they all run a maze; the hungry rats learn to find their way through the maze more quickly than the satiated rats do. Speed of learning could not be causing

[3] Barring instances where systematic bias appears to be a real possibility.

food deprivation, because *first* some of the rats were deprived of food, and *then* they all ran the maze.

Sometimes, as in experiments, before-after conditions are obviously present; they are a "given." Cases clearly "got," or were subjected to, the presumed causal variable at a certain time. Then, at a later time, some cases show an increment in the presumed effect-variable. Under these conditions, it is clear that any correlation between *A* and *B*, presumed cause and effect, is not simply due to the fact that *B* is causing *A*.

In the absence of perfectly clear-cut before-after conditions, sometimes before-after conditions may be argued for. It may appear very unreasonable to suppose that variable *B* preceded *A* in time. With the correlation between cigarette smoking and lung cancer, for example: some of the people in the sample must have started smoking relatively early in their lives; then later in their lives, some got lung cancer. It is hard to imagine how cancer could have preceded smoking in time. We do not really *know* that this did not happen, but it seems unreasonable. In such an instance as this, perhaps, a fairly strong case could be made for the presence of before-after conditions.

Quite often, of course, a causal inference is drawn from a correlation, when no such case can be made for before-after conditions. An example is a correlation that has emerged from a number of child-development studies between physical punishment and children's aggressiveness. Children who receive a lot of spankings tend to be more aggressive, fight more, argue and contend more, and so on, than do other children who are not spanked, or who are rarely spanked (Bronfenbrenner 1958). Does spanking engender aggressiveness? Or does aggressiveness provoke spankings? The child-development psychologists prefer the former explanation; but in the absence of before-after conditions in the data collection, the evidence is not so strong as it might be.

To summarize here: if variables *A* and *B* are in fact correlated, there are three possibilities with respect to the direction of the cause-effect relationship: *A* is causing *B*; *B* is causing *A*; some outside causal factor(s), *C*, is (are) causing them both in such a manner as to produce the correlation between them. How strong the evidence is for an hypothesis that says that *A* is a cause for *B*, depends on whether one or both of these other possibilities can be ruled out. If the data give us before-after conditions, then the *B*-causes-*A* possibility can be eliminated, and evidence for *A*-causes-*B* is stronger than it would be otherwise. Before evidence becomes really strong, however, we must eliminate the third possibility, which might be pictured as:

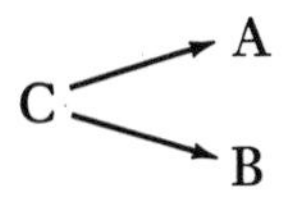


As an illustration of such an outside causal influence, imagine a cross-cultural study. A great many tribes, communities, "societies" in various parts of the world are classified with respect to presence or absence of a long list of culture traits: movies, the wheel, ancestor worship, the blowgun, chess, polygyny, witchcraft, betel chewing, and so on. Each tribe is a case, each culture trait is a variable. After the cataloguing is finished, all the variables could be correlated with each other. We would be certain to find a good many pronounced relationships where it would be hard to conceive how one of the variables could be causing the other: a positive correlation between Buddhism and rice-growing, for example; harpoons and igloos; outrigger canoes and *kava* drinking. For some of these, the correlation must hinge merely on the location of societies. Culture area must be the determining factor: in (or out of) southeast Asia, Eskimo land, Polynesia. Some societies are located in southeast Asia, others are not. The southeast-Asia cases tend to be rice growers, and they tend to be Buddhist. This produces the positive correlation between rice and Buddhism. The two traits could be said to be causally related; they are both caused by something else, a common causal factor, location in southeast Asia. In other words:

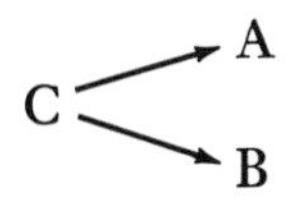

Similarly with other correlations that are not the fruit of experiments. Conceivably, the correlation between spankings and children's aggressiveness is *not* due to the fact that aggressive children provoke more spankings, or that spanking in itself makes children more aggressive. Some variable *C* residing in the parent —degree of impulsiveness or aggressiveness or some other character trait—might be causing both variables, so as to make them co-vary.

The variable-*C* possibility can be ruled out if the data come from an experiment. An experiment also rules out the *B*-causes-*A* possibility. If a correlation between variables *A* and *B* emerges from experimental data, only one possibility remains, with respect to the direction of the cause-effect relationship: *A* must be causing *B*. The trap closes.[4] It is a shame that opportunities for doing experiments on people are so limited, since this is the avenue to really powerfully documented causal hypotheses.

By an experiment, I mean a study in which variable *A*, the presumed cause-variable, is under the control of the researcher. He imposes it on, "does it to," some cases in his sample, withholds it from or "doesn't do it to" others, and then measures the presumed effect-variable. Cases are not self-selected or self-determined with respect to variable *A*; variable *A* is something that is done to some of them by the experimenter. Some experiments are performed in the presence of various "controls," others not; controls are not necessary in order for a study to qualify as an experiment, by the definition of experiment to be used here.

An example of an experiment is a well-publicized toothpaste test. A sample of children is examined for cavities. Then some of them are set to brushing their teeth with Crest, others with brand X. At the end of the study their teeth are examined again, and new cavities are noted. There is a negative correlation between increment of cavities and brushing with Crest. If the study was conducted properly and reported honestly, there is only one possible explanation for this correlation: Crest must be better than brand X. Increment of cavities could not have been determining the choice of toothpaste, because before-after conditions were

[4] This is a bit overstated. Some marginal doubts reside even in experimental data. These will be discussed soon.

present: first the children were segregated into Crest users and non-Crest users; then, at a later time, they were measured for increment of cavities. Neither could variable *C* produce the correlation, because the presumed cause was under the control of the experimenter.

If the correlation had not emerged from an experiment, then it might have been caused by variable *C*. Suppose that a sample of children had simply been surveyed: each child is asked his brand of toothpaste, each has a dental examination. The Crest users tend to have fewer cavities. Variable *C* might be the parents' degree of concern with dental hygiene: concerned parents tended to insist on certain foods, give their children fluoride and calcium supplements, etc.; they were also more responsive to the Crest advertising campaign and bought Crest. Less concerned parents were less likely to do these things. This could have produced the correlation. Whenever, as in this example, variable *A* cannot be controlled by the researcher, then a correlation may simply reflect the fact that both it and variable *B* are responding in like fashion to some possible variable *C*.

The issue is not, of course, whether or not there are other causes for variable *B*, aside from variable *A*. There must be. There could be fifty causes for dental health; if Crest were only one of these, it would still be true that Crest helps prevent cavities. Rather, the issue is: Is the correlation between *A* and *B* simply the result of something else, which is causing them both so as to make them co-vary?

Also, the issue does not concern the remoteness of any causal relationship. One or a number of intervening variables, or mechanisms, could "stand between" variables *A* and *B* in an historical chain reaction; *A* can still be a cause for *B*. Insemination is a cause for giving birth, getting married is, too; so is being a female.

Finally, the issue is not whether variables *A* and *B* respond to a similar causal influence(s). Undoubtedly they must. Both smoking and cancer, for example, must be influenced by such variables as culture-membership, locality, age. The question is: Is the correlation between them merely due to the fact that some variable *C* is making them co-vary?

In order to really "tie down" a cause-effect relationship, therefore, to demonstrate fully the direction of causation, one must do an experiment. A correlation in the absence of an experiment gives minimal evidence for the cause-effect relationship. Before-after conditions, if they can be demonstrated, strengthen the evidence somewhat (*B* cannot be causing *A*). The experiment rules out all possibilities but one, with respect to direction of causation: *A* must be causing *B*.

In performing an experiment, slips can occur, of course. The experimenter may be dishonest or slovenly; or for one reason or another, mistakes can occur so as to give evidence that *A* is causing *B* when such, in fact, is not the case. To give a rather cursory review of sources of spurious evidence from experiments, these might be divided into two types: (1) slips in sorting cases into treatment conditions, and (2) slips in the imposition of the presumed causal variable.

(1) In an experiment, some cases are assigned to an experimental group, others are put in a control group (this is the simplest model; sometimes there are more than two treatment conditions). The experimental-group subjects "get" the cause: they are the Crest users, the rats deprived of food, or whatever. The control-group cases do not receive this treatment. This assignment to treatment conditions should be by a random selection procedure: a flip of a coin or a similarly impartial method. If it is, and if the sample is fair-sized, then individual differences between the subjects—with respect to other variables which might influence variable *B*—should show a reasonably equal distribution between experimental group and control group. In the maze-running experiment, for example, the experimental group will not contain a disproportionate share of intelligent rats, nor the control group, of stupid rats; the hungry rats will not learn the maze faster simply because they are smarter. In the Crest test, the Crest users will not be selected from a town with a fluoridated water supply, while the users of brand *X* come from another town with nonfluoridated water. If a biased selection procedure is used in sorting subjects into experimental and control groups, this can produce spuriously favorable evidence.

To cite another example; suppose an after-care program is instituted for boys who emerge from a state training school (i.e., from a prison for juvenile delinquents). Some of the boys, on release, go to live in a "halfway house" for a certain length of time; they live there under supervision by state authorities, going out during the day to school or to work; eventually they leave the halfway house and go about their separate ways. Suppose, further, that someone wishes to do an evaluation study, to see if the after-care program actually does the boys any good. An experiment could be set up. Some boys, on release from prison, spend some time in the halfway house. Others do not; they go directly to their homes, or to wherever they wish to go. All the boys are "followed"; the authorites can note which ones of them get arrested or convicted again, within a given time span—perhaps within three years of release. If the boys who go through the halfway house, the experimental group, show a lower rate of recidivism, this is evidence that the after-care program is acting to prevent future crimes, that it is "helping" at least some of the boys.

If the study were done properly, the boys would be selected for inclusion in the experimental group by an impartial criterion: the flip of a coin, every third boy emerging from the prison, etc. In practice, there might be stiff resistance from the authorities to any such crassly impersonal selection procedure. The halfway house may be so small that it can only accommodate a fraction of the boys who emerge from prison. For humanitarian reasons, the director of the halfway house might wish to choose those boys who, it is judged, need the after-care treatment the most: boys who have no other homes to go to, perhaps; boys whose home environments seem particularly pathogenic. Or for practical treatment considerations, he may wish to choose those boys who look like the best risks. The environment provided by the halfway house must depend very much on what sorts of boys are living in it; particularly delinquent types, "bad apples," might poison the environment for all the boys.

If such personalized, clinical considerations influence the selection procedure, then any forthcoming evidence for the efficacy of the halfway house is tainted. Perhaps the boys who went through the after-care program showed a lower rate of recidivism than other boys did, not because of the after-care program, but because they were the sort of boys they were.

(2) Perhaps the major danger of spuriously favorable evidence from experiments is what might be termed the contaminated cause. When the experimenter "gives" variable *A* to the experimental-group subjects, he inadvertantly "gives" them another variable too. Let us call this $A_1$. And it is really $A_1$, not *A*, which produces the effect. A classic instance of this occurred in one of the old Western Electric studies (Homans 1951). A group of female workers who assembled a small electrical component were taken aside, put in a special room within the plant, and made the subjects of a series of studies of the effects of various working conditions on productivity. Lighting was improved; the hours of work were changed; various other possible improvements in working conditions were introduced, one by one. Each time one of these possible production aids was introduced, the girls were watched closely, and were questioned about how they felt about the change; and their production rates were noted. After each such improvement, their productivity increased. But as the study continued, the researchers found that *any* change seemed to help. When the lighting was improved, productivity rose; when the good lighting was replaced by bad, productivity rose still higher. They finally concluded that it was not the good lighting, better hours, etc., as such, that made the difference. It was simply the fact that the girls were receiving special attention. Whereas before they had worked as cogs in a vast industrial machine, now they were quasi celebrities; various official-looking persons were showing concern about their work and how they felt about it. This inspired them to work faster and faster, better and better.

Another example: flatworms have been taught a simple experimental task (that is, conditioned to a particular stimulus), then ground into a paste and fed to other flatworms. These worms, in turn, are taught the same task. They learn it faster than do other worms who were without benefit of such an instructive diet. Were the worms actually able to ingest a learned habit? Apparently not. The paste may have given them some increment of a stimulating chemical substance (RNA), which spurred them on to attack their task with greater vigor, thus learning it faster. The level of this chemical was raised in the worms they had eaten, not as a result of learning the task as such, but simply because, in the course of learning it, they were more active, more stimulated, than the ordinary laboratory worm. In other words, variable $A$ is eating worms who had learned the task; variable $A_1$ is eating worms who had lived active lives. $A_1$ appears to be the cause, the reason for the positive correlation between $A$ and $B$ (Hartry and Morton 1964).

Making allowance for occasional tricks like these that experimental data can play on us, one is bound to hold the experimental model in great respect. It is the full solution to the direction-of-causation problem. The main difficulty with experiments is that we cannot have more of them.

## Holding Constant

When, as is so often the case, a particular hypothesis cannot be experimentally tested, a poor second-best may be achieved by matched groups or multivariate analysis. If the researcher cannot virtually rule out all possible variable C's by means of experimentally manipulating the cause-variable himself, he can at least rule out certain possible variable C's by resort to holding-constant operations.

To illustrate multivariate analysis, let us return to the example hypothesis "Married students are better students." Does getting married, in itself, tend to make people settle down and study better? Suppose we had data indicating that this is indeed the case:

TABLE XIII

MARRIED STUDENTS ARE BETTER STUDENTS

| | *Grade-point average* | |
|---|---|---|
| | "B" or above | Under "B" |
| Married students | 200 | 250 |
| Unmarried students | 500 | 800 |

There is a weak but definite positive correlation between being married and getting good grades in school. There must be some sort of causal relation between the two variables. What is it? Could grade-point average be a determinant of marital status? (In other words, *B*-causes-*A*.) This seems unlikely. Could the causal agent be some outside variable? Possibly. Perhaps age is the determining factor. Older persons are more likely to be married, and maturity is an aid to scholarship. Let us see:

TABLE XIV

OLDER STUDENTS ARE MARRIED STUDENTS ARE BETTER STUDENTS

| | *Young students (under 20)* | | *Old students (20 and over)* | |
|---|---|---|---|---|
| | *Grade-point average is "B" or above?* | | *Grade-point average is "B" or above?* | |
| | Yes | No | Yes | No |
| Married | 50 | 100 | 150 | 150 |
| Single | 300 | 600 | 200 | 200 |

In Table XIV, the age-variable has been held constant. Students in the sample were divided into two groups: young and old. Then within each group the correlation between grades and marital status was rerun. When this sort of breakdown is made, the positive correlation disappears. In each of the two groups, there is a zero correlation between grades and marital status; the married students are no more likely than the unmarried ones to make better grades. This would indicate that getting married does *not* improve one's schoolwork. The correlation in Table XIII was an artifact of an "outside" causal agent, a variable *C*, age.

If, on the other hand, when age was held constant, the positive correlation between marriedness and grades held firm—within both the "young" and "old" groups—then we have evidence that *A* (marriage) is a cause for *B* (good grades). And our evidence is a bit stronger than it was before the multivariate analysis was run: one possible variable *C*, age, has been ruled out.

If we had measures for them, we might likewise eliminate—or test for—other possible variable *C*'s: church membership, ethnicity, social-class position, rural versus urban home background, IQ, fraternity-sorority membership, and so on. However, we could never thus eliminate all possible variable *C*'s. Even if our hypothesis survived all these tests, it is still conceivable that some other, unmeasured, variable—security need, perhaps—is causing *both* marital status *and* grade-point average and, hence, producing the correlation.

The term "multivariate analysis" has been assigned to a variety of tabular and mathematical treatments which permit one to look for the effects of "outside" variables on a correlation. One can "hold constant" some possible variable *C*'s, either singly (as in the crude example, above) or collectively (as with analysis of variance), and thus see, when this is done, if the correlation between variables *A* and *B* holds firm, or if it becomes much weaker, or if it disappears.[5] All such treatments are inferior to the experiment, for purposes of demonstrating direction of causation at any rate. A variable cannot be statistically controlled unless it has been measured; possible effects of unmeasured and unmeasurable variables remain unknown. With the experiment, on the other hand, *all possible* variable *C*'s are ruled out. The presumed causal variable, variable *A*, is something the experimenter does to the subjects; how the experimental subjects score on it depends solely on what he does to them. Any resulting correlation cannot be due to the fact that some variable *C* is causing both variables *A* and *B*, in such a manner as to make them co-vary.

An alternative to multivariate analysis—as a means for "controlling for" certain possible outside causal agents—is matched groups. Rather than having statistical controls, one builds some controls into his sample selection. To return to the delinquency research: there are certain demographic predictors of crime. Boys from "bad" neighborhoods, boys from poor families, boys from broken homes: such boys are more likely than more fortunate boys to turn to crime. If one wishes to test hypotheses

[5] Two references on multivariate analysis: Lazarsfeld 1955; Zeisel 1957.

about more purely psychogenic causes for delinquency, such social-background variables stand as possible variable *C*'s. Bandura and Walters (1959), for example, found that the delinquents more than the nondelinquents in their sample tended to have estranged, distant relationships with their fathers. From this correlation they drew the causal inference: estranged relationship with father is a determinant of delinquency. Perhaps variable *C* is something about life in the slums which tends to put special barriers between father and son, and also tends to tempt the son into crime. In the Bandura-Walters study this sort of possibility was ruled out by the sample selection. All the boys, delinquent and nondelinquent, were drawn from intact, non-slum, middle-class homes.

In other words, the matched-groups technique represents an attempt to equalize the two groups in one's sample—those cases that "have" the presumed causal variable and those that do not —with respect to certain possible outside causal agents. Like multivariate analysis, it is better than nothing, but it is intrinsically weaker than the experiment. Some, but not all possible, variable *C*'s can be so controlled.

## "Reasonable" Causal Inferences

In the absence of an experiment, or of any holding-constant operations, or even of before-after conditions, causal inferences are still made from correlations. When there is no evidence with respect to the direction of the causal relationship, then theoretically one's evidence from such a correlation, that *A* is causing *B*, is not terribly strong, since it is just one of three possibilities. In practice, the convincingness of such correlational evidence hinges on considerations of "reasonableness"—that is, on nonempirical criteria. For some correlations, the *A*-causes-*B* explanation seems eminently reasonable; *B*-causes-*A* and *C*-causes-*A*-and-*B* seem unreasonable; such correlations can inspire considerable confidence that *A* is in fact a cause for *B*. With others, one or both of the alternative possibilities may not seem so unlikely; therefore the *A*-causes-*B* interpretation inspires less conviction.

To illustrate various levels of convincingness by the criterion of reasonableness, let us turn to marital-adjustment research. What causes one marriage to succeed, another to fail? Why are some marriages reasonably happy affairs, while others are unhappy?

1. Similarity of spouses, with respect to social background, is one predictor of marital adjustment. If husband and wife were brought up in the same religion, if they had about the same amount of schooling, if their families' social-class positions were similar: all this presages a successful marriage.
2. The spouses' relationships with their own parents is another predictor. If your fiancé is getting along badly with her (or his) parents, this makes the fiancé a relatively bad risk.
3. Happiness of parents' marriage is a third predictor. If your parents are happily married, you stand a better chance of making your own marriage work.
4. People who have no brothers or sisters are poor risks as potential spouses. Marry a girl with a brother or sister. The best risk is a girl with a *younger* brother or sister.
5. Early marriages tend to be unhappy marriages. Don't marry when you are very young; wait a while.
6. Level of education is a relatively strong predictor. The better-educated a couple is, the better their chances for marital adjustment.
7. Girls, do not marry a traveling man. Traveling salesmen, railroad workers, transcontinental truck drivers, men whose jobs take them away from home a good deal: these are poor risks.
8. Marry someone you have known for a long time. The longer the period of prior acquaintance, the longer the dating period and the engagement, the better the chances for good marital adjustment.

These were all presented as facts. Actually, they are merely correlations, drawn from one questionnaire-based survey done in Illinois thirty years ago (Burgess and Cottrell 1939). Also, they are all inferred-variable hypotheses. Disregarding for the moment the validity problems and any possible sampling problem, how convincing are these correlations as indicators of causes for marital happiness/unhappiness?

First of all, the *B*-causes-*A* possibility appears to be highly unlikely; a strong case can be made for before-after conditions. *First* the couples were engaged (for long or short periods); went to school (for long or short periods); had or did not have brothers and sisters; came from similar or dissimilar family backgrounds; married early or late. *Then* some of them had happy marriages, some unhappy. Degree of marital adjustment could hardly be causing the "predictors"—age at marriage, level of education, siblings, and so on—since it must have come later in time. Perhaps before-after conditions are a bit more clear-cut for some of the correlations than for others. For correlation 6, for example, some respondents may have continued in school after they were married. For correlation 7, some men may have taken to the road only after their marriages. For correlation 4, on the other hand, before-after conditions seem perfectly clear-cut; they must have obtained for the entire sample.

At any rate, one might rule out the *B*-causes-*A* possibility as highly unlikely for all these correlations, using in one's argument the claim that before-after conditions must have been present. And for some of the correlations, such as 4, one might do this a bit more confidently than for others, such as 6 or 7.

The *C*-causes-*A*-and-*B* possibility remains. For correlation 8, variable *C* might be some character trait such as caution versus impulsiveness, which is a determinant both of the length of engagement and the marriage's subsequent stability. For correlation 7, variable *C* might be some other trait in some of the men: restlessness, perhaps, causing both choice of traveling job and marital troubles, so as to produce the correlation. For correlation 6 no outside causal influence is apparent. For correlation 5, variable *C* might be caution versus impulsiveness, again. For correlation 4 it is practically impossible to think of an outside causal influence: what could be causing *both* whether one had siblings *and* one's future success in marriage, in such a manner as to produce the correlation?

One can think about the correlations in this fashion, and thereby rate them for how convincing they are as evidence for particular causal inferences. All of them seem fairly convincing to me. That is, I would be more concerned about the inferred variables than about direction of causation. Direction of causation has not really been demonstrated, though; there was no experiment, not even any holding constant. A less credulous judge might be less thoroughly convinced.

Hypotheses of this order can be contrasted with others where no such case can be made for before-after conditions. A previous example was the correlation between physical punishment and children's aggressiveness. It is equally plausible to me that the correlation merely reflects the fact that aggressive children provoke more spankings, and that physical punishment makes children more aggressive. Therefore, I could not feel very confident about either of these causal inferences.

With some correlations, I think, the causal inference can be made with complete confidence. An experiment is not needed to show the direction of causation. This happens when the causal variable is something which could not conceivably be the result of experience, a variable such as sex or race. If women have fewer accidents than do men, this must be because sex is a determinant of accident rate. Accidents could hardly be causing the drivers' sex. What could determine *both* sex *and* proneness to auto accidents, so as to produce the correlation? Similarly, American Negroes have a lower life expectancy than do whites. The only possibility, with respect to direction of causation, must be that *A* causes *B*. Race must be a real, if remote, determinant of life expectancy.

Twin-studies, likewise, occupy this privileged position. A group of identical (i.e., monozygotic, one-egg) twins can be compared with a group of fraternal (dizygotic, two-egg) twins. The researcher calculates expectancy rates: the likelihood that if a person has a twin who is schizophrenic, or a criminal, or has a very high (or low) IQ, that person will show the same characteristic. Identical twins—those who are genetically most similar to each other—show higher expectancy rates than do fraternal twins. This is rather convincing evidence that schizophrenia, criminality, and IQ are caused, in part, by genetic inheritance. The direction-of-causation problem has been fully handled: schizophrenia (etc.) could certainly not be causing degree of genetic similarity. What could possibly be causing both degree of genetic relatedness and schizophrenia, so as to make them co-vary? (Fuller and Thompson 1960)

Such "privileged" causal variables shade off into others, where it is just barely conceivable—but extremely unlikely—that the direction of causation has been misread. Ordinal position and number of siblings—as with correlation 4, above—would appear to be one of these. Locality, at times, is another. Vermonters, for example, tend to vote Republican. Living in Vermont, in itself, must be one determinant of partisan vote. How else could this be explained?

## Panel Studies

Earlier in the chapter I stated my impression that the majority opinion among social scientists was that minimal evidence for a causal statement is an observed correlation between the presumed cause-variable and effect-variable. This should be qualified. Panel studies are taken very seriously as causal evidence. They do, in a sense, show "covariance." However, it could be argued that they do not, strictly speaking, show correlation between variables *A* and *B*.

In a panel study, a group of cases is measured for variable *B*. Then variable *A* "happens to them." Then they are remeasured for variable *B*, and any increments are noted.[6] Sometimes variable *A* is actually imposed on the cases by the researcher; then the study takes on the nature of an experiment without a control group.

Panel studies receive heavy use in market research. If an advertising firm decides upon a new promotional gambit for some product, its efficacy can be tested by means of such a before-after

[6] This, again, is the simplest type. Sometimes they are measured more often than twice (Lazarsfeld 1948).

study. Variable *B* would be the product's sales. Sales figures are gathered, and the promotional campaign is undertaken; then, after a reasonable interval, sales figures are scanned again. If sales rose after the new promotion was introduced, this is evidence that the promotion helped sales.

The special danger with causal inferences from panel studies or trend studies is that something else intervened or changed, between the time of first measurement and the second measurement, and this "something else" is the real reason for any increment in variable *B*. A temporary fluctuation in the national economy, for example, might have been the real cause for the rise in sales. With some panel studies, such an extraneous causal factor is a real possibility; with others, the danger appears to be remote.

This concludes the discussion of evidence for causal generalizations, and the treatment of the direction-of-causation problem. For an alternative conceptualization of models for causal inference, the reader is referred to Samuel Stouffer's lucid and penetrating article, "Some Observations on Study Designs." (1950: 356–359)

We now turn to the explanation for the single case.

## The Single Case

This is the type of causal hypothesis that takes precedence in everyday talking and thinking, and in nonscientific writings: "The alarm clock woke me up"; "I have to get up early tomorrow, so I must set the alarm"; "The car stopped because I applied the brakes"; "The atomic bomb destroyed Hiroshima"; "Before I get into the movie, I must buy a ticket."

All such single-case explanations refer back to causal generalizations: "Alarms wake people"; "Braking stops cars"; "Bombs destroy things"; "To get into a movie, one must first buy a ticket." Our scheme of reality, which permits us to go about our daily activities, is comprised of a great many such causal laws, in which we place our faith. Believing them, we "know what to do" in various contexts: when coming to a stoplight, when arriving at a theater, and so on. They also enable us to explain events after they occurred: why one woke up when he did, why the face of Hiroshima was so drastically changed in 1945, and so on.

Probably rather few of these guiding principles have actually been documented by research. If they could be said to be supported by evidence, the evidence is, in the main, impressionistic. There is much to be said for not applying any "scientific" epistemology, such as the one in use here, to this sort of "common knowledge." If we were to be as severe in our judgments of single-case explanations and their explanatory laws as we are in judging research reported in journal articles, we would become virtually immobilized by skepticism and doubts.

If the single-case explanation is true, then the principle on which it rests must be true. If it is true that the alarm waked you, then it must be true that alarm clocks wake people.[7]

This is, perhaps, open to argument. One might claim, for certain of such explanations, that no general principle is needed. The case "explains itself." Thus with Hiroshima: people observed the dropping of the bomb and the subsequent devastation. This observation of co-occurrence for a single case *is* the evidence.

The counterargument would be that observation of co-occurrence, for a single case, is no real evidence at all. The coincidence of cause and effect, in a single case, can very well be a true coincidence, a chance happening. Likelihood of chance co-occurrence, with a single case, should be quite high. Also, of course, co-occurrence is not correlation. To permit the customary minimal evidence, a correlation must be observed for a sample of cases. Theoretically at least, such a sample is always available. For the bomb example, the sample might be a collection of days in particular cities:

TABLE XV

| | The bomb was dropped | The bomb was not dropped |
|---|---|---|
| The city was destroyed | 1 | 1,000 |
| The city was not destroyed | 0 | 50 million |

[7] The causal principle, phrased as a non-necessary-cause-effect generalization, must be true.

In practice, of course, we routinely explain events without conscious recourse to general principles of causal laws. Perhaps we do this improperly, without any real evidence. In some instances, though, as with the bomb example, chance co-occurrence does appear to be unlikely, to say the least.

At any rate, here I shall adhere to the conventional philosophic position, that all single-case explanations do "rest on" general causal laws (Gibson 1960:29–42; Kemeny 1959:49; Popper 1959:60). Such a law can always be invoked, although sometimes in practice there will be some ambiguity or range of choice with respect to what should be the appropriate "controlling principle." Evidence in support of a single-case explanation means, first of all, evidence in support of the explanatory principle: an observed correlation, for a sample of cases, between bomb detonation and subsequent destruction, between the sounding of an alarm clock and subsequent waking. Also, the single-case explanation requires something extra: a test for negative cases. All single-case explanations can be construed as necessary-cause statements ("If the alarm had not sounded, then, I would not have awakened when I did"). A test for negative cases, in this instance, would involve noting the percentage of times when waking *did* occur (at a particular point in time), when an alarm clock did *not* go off. (This is discussed in Chapter 2. Certainly if such a test were done, the odds for waking at a particular moment without the alarm would turn out to be very low. The test for negative cases would return evidence favorable to the hypothesis, "The alarm waked me.")

Single-case explanations such as these, whose explanatory principles have not been documented by research, which are only "supported" by impressionistic evidence, are also in jeopardy with respect to source-of-doubt G, the relevance problem. *Is* there any evidence? At best, the correlation and test for negative cases are dimly pictured in one's memory. This "picture," of course, does not have the focus of a table given in a research report. How many cases observed, disposition of each case, strength of the correlation, number of exceptions—these cannot be recalled. Considerable ambiguity may surround the explanatory principle itself: what general causal law *does* explain this single case?

The relevance problem is perhaps least serious when Ego, himself, has observed some cases which document any such explanatory principle, and when the sorting criteria are fairly explicit. For the homelier, everyday explanations, concerning alarm clocks, ticket-buying, automobile-braking, Ego might be said to "have evidence." He has done it himself, in the past, and has seen the results. What he did, what the results were, can often be specified clearly enough.

For the more profound single-case explanations—such as those offered by historians, news analysts, psychoanalysts, social theorists, speculative writers of all sorts—the relevance problem is so grave that generally, I think, it could legitimately be said that there is no evidence at all.

## Explanation

If all explanations were to be arranged into types, one possible typology might run like this:

1. Single-case explanations: "Why did he commit suicide?" "Because he was not a Catholic."
2. Causal generalizations, which are, in effect, explanations for correlations: "Why do Catholics commit suicide less frequently than Protestants do?" "Because Catholicism prevents suicide."
3. The third type will be termed here a compound hypothesis; it further explains a causal generalization by pointing to a mechanism through which the cause works its effect. "Why does Catholicism prevent suicide?" "Because Catholicism fosters social integration, which in turn is a preventive of suicide."
4. More lengthy explanations; sometimes, in order to explain whatever one wants to explain, one may have to string together a long series of hypotheses.
5. Finally, a residual category for the occasional noncausal explanation. This includes such rare and esoteric types as: (a)

explanation by tautology ("Why is *X* equal to *A* plus *B*?" "Because *B* is equal to *X* minus *A*"); (b) explanation by reference to a supposedly perfect co-occurrence ("Why is that egg greenish-blue?" "Because it is a robin's egg, and all robins' eggs are greenish-blue"); (c) mathematical models which describe the workings of systems (these could, perhaps, be viewed as explanations).

Considering just causal explanations, the first four types: how do these compare with each other with respect to likelihood of truth? In the light of the principle of multiple contingency—the number of subsidiary hypotheses that must be true if the entire explanation is true—causal generalizations, the second type, are more to be trusted than the other types. In particular, the non-necessary causal generalization, which requires no test for negative cases, rests on the fewest subsidiary hypotheses and makes the most modest demands for evidence. For the single-case explanation: the general principle it invokes might indeed be true, yet it might not account for the case in question. (Perhaps I would have awakened, then, even if the alarm had not gone off.) A compound hypothesis can be broken down into a number of part-hypotheses, usually three. For it to be true, each part-hypothesis must be true. For the example above: it must be true that Catholicism fosters social integration, that social integration prevents suicide, and that Catholicism prevents suicide. Likewise, the more lengthy explanations (the fourth type) rest on still more part-hypotheses or subsidiary hypotheses. For one of these to be true, all the parts must be true. The longer the explanation, the more chances it has of being wrong.

By the principle of multiple contingency alone, then, the non-necessary causal generalization—a single hypothesis, citing but two variables—is the type of explanation that stands the best chance of being true. If a particular explanation is to be judged on the evidence, then many other considerations also have a bearing on its truth value, of course: the validity problem, the sampling problem, direction of causation, and so on. The relevance problem also enters in: how clear is it that any observations can be related to the explanation, as evidence? As stated before, this depends to a considerable extent on whether any such observations were the fruit of research, or whether any "evidence" is impressionistic.

With respect to the relevance problem, too, the causal generalizations (the type-2 explanations) would seem to be in better shape, generally, than causal explanations of other types. At least, a good many of these have been documented by research. The other types of explanation are more likely to rest in whole or in part on impressionistic evidence, or on no evidence whatever; at the very least, this is true of explanations for human behavior.

Evidence or no, explanations of all types press for use. Each of us carries about in his head an enormous store of explanations. The sum total of these might be termed one's "understanding." Driven by a need for understanding, one finds new things to be explained, acquires explanations for them, and adds to the store. The more curious and perceptive one is, the greater the number of things he notices which call for explanation; the more there is to understand. Similarly, the more erudite one is, the more explanations he picks up secondhand; too, the more "facts" that will be forced on him, the more questions suggested, which call for explanation. Also, the more inventive, clever, and creative the person, the richer his production of explanations.

Perhaps there is some fairly basic human need for intellectual closure, which insures that "facts" which really beg a question will not go unexplained. No matter what the status of real knowledge concerning a fact, the fact will be explained, by someone. Thus, until fairly recently, little was known about the causes of illness. Yet every malaise had its explanation. If one studies primitive peoples, he is struck by the intellectual clutter in which such persons live. Not only must they cope with a real world—yams and pigs and digging sticks and babies. They must also deal with a teeming unreal world of their own making: ghosts, witches, countless spirits and supernatural agents—numerous causal agents whom they have created with their explanations. Prescientific explanations for illness—in terms of spirit possession, bewitchment, violation of taboos—seem quaint to us now, since medical research has removed much of this clutter. Yet in areas outside the reach of scientific research, much of our understanding is no doubt illusory too, in the manner of the primitive explanations for illness.

Merely answering a question with an explanation can at least create the illusion of understanding. This, apparently, is comforting. Explanation reaches far beyond the range of evidence. If this results in some harmful illusions, it has its brighter side too. If man were by nature empirically minded, faithful to the needs of evidence, his map of reality would resemble a jigsaw puzzle with most of the pieces missing. His mental life would be arid, his sensibilities blunted, his range of awareness limited: no Freud, no notion of the unconscious or even of personality; no Toynbee or Marx, no scheme to make any overall sense out of history; no social theory, little philosophy, no speculative tradition, few insights of much import; limited awareness. Just science—a grim prospect. Happily, we are not so constrained. We explain, and evidence be damned.

Typically, explanation is given after the fact. First something happens; then it is explained. One awkward feature of such explanations is that frequently—if the explainer is sufficiently clever, or if there is a number of explainers—there are *many* explanations for the same fact. For example, one popular focus of explanation among social theorists is the universality of incest taboos. All known societies have rules against sexual intercourse and marriage between brother and sister, father and daughter, mother and son, and various other relatives. At last count (Stephens 1967), there were at least a dozen competing explanations for this fact. How does one choose from such a wealth of explanations? Occasionally bona fide evidence is available which can be used in the choice. Often, as in this case, no real evidence is at hand. The explanations are all untestable. In this event, if a choice must be made, it must hinge on personal taste, vague notions of "reasonableness." Some explanations might be rejected on grounds that they "don't make sense"; i.e., in some dimly perceived fashion, they are felt not to jibe with one's other beliefs. Several other explanations might be tentatively accepted. They may appear as if they may "have some truth in them"; i.e., they point to various contributing causes for incest taboos. Or, one can fix on one explanation, the most "reasonable" one, and reject all the rest.

Some "facts" do not present an unlimited number of alternative explanations. If all we wish to do is to explain a correlation between two variables, *A* and *B*, then there are only four possibilities: *A* causes *B*; *B* causes *A*; an outside influence, *C*, causes them both, so as to produce the correlation; or coincidence. If, however, one wishes to go beyond such a limited explanation and cite mechanisms, then he is in the realm of compound hypotheses, and many more possibilities—alternative explanations—are opened up.

Sometimes only one explanation for a particular "fact" comes to mind. Then, of course, the explainer is not faced with this problem of choice. Quite likely, though, he enjoys this secure position merely because his imagination is limited. If he were more inventive, or if other explainers were put to the task, more explanations could be produced.

How fallible is the criterion of reasonableness, as a method for choosing explanations in lieu of evidence? One can only guess. This must depend on the time and place, who the judge is, the state of evidence for whatever set of beliefs, in the judge's mind, are related to the explanation. In general, reason is likely to be extremely treacherous. Often the reasonable explanation is the wrong one. An unreasonable explanation—wildly improbable, in the context of the judge's belief system, clashing with his "experience"—may turn out to be the right one. (Why does the sun rise and set? Why do people catch cold? What causes rainbows? Why do blue-eyed parents frequently have blue-eyed children?) The history of the natural sciences is littered with defunct reasonable explanations. As the sciences unfold, the emerging picture of the physical world becomes stranger and stranger, more and more bizarre, increasingly at odds with the world that we "know" through our sensory apparatus.

With scientific advance, not only do reasonable explanations fall by the wayside; many of the "facts" which seemed so well explained become casualties also. Many a well-known fact about human behavior, with which we had grown comfortable, has been revealed to be a fiction when someone finally got around to testing it.[8] Everyone knows, for example, that—in our society, at any rate—living with in-laws puts a strain upon a marriage. There are various good reasons why this is so. Yet it is not so. In the Burgess-Cottrell (1939) sample, at any rate, couples who lived with the parent(s) of husband or wife scored just as high on marital adjustment as did the couples who lived by themselves. It would be possible to assemble a list of research findings, word them in reverse ("Burgess and Cottrell found that couples who lived with in-laws had poor marital adjustment"), and present them to people who were unaware of the true findings. For each bogus finding, the naive explainers could produce interpretations (why it is that in-laws create trouble). If they were, say, eager and theoretically oriented graduate students, they should be able to come up with a number of interpretations for each "fact." Then the "facts" could be turned around, the true findings given, and the explainers could be set to re-explaining the findings. If such an exercise were to be performed,[9] quite likely the first set of explanations would be just as reasonable, give just as strong a subjective feeling of "making sense," as the second set of explanations.

## Compound Hypotheses

An explanation frequently raises still more questions, which call for explanations of their own. So the reason Protestants show a higher rate of suicide is that Catholicism acts to prevent suicide. This is not in itself very satisfying. *Why* does Catholicism prevent suicide? What is the mechanism? What is (are) the intervening variable(s)? Answers to these questions might then be given, which may be more or less elaborate. If such an answer is

[8] I.e., the research evidence was unfavorable.

[9] It has been done. Appreciation to Alvin Zalinger (Department of Sociology, Boston University).

fairly short, citing just one or two intervening variables, it may be possible to state it in a single sentence: "Catholicism prevents suicide because it fosters social integration, and social integration is a preventive of suicide"; or "Catholics are especially afraid of supernatural punishment for suicide, and this keeps them from killing themselves." This sort of explanation will be termed a compound hypothesis.

We might call the intervening variable "variable *Y*." "Why do women have fewer auto accidents than do men?" "Because they don't drive as much." Sex (variable *A*) is a determinant of how much one drives (variable *Y*), which is in turn a determinant of the accident rate (variable *B*). A relatively remote causal relation, between sex and accident rate, is explained by citing two less remote, intervening, causal relations: between sex and miles driven and between miles driven and accident rate. Such a compound hypothesis states three cause-effect relationships: between variables *A* and *Y*, *Y* and *B*, and *A* and *B*.

Another example: in the illustration of the educated worms, earlier in the chapter, how did eating worms who had led active lives enable faster learning? Activity apparently produced an increment of a chemical substance within the worms (RNA). When the active worms were ground up and fed to other planaria, this increment was passed on to the cannibal worms. Level of RNA is a determinant of memory, speed of learning. In other words, variable *A* (eating worms who had led active lives) causes variable *Y* (RNA increment) causes variable *B* (faster learning).

A final example might be drawn from the infant-stress experiments. Why do rats who are "stimulated" in infancy—shocked, frightened, roughed up—grow up to become unusually large, healthy, "smart," generally superior rats? The mechanism is a physiological one of some sort, which appears to have something to do with a stimulation of the endocrines (variable *Y*) caused by this sort of stimulation during infancy, which in turn causes the superior development (Levine 1960; Denenberg 1963; Bovard 1958).

The citing of a mechanism can intensify one's conviction that

*A* is really a cause for *B*. With these animal experiments, for example, the mechanism, when supplied, helps the whole thing "make sense." The experimental findings seem less occult, less peculiar looking, once they are so explained.

When behavior is being explained, the statement of mechanism is more likely to be convincing if the mechanism is a biological one, rather than psychological. For one thing, a reduction to chemical changes can give one the comfortable feeling that he has penetrated to the "basic process," that the explanation is, in a sense, more complete. Also, the biological mechanism may actually have been observed; at any rate, a rather impressive index of the intervening variable may be available, so that the entire compound hypothesis can be tested, with a minimum of inference. If one has a measure for variable *Y*, he can actually see if variables *A* and *Y*, *Y* and *B*, and *A* and *B* are positively correlated.

If, on the other hand, the mechanism is a psychological one—if the intervening variable is something that goes on in the human mind, even if it is some aspect of behavior—then, ordinarily, it cannot be directly measured. Either the psychological mechanism is simply invoked, with no evidence at all, or evidence may come by way of an index—a personality test, perhaps—which is likely to inspire less faith than the physiologist's indicators. Occasionally, of course, the intervening variable may be observed, and the compound hypothesis can be fully tested, as with "Women have fewer accidents because they drive less."

As an example of explanation by invocation, we might turn to a cross-cultural study by G. P. Murdock. He found a pronounced positive correlation between sororal polygyny and polygynous households. If, in polygynous families, the co-wives are also sisters to each other, then usually they will all be housed under one roof, in one big polygynous household. If, on the other hand, they are not sisters, each co-wife will usually have her own house (or hut); each co-wife lives apart, and the husband will visit first the hut of one wife, then the hut of another (or he will stay in still another house of his own). Murdock views the separate-huts arrangement as a way of handling conflict between co-wives. The wives have a tendency to fight with each other;

one way to achieve some minimum of domestic peace is to put fighting or potentially hostile co-wives in separate houses. However, if the co-wives are also sisters, they are better able to get along with each other (for still other reasons, which he states). Thus sisters who are also co-wives are in less need of the separate-huts treatment. If they get along well enough, they might actually want to live together; the bonds of sisterhood may be stronger than any sexual or domestic rivalry. In capsule: sororal polygyny (variable *A*) is associated with polygynous households (variable *B*) because sororal polygyny tends to result in a minimum of hostility between co-wives (variable *Y*), and this in turn enables the large polygynous households (Murdock and Whiting 1951). In other words, A——→Y——→B. Murdock has evidence for A——→B. This is the correlation, in the cross-cultural data, between sororal polygyny and polygynous households. However, the cross-cultural data do not permit him to "observe" or measure the intervening variable, fighting potential. Thus he has no evidence that *A* is a cause for *Y*, or that *Y* is a cause for *B*.

## Magic and Evidence

As a final exercise, we might review a famous explanation offered by Bronislaw Malinowski (1948). This, too, is an undocumented explanation. Perhaps it should be viewed as a special variety of explanation for a single case (actually, two cases seem to be involved). Malinowski observed a certain phenomenon during his field work in the Trobriands. He explained it as an instance of a general causal law. The law should probably be construed as a high-level law.

The explanation accounted for the occurrence of fishing magic. His Trobriand Islanders did two types of fishing: lagoon fishing and deep-sea fishing. When fishing in the lagoons, they merely poisoned the water and then walked or paddled out into the shallows and picked up the fish. The procedure was fairly routine; size of the catch was to some extent predictable. There was no magic, Malinowski says, associated with fishing in the lagoons. They also fished on the open sea, in rather fragile outrigger canoes. There was some danger; occasionally the fishermen did not come back. Size of catch was also less predictable: sometimes they were lucky and made a great haul; at other times they did not. An enormous amount of ritual, incantations, charms, taboos, and so on, was associated with these deep-sea fishing trips. There was even a great deal of magical rigamarole involved in making one of the outrigger canoes. Since Malinowski was a sensitive observer, this difference between the two types of fishing did not go unnoticed. It provoked a brilliant insight, a law, which could be used to explain the Trobriand fishing magic, and which could apply equally well to the distribution of supernaturalism across numerous activities and situations, not just within the Trobriand Islands, but for mankind generally—why, for example, soldiers become more religious when they go to the front; why various little rituals, lucky charms, magical acts, characterize gamblers and professional baseball players; why this is less likely to characterize more prosaic and less "chancy" occupations.

The law, briefly stated, is this: Magic (or supernaturalism associated with a particular activity) arises in situations of uncertainty, when much is at stake and the issue is in doubt. In other words: If much hinges on the outcome, and if the activity is "chancy"—with luck or uncontrollable forces playing a major role—then the actor will turn to supernatural control methods which can at least give him the feeling that he has more control over the outcome. The law could, in fact, be construed in a variety of ways as to just what it "says," what the case is and what the variables are. The case could be construed as a situation in which someone is working to achieve a particular result. There would appear to be two causal variables: One is how much is at stake; the other is the unpredictability of the outcome. Perhaps the law should be viewed as stating an interaction effect: when both of these causes are present (in some unspecified magnitude), one gets magic. Otherwise one doesn't; at least, one is less likely to find magic. Magic is the effect. Probably one, several, or all three of the variables should be viewed as abstract variables. The term "magic"—and perhaps the other two terms, "much at stake" and "issue in doubt"—stands for a class of lower-order observed variables; and the parameters of that class, its boundaries, have been left undetermined. By "magic" Malinowski must mean such things as wearing amulets, uttering incantations, carrying charms, and—what else? Observing taboos? Prophylactic acts of various sorts? Prayer? Visions and seances? Ritual? For the two causal variables: at the very least, it must have been unspecified, in his mind, what a case must "have" or "show" in order to qualify as "high" or "present" for "much at stake," or for "issue in doubt."

He fitted the Trobriand fishing magic to his law, thereby explaining it. We might say that he observed two cases: the lagoon fishing and the deep-sea fishing. The lagoon fishing was classified "low" or "absent" for all three variables; the deep-sea fishing was classified "high" or "present" for all three. Thus the explanation: the reason magic surrounded deep-sea fishing, but did not enter into lagoon fishing, was that fishing in the deep sea was dangerous and chancy—much was at stake; the issue was in doubt. With lagoon fishing, there was no danger and there was less fluctuation of size of catch, less of a luck factor.

Is the explanation true? If the explanatory principle is construed as a high-level law, then it cannot be judged for likelihood of truth. There would seem to be no "evidence" that the explanation is true. If, on the other hand, we decided to view the explanatory principle as merely an inferred-variable hypothesis which is *not* a high-level law, *then* what is the evidence? What observations have been made that uphold the law? Since any evidence must be impressionistic, it is surrounded with the usual ambiguity. We might say that the only evidence is the Trobriand case. The phenomenon that Malinowski observed both was explained by the law *and* stood as the sole evidence for the law. Or we might admit other supposed observations as evidence, made by someone, somewhere: superstitious ballplayers and gamblers, non-superstitious accountants and file clerks.

Since the variables are ill-defined, since any evidence is impressionistic, any attempt to weigh evidence would dissolve into a muddle. One would no doubt decide that the Malinowski hypothesis cannot really be related to evidence.

Any such analysis is, of course, an unnatural act. Malinowski is being judged by an alien set of rules. If these rules were his rules, he never would have offered the explanation in the first place.

We must ride two horses. On the one hand there is our scientific training, our awareness of the requirements of evidence; on the other, a need for intellectual sustenance, for some freedom to speculate, and a need to fit what we "see" and "find" to general orientations, broad explanatory principles—a need to "theorize." The equestrian must be nimble. The horses take off in opposite directions. In a given professional act—a piece of writing, say—it is possible to behave like a 100 percent hard-nosed scientist, or like a 100 percent free-flying speculator. But the whole man must somehow come to terms with each of the conflicting claims. The proper scientist finds, when he leaves his laboratory, that well-documented hypotheses will not take him very far. In his everyday activities and in his private thoughts—outside the laboratory—he must be almost as credulous and superstitious as the rest of us. Likewise, the more sophisticated speculative writer has some understanding of scientific procedures and the demands of evidence. He can, perhaps, temporarily suspend this awareness, in order to free himself to speculate. But this awareness, no matter how it is handled, must be with him, and it must affect the way he feels about his work.

The practice of social science, it is said, requires tolerance for ambiguity. The supreme ambiguity is, perhaps, this duality itself: operating "scientifically" in some contexts, having to be "unscientific" in others. In alternately moving into, then out of, the scientist's role, a major mental adjustment must take place. Rules of evidence must be put aside, or not taken seriously, or temporarily forgotten, when "theorizing" or elaborate explaining is undertaken. Or, the speculations must be entertained in a playful fashion, not themselves taken seriously—if this is possible.

In the scientific work itself, the dilemma expresses itself in the conflict between significance and likelihood of truth, between profundity and relative certainty. One can confine one's work to the sorts of hypotheses which, by their nature, can be strongly documented, well tested. Or one can pursue the more difficult hypotheses: ones that present many sources of doubt, that can only be "tested" in a roundabout and problematic manner. The continuum is a broad one, and there is considerable range of choice; one can be more or less inferential or fact-oriented, liberal or conservative. The disciplines and subdisciplines, and we ourselves, fall at various points along this scale. The conflict has many possible compromise resolutions; it has no full solution.

## *Selected References*

Causality—philosophic issues:

"Causality, Determinism, Indeterminism, and Probability," sec. V, in Herbert Feigl and May Brodbeck, eds., *Readings in the Philosophy of Science.*

Mario Bunge, "Causality, Chance and Law," *American Scientist,* Vol. 49 (1961), pp. 432–448.

Quentin Gibson, *The Logic of Social Enquiry,* pp. 29–42, 140–150.

Direction of causation—closing the trap:

Samuel Stouffer, "Some Observations on Study Design," *The American Journal of Sociology,* Vol. 55 (1950), pp. 356–359.

Holding constant by tabular breakdowns:

Hans Zeisel, *Say It with Figures,* chaps. 6–9

Multivariate analysis:

Paul Lazarsfeld and Morris Rosenberg, *The Language of Social Research,* sec. 2.

Panels:

Paul Lazarsfeld, "The Uses of Panels in Social Research," *Proceedings of the American Philosophic Society,* Vol. 92 (1948), pp. 405–410.

Hans Zeisel, *Say It with Figures,* chap. 10.

The contaminated cause—a specimen:

Martin Orne and Frederick Evans, "Social Control in the Psychological Experiment: Antisocial Behavior and Hypnosis," *Journal of Personality and Social Psychology*, Vol. 1 (1965), pp. 189–200.

Programming experiments in the laboratory:

Murray Sidman, *Tactics of Scientific Research*.

# REFERENCES


ANASTASI, ANNE, *Differential Psychology*. New York, Macmillan, 1958.

———, *Psychological Testing*. New York, Macmillan, 1954.

ANGELL, ROBERT, *The Integration of American Society*. New York, McGraw-Hill, 1941.

AYER, A. J., *The Problem of Knowledge*. London, Macmillan, 1956.

BALES, ROBERT F., "A Set of Categories for the Analysis of Small Group Interaction." *American Sociological Review*, Vol. 15 (1950), pp. 257–263.

BANDURA, ALFRED, and R. H. WALTERS, *Adolescent Aggression*. New York, Ronald, 1959.

BECK, L. W., "Constructions and Inferred Entities." *Philosophy of Science*, Vol. 17, 1950.

BERELSON, BERNARD, *Content Analysis in Communications Research*. Glencoe, Ill., Free Press, 1952.

———, and GARY STEINER, *Human Behavior: An Inventory of Scientific Findings*. New York, Harcourt, Brace, 1964.

BOVARD, EVERETT, "The Effects of Early Handling on Viability of the Albino Rat." *Psychological Review*, Vol. 65 (1958), pp. 509–545.

BRECHER, RUTH, and EDWARD BRECHER, "Smoking and Lung Cancer." *Consumer Reports*, June, 1963.

BRONFENBRENNER, URIE, "Socialization and Social Class through Time and Space." In E. E. Maccoby, T. M. Newcomb, and E. L. Hartley, eds., *Readings in Social Psychology*, New York, Holt, Rinehart & Winston, 1958.

BROWN, ROGER, *Words and Things*. New York, Free Press, 1958.

BUNGE, MARIO, "Causality, Chance and Law." *American Scientist*, Vol. 49 (1961), pp. 432–448.

BUROS, OSKAR, *The Sixth Mental Measurements Yearbook*. Highland Park, N.J., Grayphone Press, 1965.

BURGESS, ERNEST, and LEONARD COTTRELL, *Predicting Success and Failure in Marriage*. Englewood Cliffs, N.J., Prentice-Hall, 1939.

CAMPBELL, ANGUS, PHILIP E. CONVERSE, WARREN E. MILLER, and DONALD E. STOKES, *The American Voter*. New York, Wiley, 1964.

CAMPBELL, ANGUS, and GEORGE KATONA, "The Sample Survey: A Technique for Social Science Research." In Leon Festinger and Daniel Katz, eds., *Research Methods in the Behavioral Sciences*, New York, Holt, Rinehart & Winston, 1953.

CARNAP, RUDOLPH, "Testability and Meaning." *Philosophy of Science*, Vol. 3 (1936).

CARTWRIGHT, DORWIN, "Analysis of Qualitative Material." In Leon Festinger and Daniel Katz, eds., *Research Methods in the Behavioral Sciences*, New York, Holt, Rinehart & Winston, 1953.

CASTON, NANCY, "Effect of Bulletin Board Notices on School Children's Attendance at a Performing Arts Series." MS., College of Education, University of Kansas.

CHEIN, ISIDORE, "An Introduction to Sampling." In Claire Selltiz, Marie Jahoda, Morton Deutsch, and Stuart W. Cook, eds., *Research Methods in Social Relations*, New York, Holt, Rinehart & Winston, 1966, appendix B, pp. 509–545.

CICOUREL, AARON, *Method and Measurement in Sociology*. New York, Free Press, 1964.

COHEN, MORRIS, *Reason and Nature*. New York, Harcourt, Brace, 1931.

———, and ERNEST NAGEL, *An Introduction to Logic and Scientific Method*. New York, Harcourt, Brace, 1934.

COOMBS, CLYDE, *A Theory of Psychological Scaling*. Ann Arbor, University of Michigan Press, 1952.

COPI, I. G., *Introduction to Logic*. New York, Macmillan, 1961.

CRONBACH, L. J., and PAUL MEEHL, "Construct Validity in Psychological Tests." *Psychological Bulletin*, Vol. 52 (1955), pp. 281–302.

CROWNE, DOUGLAS, and DAVID MARLOWE, *The Approval Motive*. New York, Wiley, 1964.

———, "A New Scale of Social Desirability Independent of Psychopathology." *Journal of Counselling Psychology*, Vol. 24 (1960), pp. 349–354.

CUTRIGHT, PHILLIPS, "National Political Development: Its Measurement and Social Correlates." In Nelson Polsby, Robert Dentler, and P. A. Smith, eds., *Politics and Social Life*, Boston, Houghton Mifflin, 1963.

DAVIS, ALLISON, and ROBERT J. HAVIGHURST, "Social Class and Color

Differences in Child Rearing." *American Sociological Review*, Vol. 11 (1946), pp. 698–710.

DAVIS, JAMES, "Great Books and Small Groups: An Informal History of a National Survey." In Philip E. Hammond, ed., *Sociologists at Work*, New York, Basic Books, 1964.

DENENBERG, VICTOR, "Early Experience and Emotional Development." *Scientific American*, Vol. 208 (June, 1963).

———, and G. G. KARAS, "Effects of Differential Handling upon Weight Gain and Mortality in Rat and Mouse." *Science*, 1959.

DEUTSCH, KARL, "Shifts in the Balance of International Communication Flows." *Public Opinion Quarterly*, Vol. 20 (1956), pp. 143–160.

EDWARDS, ALLEN, *Techniques for Attitude Scale Construction.* New York, Appleton-Century-Crofts, 1957.

FEIGL, HERBERT, "Notes on Causality." In Herbert Feigl and May Brodbeck, eds., *Readings in the Philosophy of Science*, New York, Appleton-Century-Crofts, 1953.

———, and MAY BRODBECK, eds., *Readings in the Philosophy of Science*. New York, Appleton-Century-Crofts, 1953.

FESTINGER, LEON, *A Theory of Cognitive Dissonance*. New York, Harper & Row, 1957.

FINNEY, D. J., "The Fischer-Yates Test of Significance in 2 x 2 Contingency Tables." *Biometrika*, Vol. 25, Parts I and II (June, 1948).

FISHER, J., "The Twisted Pear and the Prediction of Behavior." *Journal of Consulting Psychology*, Vol. 23 (1959), pp. 400–405.

FLESCH, RUDOLPH, *The Art of Plain Talk*. New York, Harper & Row, 1946.

FRANCK, KATE, and EPHRAIM ROSEN, "A Projective Test of Masculinity-Femininity." *Journal of Consulting Psychology*, Vol. 13 (1949).

FREUD, SIGMUND, *A General Introduction to Psychoanalysis*, trans. by Joan Riviere. New York, Liveright, 1935.

FULLER, JOHN, and ROBERT THOMPSON, *Behavior Genetics*. New York, Wiley, 1960.

GARFINKEL, HAROLD, *Studies in Ethnomethodology*. Englewood Cliffs, N.J., Prentice-Hall, 1966.

GIBSON, QUENTIN, *The Logic of Social Enquiry*. New York, Humanities Press, 1960.

GOUGH, HARRISON, "Clinical versus Actuarial Prediction in Psychology." In Leo Postman, ed., *Psychology in the Making*, New York, Knopf, 1962.

GREEN, BERT, "Attitude Measurement." In Gardner Lindzey, ed., *Handbook of Social Psychology*, Reading, Mass., Addison-Wesley, 1954.

GUTTMAN, LOUIS, in Samuel Stouffer *et al.*, eds., *Measurement and Prediction*, Princeton, Princeton University Press, 1950, chaps. 2, 3, 6, 8, 9.

HAYAKAWA, S. I., *Language in Thought and Action*. New York, Harcourt, Brace, 1949.

HEMPEL, C. G., "Fundamentals of Concept Formation in Empirical Sciences." In O. Neurath *et al.*, eds., *International Encyclopedia of Unified Science*, Vol. 2, No. 7, Chicago, University of Chicago Press, 1952.

HEYNS, ROGER, and ALVIN ZANDER, "Observation of Group Behavior." In Leon Festinger and Daniel Katz, eds., *Research Methods in the Behavioral Sciences*, New York, Holt, Rinehart & Winston, 1953.

HOMANS, GEORGE, *Social Behavior: Its Elementary Forms*. New York, Harcourt, Brace, 1961.

———, "The Western Electric Researches." In Dean Hoslet, ed., *Human Factors in Management*, New York, Harper & Row, 1951.

HYMAN, HERBERT, *Survey Design and Analysis*. New York, Free Press, 1955.

KAHL, JOSEPH, and JAMES DAVIS, "A Comparison of Indexes of Socio-Economic Status." *American Sociological Review*, Vol. 20 (1955), pp. 317–325.

KANTOR, J. ROBERT, "Events and Constructs in Psychology." *Psychological Record*, Vol. 7 (1957), pp. 55–60.

KAPLAN, ABRAHAM, *The Conduct of Inquiry*. San Francisco, Chandler, 1964.

———, "Definition and Specification of Meaning." *The Journal of Philosophy*, Vol. 43 (1946), pp. 281–288.

KATZ, DANIEL, "The Criteria: Knowledge, Conviction, and Significance." In Bernard Berelson and Morris Janowitz, eds., *Reader in Public Opinion and Communication*, New York, Free Press, 1950, pp. 50–57.

KEMENY, J. G., *A Philosopher Looks at Science*. New York, Van Nostrand, 1959.

KROEBER, ALFRED, and CLYDE KLUCKHOHN, "Culture." *Papers of the Peabody Museum of American Archaeology and Ethnology*, Vol. 47 (1952).

LARRABEE, H. A., *Reliable Knowledge*. Boston, Houghton Mifflin, 1945.

LAZARSFELD, PAUL, "Interpretation of Statistical Relations as a Research Operation." In Paul Lazarsfeld and Morris Rosenberg, eds., *The Language of Social Research*, New York, Free Press, 1955.

———, in Samuel Stouffer *et al., Measurement and Prediction*, Princeton, Princeton University Press, 1950, chaps. 10, 11.

———, "The Uses of Panels in Social Research." *The Proceedings of the American Philosophic Society*, Vol. 92 (1948), pp. 405–410.

———, and ALLEN BARTON, "Qualitative Measurement in the Social Sciences." In Daniel Lerner and Harold Lasswell, eds., *The Policy Sciences: Recent Developments in Scope and Method*, Stanford, Stanford University Press, 1951.

———, and MORRIS ROSENBERG, *The Language of Social Research*. New York, Free Press, 1955.

LEVINE, SEYMOUR, "Stimulation in Infancy." *Scientific American*, 1960.

———, "Psychophysical Effects in Infantile Stimulation." In E. L. Bliss, ed., *Roots of Behavior*, New York, Hoeber, 1962.

———, J. A. CHEVALIER, and S. O. KORCHIN, "The Effects of Early Shock and Handling in Infancy on Later Avoidance Learning." *Journal of Personality*, Vol. 24 (1960).

LEWIS, C. I., *An Analysis of Knowledge and Valuation*. La Salle, Ill., Open Court, 1945.

LINDESMITH, ALFRED, *Opiate Addiction*. Evanston, Principia Press, 1948.

LIPPIT, RONALD, and ALVIN ZANDER, "Observation and Interview Methods for the Leadership Training Study." Boy Scouts of America, 2 Park Ave., New York, mimeographed, 1943.

LIPSET, SEYMOUR, *Political Man*. New York, Doubleday, 1960.

LOEVINGER, JANE, "A Systematic Approach to the Construction and Evaluation of Tests of Ability." *Psychological Monographs*, Vol. 61 (1947).

MACCOBY, ELEANOR, and P. K. GIBBS, "Methods of Child Rearing in Two Social Classes." In W. E. Martin and C. B. Stendler, eds., *Readings in Child Development*, New York, Harcourt, Brace, 1954.

MALINOWSKI, BRONISLAW, *Magic, Science and Religion*. Boston, Beacon, 1948.

MARX, MELVIN, "Intervening Variable or Hypothetical Construct?" *Psychological Review*, Vol. 58 (1951), pp. 235–247.

MC CORD, WILLIAM, JOAN MC CORD, and IRVING ZOLA, *Origins of Crime*. New York, Columbia University Press, 1959.

MAC CORQUODALE, KENNETH, and PAUL MEEHL, "On the Distinction between Hypothetical Constructs and Intervening Variables." *Psychological Review*, Vol. 58 (1951), pp. 235–247.

MC CULLOUGH, CELESTE, and LOCHE VAN ATTA, *Statistical Concepts: A Program for Self-Instruction*. New York, McGraw-Hill, 1963.

MAC IVER, ROBERT M., *Society*. New York, Holt, Rinehart & Winston, 1937.

———, *Social Causation*. Boston, Ginn, 1942.

MC QUITTY, LOUIS, "Elementary Linkage Analysis for Isolating Orthogonal and Oblique Types and Typal Relevancies." *Educational Psychology Measurement*, Vol. 17 (1957).

MEEHL, PAUL, *Clinical versus Actuarial Prediction*. Minneapolis, University of Minnesota Press, 1954.

MOULTON, RAY, and JUSTUS SCHIFFERES, *The Autobiography of Science*. Garden City, N.Y., Doubleday, 1945.

MURDOCK, GEORGE PETER, *Social Structure*. New York, Macmillan, 1949.

———, and JOHN W. M. WHITING, "Cultural Determination of Parental Attitudes: The Relationship between Social Structure, Particularly Family Structure, and Parental Behavior." In Milton Senn, ed., *Problems of Infancy and Childhood*. New York, Josiah Macy Foundation, 1951.

NAGEL, ERNEST, *Freedom and Reason*. New York, Free Press, 1951.

———, *The Structure of Science*. New York, Harcourt, Brace, 1961.

ORNE, MARTIN, and FREDERICK EVANS, "Social Control in the Psychological Experiment: Antisocial Behavior and Hypnosis." *Journal of Personality and Social Psychology*, Vol. 1 (1965), pp. 189–200.

PLUTCHIK, R. A., "Operationism as Methodology." *Behavioral Science*, Vol. 8 (1963), pp. 234–241.

PARTEN, MILDRED, *Surveys, Polls and Samples: Practical Procedures*. New York, Harper & Row, 1950.

POPPER, KARL, *The Logic of Scientific Discovery*. New York, Basic Books, 1959.

RAO, C. R., *Advanced Statistical Methods for Biometric Research*. New York, Wiley, 1952.

RAPOPORT, ANATOL, "Various Meanings of 'Theory.'" *American Political Science Review*, Vol. 52 (1958), pp. 972–988.

ROUECHE, BERTON, "Annals of Medicine: In the Bughouse." *The New Yorker*, November 27, 1965.

RUSSELL, BERTRAND, *Mysticism and Logic*. London, Allen & Unwin, 1929.

SEARS, ROBERT R., ELEANOR MACCOBY, and HARRY LEVIN, *Patterns of Child Rearing*. Chicago, Harper & Row, 1957.

SECORD, PAUL, and CARL BACKMAN, *Social Psychology*. New York, McGraw-Hill, 1964.

SHEPLER, B. F., "A Comparison of Masculinity-Femininity Measures." *Journal of Counselling Psychology*, Vol. 15 (1951), pp. 484–486.

SHERIF, MUZAFER, "Superordinate Goals in the Reduction of Intergroup Conflict." *American Journal of Sociology*, Vol. 63 (1958), pp. 349–356.

SIDMAN, MURRAY, *Tactics of Scientific Research*. New York, Basic Books, 1960.

SPENCE, KENNETH W., "The Nature of Theory Constructions in Contemporary Psychology." *Psychological Review*, Vol. 51 (1944), pp. 47–68.

STEPHAN, FREDERICK, and PHILIP J. MC CARTHY, *Sampling Opinions*. New York, Wiley, 1958.

STEPHENS, WILLIAM N., "Family and Kinship." In Neil Smelser, ed., *Sociology*, New York, Wiley, 1967.

STEVENS, S. S., "Mathematics, Measurement and Psychophysics." In S. S. Stevens, ed., *Handbook of Experimental Psychology*, New York, Wiley, 1951.

STOUFFER, SAMUEL, "Some Observations on Study Design." *The American Journal of Sociology*, Vol. 55 (1950), pp. 356–359.

———, "Sociological Factors Favoring Innovations." In L. H. Clark, ed., *Consumer Behavior: Research on Consumer Reactions*, New York, Harper, 1958.

———, E. F. BORGATTA, D. G. HAYS, and A. F. HENRY, "A Technique for Improving Cumulative Scales." *Public Opinion Quarterly*, Vol. 16 (1952), pp. 273–291.

TORGERSON, WARREN S., *Theory and Methods of Scaling*. New York, Wiley, 1957.

THURSTONE, L. L., *Multiple-Factor Analysis: A Development and Expansion of the Vectors of the Mind*. Chicago, University of Chicago Press, 1947.

———, and E. J. CHAVE, *The Measurement of Attitude*. Chicago, University of Chicago Press, 1929.

UNDERWOOD, BENTON J., *Psychological Research*. New York, Appleton-Century-Crofts, 1957.

WEAVER, W., "The Imperfections of Science." *American Scientist*, Vol. 49 (1961), pp. 99–113.

WRIGHT, CHARLES R., and HERBERT HYMAN, "The Evaluators." In Philip E. Hammond, ed., *Sociologists at Work*, New York, Basic Books, 1964.

ZEISEL, HANS, *Say It with Figures*. New York, Harper, 1957.

ZETTERBERG, HANS, *On Theory and Verification in Sociology*, Totowa, N.J., Bedminster, 1963.

# INDEX

# Index

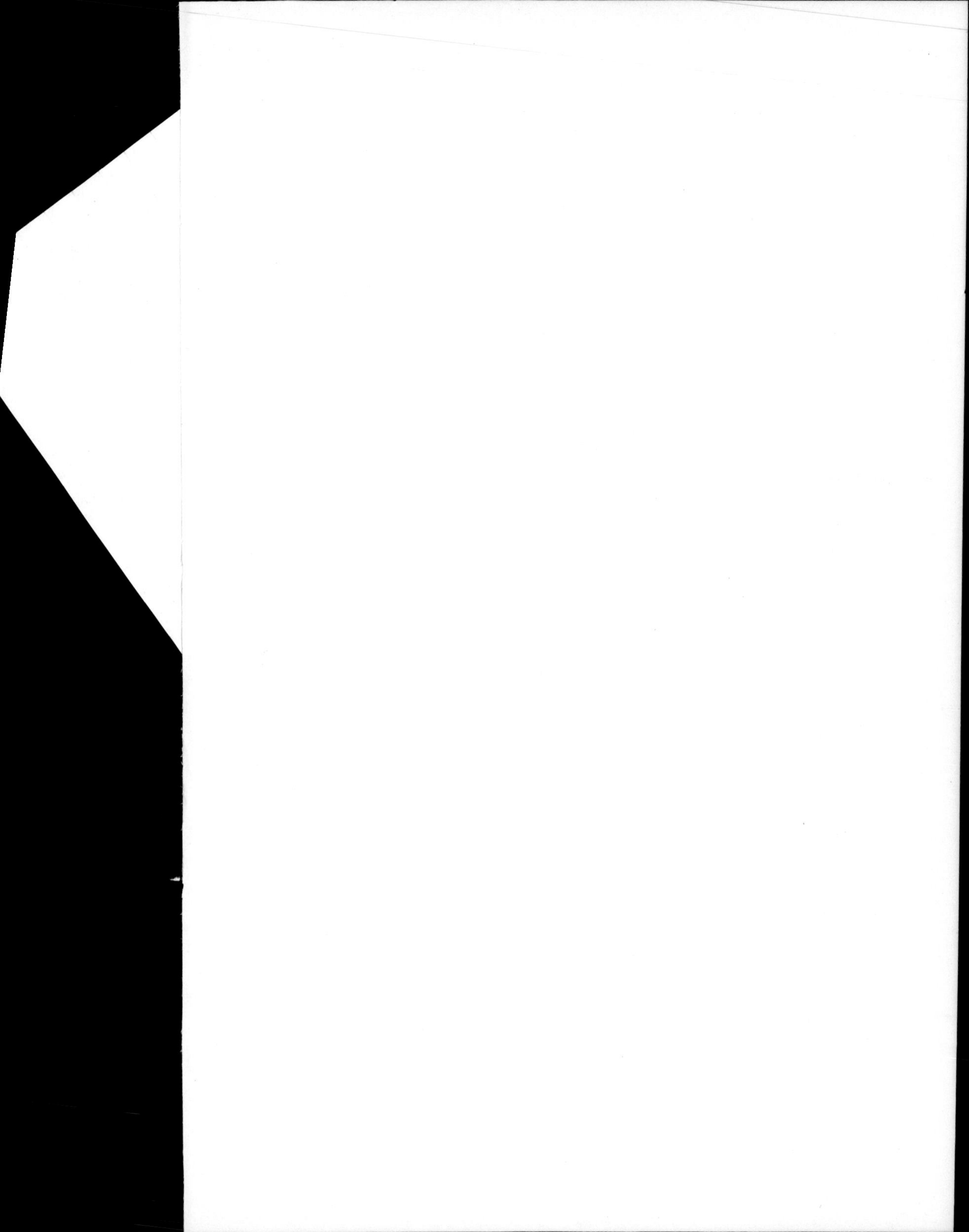

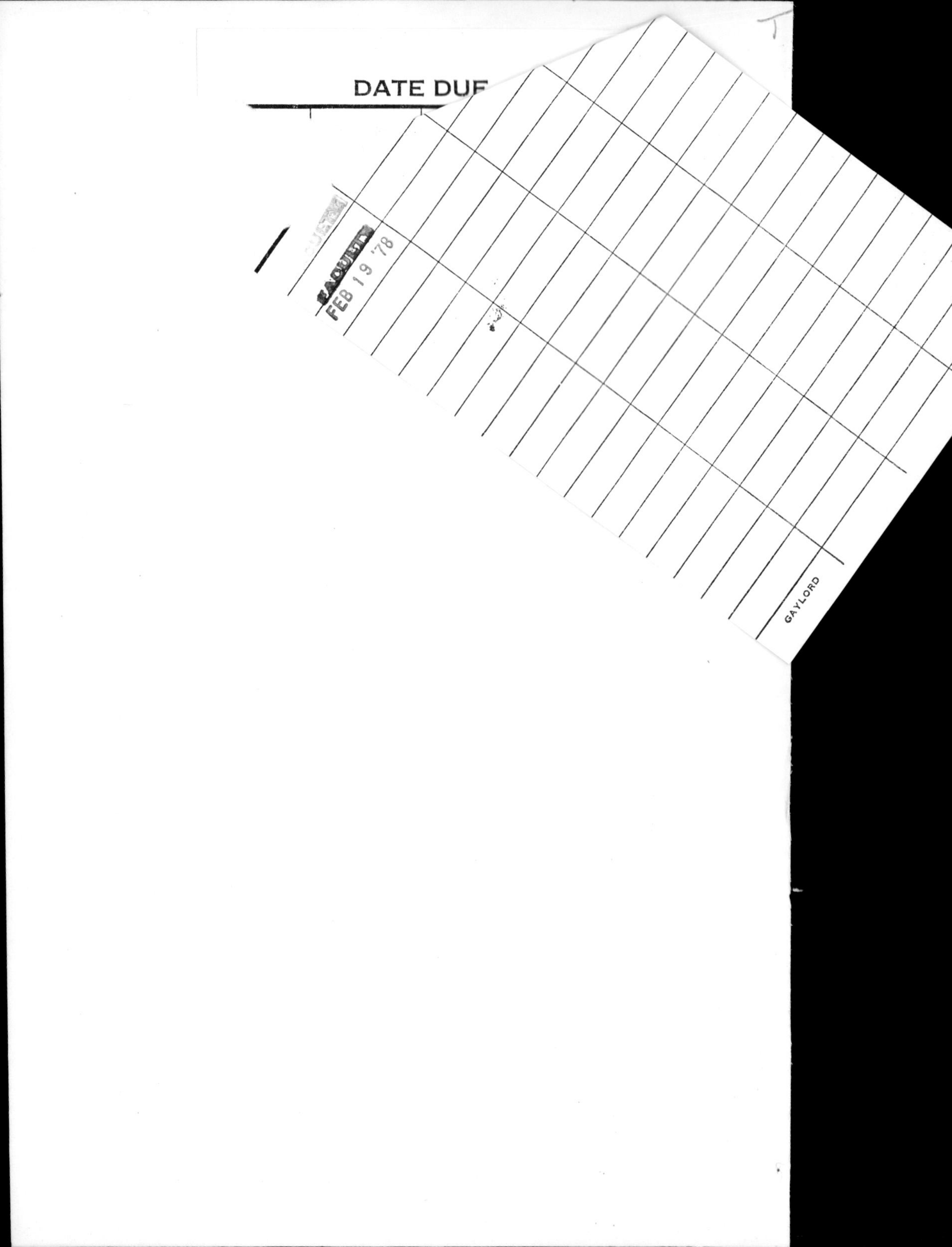
DATE DUE
FEB 19 '78
GAYLORD